GOTHIC CINEMA

Arguing for the need to understand Gothic cinema as an aesthetic mode, this book explores its long history, from its transitional origins in phantasmagoria shows and the first 'trick' films to its postmodern fragmentation in the Gothic pastiches of Tim Burton.

But what is Gothic cinema? Is the iconography of the Gothic film equivalent to that of the horror genre? Are the literary origins of the Gothic what solidified its aesthetics? And exactly what cultural roles does the Gothic continue to perform for us today? *Gothic Cinema* covers topics such as the chiaroscuro experiments of early German cinema, the monster cinema of the 1930s, the explained supernatural of the old dark house mystery films of the 1920s and the Female Gothics of the 1940s, the use of vibrant colours in the period Gothics of the late 1950s, the European exploitation booms of the 1960s and 1970s, and the animated films and Gothic superheroes that dominate present times. Throughout, Aldana Reyes makes a strong case for a medium-specific and more intuitive approach to the Gothic on screen that acknowledges its position within wider film industries with their own sets of financial pressures and priorities.

This groundbreaking book is the first thorough chronological, transhistorical and transnational study of Gothic cinema, ideal for both new and seasoned scholars, as well as those with a wider interest in the Gothic.

Xavier Aldana Reyes is Reader in English Literature and Film at Manchester Metropolitan University and a founder member of the Manchester Centre for Gothic Studies. He is the author of the books *Spanish Gothic* (2017), *Horror Film and Affect* (2016) and *Body Gothic* (2014).

Routledge Film Guidebooks

The Routledge Film Guidebooks offer a clear introduction to and overview of the work of key filmmakers, movements or genres. Each guidebook contains an introduction, including a brief history; defining characteristics and major films; a chronology; key debates surrounding the filmmaker, movement or genre; and pivotal scenes, focusing on narrative structure, camera work and production quality.

Film Noir
Justus Nieland and Jennifer Fay

Documentary
Dave Saunders

Romantic Comedy
Claire Mortimer

Westerns
John White

Fantasy
Jacqueline Furby and Claire Hines

Crime
Sarah Casey Benyahia

Science Fiction
Mark Bould

Bollywood
A Guidebook to Popular Hindi Cinema, 2nd Edition
Tejaswini Ganti

European Art Cinema
John White

Hollywood Musicals
Steven Cohan

Gothic Cinema
Xavier Aldana Reyes

For more information, visit: https://www.routledge.com/Routledge-Film-Guidebooks/book-series/SE0653

GOTHIC CINEMA

XAVIER ALDANA REYES

LONDON AND NEW YORK

First published 2020
by Routledge
2 Park Square, Milton Park, Abingdon, Oxon OX14 4RN

and by Routledge
52 Vanderbilt Avenue, New York, NY 10017

Routledge is an imprint of the Taylor & Francis Group, an informa business

© 2020 Xavier Aldana Reyes

The right of Xavier Aldana Reyes to be identified as author of this work has been asserted by him in accordance with sections 77 and 78 of the Copyright, Designs and Patents Act 1988.

All rights reserved. No part of this book may be reprinted or reproduced or utilised in any form or by any electronic, mechanical, or other means, now known or hereafter invented, including photocopying and recording, or in any information storage or retrieval system, without permission in writing from the publishers.

Trademark notice: Product or corporate names may be trademarks or registered trademarks, and are used only for identification and explanation without intent to infringe.

British Library Cataloguing-in-Publication Data
A catalogue record for this book is available from the British Library

Library of Congress Cataloging-in-Publication Data
A catalog record has been requested for this book

ISBN: 978-1-138-22755-2 (hbk)
ISBN: 978-1-138-22756-9 (pbk)
ISBN: 978-1-315-39538-8 (ebk)

Typeset in Joanna
by Taylor & Francis Books

This book is dedicated to Chris Barker.
Imzadi

CONTENTS

List of figures — viii
Acknowledgements — xi

Introduction — 1
1 **Transitional origins** — 43
2 **Monstrous shadows** — 72
3 **Franchise Gothic** — 99
4 **The explained supernatural** — 126
5 **Gothic in technicolour** — 154
6 **Exploitation Gothic** — 181
7 **Late dispersions** — 209

Index — 239

FIGURES

I.1 Adaptations of first wave Gothic novels, such as the partially animated *Otrantský zámek* (*Castle of Otranto*, 1977), have been scarce.   3

I.2 The retrojected Gothic aesthetic of *Crimson Peak* (2015) is perfectly compatible with the visceral thrills normally associated with horror.   11

I.3 Supernatural elements combine with a period setting and a dark aesthetic to denote the Gothic in *Viy* (*Spirit of Evil*, 1967).   22

1.1 The setting of *La Légende du fantôme* (*The Black Pearl*, 1908) is suggestive of archaism and superstitious magic, key elements of the early Gothic film.   47

1.2 The tricks, set and formulae of a film like *La Fée Carabosse, ou Le Poignard fatal* (*The Witch*, 1906) evince the intermedia origins of Gothic cinema.   54

1.3 *Frankenstein* (1910) is the first cinematic adaptation of Mary Shelley's classic and one of many transitional narrative films of the period. 59

2.1 Double exposure was used in *Der Student von Prag* (*The Student of Prague*, 1913) to give the illusion that Balduin (Wegener) is playing a game of cards against his doppelgänger. 76

2.2 Gothic cinema began to frame monsters as dangerous and inextricable from the mise-en-scène in films like *Nosferatu, eine Symphonie des Grauens* (*Nosferatu*, 1922). 85

2.3 Expressionism's dramatic interplay between light and darkness is evident in this still from *Dos monjes* (*Two Monks*, 1934), which depicts a (hallucinated) masked monk. 91

3.1 Grandiose and antiquated sets were a key component of early Universal melodramas like *The Phantom of the Opera* (1925). 103

3.2 The cliff-perched medieval castle, with its signature ruined entrance, became as iconic as Bela Lugosi's interpretation of the count in *Dracula* (1931). 108

3.3 Boris Karloff reprised his iconic 'monster' role for the second and last time in *Son of Frankenstein* (1939), an example of Gothic franchising. 111

4.1 In *The Bat* (1926), the trappings of the Gothic castle travelled virtually unchanged into the structures of the mysterious old dark house. 133

4.2 Portraits establish female lineages and act as forewarnings in Female Gothics like *Gaslight* (1944). 143

5.1 The colourful and sensational opening credits for *Dracula* (1958) were a veritable statement of aims for Hammer's brand of Gothic cinema. 155

5.2 The tortuous mindscapes of Poe's characters found cinematic equivalents in the set design and vivid colours of *House of Usher* (1960). 171
6.1 The incipient eroticism characteristic of the continental Gothic is manifest in *I vampiri* (*The Vampires*, 1957), Italy's first sound horror film. 187
6.2 The knights Templar in *La noche del terror ciego* (*Tombs of the Blind Dead*, 1972) stage the Gothic confrontation between the liberal present and ossified moral attitudes. 195
7.1 In *La chiesa* (*The Church*, 1989), a cross made out of murdered heretics symbolises religion-fuelled cruelty. 213
7.2 The vengeful ghost, a central figure in *Kaidan* (2007), continues to be one of the most enduring and transnational monsters associated with the Gothic. 223
7.3 The light-hearted pastiche of animated films like *Frankenweenie* (2012) illustrates the Gothic's postmodern evolution. 228

ACKNOWLEDGEMENTS

I would like to thank the British Academy and the Leverhulme Trust for their generous support of this book, which took the shape of a British Academy Small Grant (2018–20) to cover some vital research trips to the Unites States. I really appreciate the faith they put in me and in this project.

I am very grateful for the expertise and assistance of Rosemary Hanes and her team at the Library of Congress's Moving Image Section and of Andrea Battiste, Rachel Bernstein, Marisa Duron, Christina Ha, Louise Hilton, Jeffrey S. Miller, Amber Sykes, Faye Thompson, Kevin Wilkerson and Wyneisha Williams at the Academy of Motion Picture Arts and Sciences at the Margaret Herrick Library. My thanks, too, to everyone who helped me with the grant application, from my mentor Dale Townshend to the RKE team at Manchester Metropolitan University, especially Becky Hewlett and Germaine Loader.

I would also like to thank Routledge for their effusive response to, and investment in, *Gothic Cinema*. Natalie Foster and Jennifer Vennall, in particular, were very helpful during the early and late stages of the project, and I am really appreciative of the fact that they allowed me to develop this book exactly as I imagined it. I am indebted to the three anonymous reviewers for their comments and advice on the early book proposal.

I have had the good luck of road-testing some of my ideas at a number of talks and conferences over the last few years. For their encouragement and feedback, I would like to thank the organisers of the Gothic film season at The Dukes (Lancaster, 2014), the 'Temporal Discombobulations: Time and the Experience of the Gothic' conference (University of Surrey, 2016), the second 'Gothic Feminism' conference (University of Kent, 2017), the 'Monsters Film Festival' (University of Reading, 2017) and the fourteenth International Gothic Association conference (Lewis University, 2019), especially Johnathan Ilott, Karen Graham, Evan Gledhill, Frances Kamm and Jamil Mustafa.

Halfway through the writing of this book, I suffered a transient ischemic attack that affected feeling and movement on the left side of my body. At one point, I was completely unable to type with my left hand and thought I would never finish this book or ever write for publication again. To say that 2017 was a challenging year would be an understatement, but I managed to pull through thanks to my partner, family, friends and colleagues, as well as to an incredible group of physiotherapists and fellow patients. Collectively, and perhaps Gothically, they 'brought me back' from the dark side, and for this I will never be able to thank them enough.

Although I only started writing what would become *Gothic Cinema* in 2016, its gestation period goes much further back. In fact, I think this is the book I have always wanted to write but only recently found the courage to tackle. Two moments were key in sparking the creative fuse. The first of these was an invitation I received to give a paper at the British Film Institute's 'Gothic: The Dark Heart of Film' season in 2013, an event I thoroughly enjoyed and which made the cinematic Gothic visible in a remarkable way. When the organisers asked me if I had a book on the subject they could promote, it suddenly hit me that I probably could and definitely should. The second wake-up call came while co-delivering the 'Introduction to Gothic Cinema' course at

Cornerhouse (now HOME) in the autumn of 2014. The experience was transformative and the excitement of the attendees truly infectious. Once more, I had to reply in the negative when people asked me if there was something I had written on the topic they could read and, once more, I thought to myself that there was no good reason for this. My thanks, then, to Rhidian Davis at the BFI, Rachel Hayward at HOME and to my colleague and co-teacher Linnie Blake. As anyone who works in academia knows, sector-specific pressures can sometimes make finding the time to research and write a real challenge, and there is a vast difference between the projects one would like to work on and the projects one should prioritise. I am delighted that, despite various hurdles, I managed to make *Gothic Cinema* happen. Regardless of its shelf life, this book will always have a special place in my heart.

Finally, I would like to thank my students, especially those who took the 'Screening the Gothic', 'Gothic and Modernity', 'Twentieth-Century Gothic' and 'Post-Millennial Gothic' MA units and the third-year specialist 'Modern Gothic' BA unit between 2013 and 2019 at Manchester Metropolitan University. Whether consciously or not, their probing questions about the Gothic and its limits helped shape my thinking around the subject. I am also very grateful for the Gothicists at the Manchester Centre for Gothic Studies for continuing important conversations outside the classroom. I am very lucky to work with such a great community of supportive, passionate and rigorous thinkers.

INTRODUCTION

From August 2013 to January 2014, the British Film Institute, Britain's most prestigious organisation in the promotion and preservation of film, ran a very widely publicised season entitled 'Gothic: The Dark Heart of Film'. Its scale was vast: 150 films were played in around 1,000 screenings throughout the UK and the season became the longest yet in BFI Southbank history. 'Gothic' also included talks from invited guests, specialist lectures and workshops, new DVD releases, an educational programme, an issue of the affiliated magazine *Sight and Sound* containing a special feature on Gothic cinema and even an accompanying compendium (Bell 2013), the first to transnationally encompass the history of the Gothic on screen beyond specific periods. The season was very successful and received coverage in major newspapers and tabloids like *The Guardian*, *Evening Standard* and *Metro*, and was also the subject of an article by the BBC.[1] It seemed that, after many years of existing on the cultural periphery as a term used mostly by scholars and architects, the Gothic had finally become a cinematic force to be reckoned with. Gothic cinema's resurgence did not end there, however, for the British Library, another mainstay of British culture, also launched a massive exhibition, 'Terror and Wonder: The Gothic Imagination', in

October of 2014 that lasted until January 2015. Like the accompanying book of the same title (Townshend 2014), its exhibits centred on literature but also included films, a decision that demonstrates their value to contemporary perceptions of the Gothic.

For all the wealth of interest these events generated, the term 'Gothic' remained somewhat vague in its application to cinema. Possible thematic clusters such as 'monsters', 'black magic', 'hauntings' and 'tainted love relationships' were identified by the BFI exhibition, but an overall definition proved elusive. The foreword to the *Gothic* companion assumed a species of transliteration from page to screen when it argued that 'Gothic film … propelled a long-marginalised and sometimes subversive form of literature from the past into the wider cultural bloodstream, and in the process turned it into myth' (Frayling 2013: 5). This idea would be attractive were it not for the fact that only a handful of novels in the Gothic canon – notably, what Kamilla Elliott calls the 'triptych' (2007: 223) made up by Mary Shelley's *Frankenstein* (1818), Bram Stoker's *Dracula* (1897) and Robert Louis Stevenson's *Strange Case of Dr Jekyll and Mr Hyde* (1886) – have gained mythical status and that none of them were published before 1818, only two years before the surge of interest in the Gothic in the late eighteenth and early nineteenth century began to fade.[2] The dearth of successful film adaptations of the works of Horace Walpole, Ann Radcliffe, Clara Reeve, William Beckford, Matthew Lewis and Charles Maturin, all of them key figures of the literary Gothic tradition, makes a direct equivalence tricky.[3] As I argue in this book, new film techniques, projection technologies and audience needs have all played a much more defining role in the development of Gothic cinema, from early ghostly experimentations with optical illusions to the erotic repurposing of certain figures in the late 1960s and early 1970s. Rhidian Davis's proposition that Gothic cinema 'was a host of half-breed human-supernatural creatures and a visceral desire for terror that came to life on film, not the torturous prose of the gothic novel, the corpus of which was ransacked for its vital organs' (2013: 24) hints at a more apparently intuitive understanding of Gothic cinema that foregrounds the presence of monsters and specific sensations.[4] Yet both are stalwarts of the horror film more widely. Gothic cinema is normally defined as the result of comparative analogies, adaptation or intertextuality and, while such approaches are not, in themselves, mistaken in either establishing or debunking the weight of a literary lineage or the predominance of a number of associated characters and responses, their assumptions reveal just how loose the aesthetic and cultural parameters of Gothic cinema still are. A number of questions arise: is the iconography of the Gothic film equivalent to that of the horror genre? Are the literary origins of the Gothic what solidified its aesthetics? And, in any case, what exactly do we mean when we talk about 'Gothic cinema'?

Full-length studies of Gothic cinema were late to appear and have remained few and far between.[5] Although distinct pre-1970s instances do exist, such as a *Sight and Sound* tribute article in honour of director James Whale referring to his horror films as 'cartoonishly "Gothick"'

Figure I.1 Adaptations of first wave Gothic novels, such as the partially animated *Otrantský zámek* (*Castle of Otranto*, 1977), have been scarce.

(Edwards 1957: 96), it would not be until after Hammer's success with its period horrors that the term would gain scholarly currency.[6] In his *A Heritage of Horror* (1973), published one year before the last films in the *Frankenstein* and *Dracula* franchises were released, David Pirie named the studio's significant output 'the English Gothic cinema'.[7] Surprisingly thorough for the time, Pirie's study attempted to locate the coordinates of Gothic film in the literary tradition and its British origins; Dracula and Frankenstein were mentioned alongside other 'equally important Gothic prototypes from earlier writers' (1973: 9). In the book, as elsewhere, Gothic acts as a qualifier that gives a specific shape to the nightmares of horror cinema, albeit from nationally significant quarters.[8] Drawing on the work of Mario Praz in his influential *The Romantic Agony* (1930, trans. 1933) and on Devendra P. Varma's *The Gothic Flame* (1957), Pirie connected Hammer and its filmic predecessors to four authors: Walpole, Radcliffe, Lewis and Maturin. He proposed that early Gothic novels such as *The Mysteries of Udolpho* (1794), *The Monk* (1796), *The Italian* (1797) and *Melmoth the Wanderer* (1820) were responsible for the seminal stereotype of the Gothic 'Fatal Man' (Pirie 1973: 17). Crucial to Pirie's argument was not just that Hammer's horror films brought back and reified certain landscapes and characters associated with the Gothic and already overfamiliar by the nineteenth century, but that their appeal could be read as a rediscovery of the Romantic experience.[9] It is clear that, in his work, the Gothic novel was a marker of origins for source material and motifs. And yet, as Pirie himself conceded, the vast majority of Gothic horror films made by Hammer did not derive from first wave Gothic fiction (1973: 166).

Later studies of Gothic cinema have tended to follow in Pirie's footsteps. Monographs have focused on specific national histories, Britain in particular, or on phases of Gothic filmmaking, such as the Female Gothics of the 1940s (Hanson 2007). Barry Forshaw, in his *British Gothic Cinema* (2013), has also positioned Hammer as a key player for the mode and seen in the transgressions of modern Gothic films a circularity that ties them to the literary tradition. Forshaw's book also conflates, like other works have done before, Gothic with horror so that a melodrama/thriller like *Peeping Tom* (1960), set in contemporary times and about a traumatised serial killer obsessed with recording dying women, is studied alongside Hammer's period horrors. The same is true of the work of Jonathan Rigby, whose brilliant encyclopaedic surveys – *English Gothic: A Century of Horror Cinema* (2000), revised and republished in 2015; *American Gothic: Sixty Years of Horror Cinema* (2007), revised and republished in 2017; and *Euro Gothic: Classics of Continental Horror Cinema* (2016) – conglomerate under the Gothic label all manner of classical horror films.[10] This boundary remains just as porous in the aforementioned *Gothic: The Dark Heart of Film*. Thanks to its layout, which explores Gothic themes ('black magic', 'spectres of the past', 'mad science'), monsters ('the vampire', 'the werewolf', 'the living dead') and settings ('the architecture of cinema', 'haunted landscapes'), the book manages to indirectly put forward a number of thematic identifiers and tropes. Precisely how Gothic cinema differs from horror, however, is never addressed. Even more nebulous is Lisa Hopkins's suggestion in *Screening the Gothic* that 'the classic genre marker of the Gothic in film is a doubleness' that manifests at the level of narrative polarities (good and evil, innocence and power, youth and age) and 'the blurring of previously secure [ones]' (2005: xi–xii). While the double, especially the shadow self, has been crucial to the history of the Gothic on screen in countries like Germany, interpreting it as a main Gothic symptom is inaccurate (polarities and dualities appear in all manner of films) and does not help resolve the existing generic impasse.

This book provides a history of the manifestations of the Gothic on screen that acknowledges that Gothic cinema has been part of a wider film industry with its own set of financial pressures and priorities. I do not mean to de-politicise or ignore the national specificities of Gothic cinema, or to suggest that its most well-known examples might not operate psychologically in interesting ways, but rather to show that the many shapes Gothic cinema has assumed throughout its history, from the 'trick film' to the sexploitation flick and the postmodern pastiche, are primarily coloured by the implementation of new shooting techniques, shifting audience tastes and the prospect of previously untapped markets. This entails a reverse reading of the Gothic which does not seek to define it through its alleged cultural purpose, but rather takes aesthetic and thematic cues as the starting point. Before I propose a rethinking of Gothic cinema, however, it is crucial that I consider generic misconceptions, since my second aim is to begin to delimit, and thus to outline, the coordinates of Gothic cinema. Critics agree on the difficulty involved in diagnosing what is, like its literary counterpart, 'a form that has been generically mobile, repeatedly hybridising and mutating' (Conrich 1998: 76).[11] Yet the Gothic's pliability in scholarly forums, where it has become an artistic category bringing together all forms of non-realist dark cinema, including certain strands of science fiction and fantasy, is often at odds with the popular understanding of that term. In my view, Gothic cinema is marked by aesthetics, and can thus manifest across genres. The Gothic's interstitiality and indeterminacy stems, primarily, from its complex relationship with horror cinema. For this reason, it is beneficial to first disentangle the two terms and demarcate their areas of connection and divergence.

GOTHIC VS. HORROR

The ambiguity between the Gothic and horror has its roots in older theorisations of enjoyable (fictional) thrills and especially in the differentiation between 'terror' and 'horror'. For all that fearful pleasure had previously been explored by Edmund Burke, writing in 1757, and Anna Laetitia Aikin, in 1773, terror and horror were used indistinctively in early Gothic works, both literary and critical. As Dale Townshend shows (2016: 36–37), the different emotions assigned to these terms began to be teased out by James Beattie and Nathan Drake towards the end of the eighteenth century (1783 and 1798, respectively) and were further developed by Radcliffe in her posthumously published 'On the Supernatural in Poetry' (1826). This short essay defined terror as a feeling that 'expands the soul, and awakens the faculties to a high degree of life' and horror as one that 'contracts, freezes and nearly annihilates them' and is accompanied by 'uncertainty and obscurity ... respecting the dreaded evil' (Radcliffe 2000: 168). Unsurprisingly, terror is connected to the sublime when employed by canonical figures such as William Shakespeare and John Milton. Admittedly, Radcliffe's theorisation is brief – her interest lies in how the supernatural functions, rather than in the implications of the horror/terror dichotomy – so it remains necessarily underdeveloped (how exactly does horror 'freeze' our faculties, and why are its dreaded evils more ambivalent than those of terror?) and contradictory (ambiguity and obscurity seem to more naturally belong in the realm of awe-inducing terror than in paralysing horror). Be that as it may, Radcliffe's binary reading of the effects evoked by the supernatural in fiction has travelled into the contemporary perception that the Gothic cannot be premised on strong emotions or direct visual or imaginative attack.[12]

The collapse of Gothic into horror, or vice versa, is understandable: both the horror genre and Gothic aesthetics are invested in darkness and in negative affect. Generally speaking, the Gothic novel can also be seen as the first manifestation of horror literature as we know it today, as a form that harnessed horrific motifs and crystallised them into fearful, but crucially also suspenseful, entertainment.[13] In his pathopening study *The Literature of Terror* (1980), David Punter dedicated a whole chapter – appropriately entitled 'Gothic in the Horror Film' – to the phenomenon of onscreen Gothic in which he already pointed to the areas of generic slippage and spillage between the Gothic and horror. Although his examples are almost exclusively horror films, Punter was careful to signal that readers should not 'assume that all horrifying films are Gothic; but at the same time it is true that the fundamentally formulaic model which is conventionally known as "the horror film" has indeed many Gothic aspects' (1980: 346). Two of these are the dependence on Gothic literary sources and the interest in ideas of the monstrous. Even more fundamental, however, is

Punter's conclusion that 'horror film has substantially, and to a rather surprising extent, continued in the Gothic tradition of providing an image-language in which to examine social and psychological fears' (371). Both the Gothic and horror have been thought to explore social and cultural anxieties (Clemens 1999; Bruhm 2002; Blake 2008), sometimes openly but often as negotiations of the repressed – as a return of the repressed, in fact (Wood 1978, 1979; Twitchell 1985) – and its monsters as manifestations of the 'id' (Jones 1999).[14] Since the Gothic is also theoretically aligned with the uncanny (Palmer 2012; van Elferen 2012), a Freudian notion that can be applied to individual feelings irrespective of genre, the Gothic and horror remain strange, associative bedfellows.

According to the popular dyad, the Gothic is subtle and suggestive; it hints at occluded or only partially visible terrors, thus offering half-glimpses of bloodcurdling images which, because they are seldom fully shown or described, allow our imagination to run wild and fill in the gaps. The Gothic is haunting and favours mood over grisly spectacle; it is interested in recurring motifs and in setting up atmospheres of gloom and unease that may also play with shadows to create a pervasive sense of threat. It is also highly psychological and preoccupied with hallucinations, vivid dreamscapes (often nightmares) and other provinces of the warped mind. Horror, by contrast, is seen as heavily graphic and explicit: it confronts viewers with terrifying images and cinematic 'numbers'.[15] Gore (especially of the gratuitous type) and violence are its tools, which in fact makes horror more oppositional or niche as a cinematic form (it is not for everyone and harder to watch) and even dangerous or morally bankrupt, potentially of interest only to sadists or those with a strong stomach. For example, the film *The Haunting* (1963) is unmistakably Gothic, as its effects are built around an elusive sense of menace that manifests through uncanny sounds and a dramatic build-up that feeds on the insecurities of a traumatised individual. *Hostel* (2005), by contrast, is a horror film because many of its scenes portray torture in painstaking detail.

This intuitional separation between the Gothic as subtle and horror as explicit is interesting and, to a certain extent, helpful. Ostensibly, viewers need some method for discriminating between different types of emotional experiences, and the Gothic, with its specific aesthetics derived heavily from grandiose architecture and from ghostly visitations, is naturally perceived as the gentler and more complex of the two. Despite this apparently straightforward logic, the alignment of the cinematic Gothic with the horrifically acceptable or less extreme runs the risk of stigmatising more transgressive films and of denying horror (as it is understood in this taxonomy) its own potential value as more than a collection of gruesome moments. As Peter Hutchings warns, the privileging of the Gothic, until the 1990s very much in need of its own re-evaluation in academic and popular terms, may be having the simultaneous effect of rendering horror nothing more than 'a vulgar, exploitative version of [it]' (1996: 89). It is simply not true that all horror is visceral, and therefore in bad taste, unaccomplished and critically expendable, as studies in the field have shown (Hills 2005; Hanich 2010; Aldana Reyes 2016).[16] Neither is it intuitive to consider all non-visceral horror films Gothic, however much power this may bestow upon the latter. *Alien* (1979), for example, does not rely on particularly visceral numbers to generate its scares and its monster stays out of focus for most of the film, but it is definitely a horror film. Its futuristic setting, ultra-modern and, if anything, dystopian, also seems at odds with the Gothic, unless, of course, the latter is de-anchored from its temporal connections to a barbaric past, haunted castles, monastic ruins and cemeteries. The film can be much more comfortably described as science fiction horror. To refer to *Alien* as a Gothic film on the grounds that it plays like a haunted house story in space entails a rethinking of the Gothic that may stretch the term to the point where it becomes so broad as to lose all sense of specificity.[17] This is especially the case with Gothic readings of texts, a growing practice whereby Gothic concepts and affiliated theoretical notions such as the sublime (Mishra 1994) end up being the 'Gothicising' agent. In other words, it is sometimes our choice of conceptual tools that makes a film Gothic and this process can itself feel inconsequential if analyses do not move beyond the identification of individual and disparate Gothic traits. In fact, as Alexandra Warwick argues, such a process can become 'a critical step that renders Gothic absolutely ubiquitous and simultaneously nullifies it' (2007: 8).

To argue that the Gothic is not graphic is also to privilege a particular Gothic tradition and to ignore its many connections to the stage, especially the violent melodrama and the Grand Guignol.[18] In what already constitutes an attempt to homogenise a self-consciously artificial form (Kilgour 1995: 3–4), the explained supernatural and the ghostly tradition are generally granted more weighting than the explicit works of Lewis, Charlotte Dacre or Maturin.[19] A film like *The Innocents* (1961) would seem to fit this paradigm: the film is orchestrated around startle effects and dread, rather than around gratuitous or confrontational violence. Yet what makes the film Gothic is not its restraint, but its mise-en-scène and period setting, the use of chiaroscuro lighting and its resorting to certain tropes associated with the Gothic (the damsel in distress, the haunted house, madness). The recent *Crimson Peak* (2015) is a pertinent illustration of how Gothic trappings (the crumbling Victorian estate, the candle-wielding heroine, the proliferation of spectres) do not preclude a film from also being punctuated by bloody incidents. In fact, one of *Crimson Peak*'s distinguishing features is its clay-red ghosts, halfway between the ethereal and the gory, and the aggressive nature of scenes like the face-stabbing of Thomas (Tom Hiddleston).[20] This is not a novelty or a contemporary affectation, a consequence of more blood-thirsty audiences and directors, but manifests even in those late eighteenth-century texts sometimes taken to be the epitome of a subtle form of the Gothic. To illustrate this point, *The Castle of Otranto* opens with a young man squashed to death by a gigantic helmet and one of Emily St. Aubert's discoveries in *The Mysteries of Udolpho* includes a dead man 'crimsoned with human blood' whose 'features, deformed by death, were ghastly and horrible' (Radcliffe 2008: 348).[21] What makes *Crimson Peak* Gothic is, once again, its setting, characters and motifs; the violence is ancillary and simply contributes to the film's visceral feel. As I show in Chapters 5 and 6, the Gothic is indeed very compatible with blood, violence and eroticism.

Unlike the Gothic, horror is recognised as a major genre both in academia, where it is routinely included in handbooks to film genre (Neale 2000; Langford 2005; Grant 2007; Bordwell and Thompson 2016) alongside science fiction, the musical or the melodrama, and in popular culture, where it is argued to have begun to coalesce as a label in journalism as early as the 1930s (Peirse 2013: 5–9; Rhodes 2018: 93).[22] Horror is also found as a category in (film) retailers like Amazon or streaming services like Netflix, another indication that its existence extends beyond the intellectual and into the practical: audiences recognise and identify horror films as a distinct type of film experience. As I use the term, horror is a genre (self-)defined by the primary effect it seeks to have on its viewers and thus is not bound to a certain type of landscape, setting or character.[23] Matters are slightly more complicated when it comes to the Gothic, which often seeks to generate fear but is not defined solely, or primarily, by this. A film like *Rebecca* (1940), now understood to be a part of the Female Gothic cycle of films popular in

Figure I.2 The retrojected Gothic aesthetic of *Crimson Peak* (2015) is perfectly compatible with the visceral thrills normally associated with horror.

Hollywood during the 1940s (covered in Chapter 4), is ultimately governed by the elicitation of suspense. In it, the Gothic manifests largely at the level of space (Manderley as Gothic locale) and of the narrative and characters (Rebecca is never seen, but her presence haunts every corner of the mansion). The Gothic can, and does, work independently of horrific affect, but it cannot be completely disentangled from it either. This is because, although horror as a narrative element precedes the Gothic novel, being a significant component of, for example, the revenge tragedy, it crystallised as a pleasurable fictional pastime during the period that saw the consolidation of the Gothic novel and its specific chronotopic markers.

For this reason, 'Gothic' is normally found used as an adjective that inflects horror, as a subgenre. Gothic cinema defines films at the level of aesthetics and mise-en-scène, yet its specificity, beyond the referential images and situations evoked by the term 'Gothic' in literature and architecture, is less apparent. An illustration of this dynamic appears in Mark A. Vieira's survey of the horror film up to 1968, which identifies four eras (the Gothic, the psychic, the atomic and the cosmic) and where the Gothic is used to refer to 'films whose horror springs from the folklore of Central Europe' (2003: 7). A later section, entitled 'The Gothic Moderne', explores Universal's horror franchises, but does not elucidate on the terminology. The term 'Gothic' seems to speak for itself to the point of not needing to be introduced: it presumably evokes all the monsters and situations associated with early horror, such as vampires, the 'living dead', werewolves and mummies, and/or derelict castles, mad scientist laboratories, full moons and Egyptian tombs.[24] Since the two main films made by Universal Studios, *Dracula* (1931) and *Frankenstein* (1931), have their origins in stage adaptations of Gothic classics, a term that was used to refer to a certain type of literature of fear in the 1920s (Birkhead 1921; Railo 1927) and 1930s (Tompkins 1932; Summers 1938), these early films are understood as Gothic by proxy. Adaptations are crucial to any discussion of Gothic cinema because, whereas the 'Gothic' label can be ambiguous, adaptations of well-known Gothic texts present themselves as de facto Gothic, regardless of their aesthetic treatment. At the same time, Gothic cinema is palimpsestic beyond direct allusion, often stitched together from the visual remnants of previous films. If we are to move past the current theoretical dead end, Gothic cinema needs to be understood not just as the result of intertextuality but also as a mode that, while moveable, is determined by its temporality and aesthetics.

GOTHIC CINEMA AS AESTHETIC MODE

In a piece where he recasts Northrop Frye's thoughts on romance, Fredric Jameson suggests that a mode is a 'particular type of literary discourse ... [that] persists as a temptation and a mode of expression across a whole range of historical periods' (1975: 138). Conceiving of the Gothic as a mode separable from its original context makes it easier to understand its regenerative spirit, how it may be 'always already a revival of something else' (Spooner 2006: 10), as well as how it might continue to offer a counternarrative to realism beyond its entrenched conception as the dark side of the Enlightenment. In other words, current function can be removed from a putatively original one. Alastair Fowler suggests as much when he writes that there is a natural tendency for 'genres' to fragment into 'modes' (and even further into 'abstract formulations') (1971: 214). Fowler actually uses the Gothic to illustrate this proposition, arguing that the 'gothic novel or romance', exemplified by Reeve's *The Old English Baron* (1788), 'yielded a Gothic mode that outlasted it and was applied to forms as diverse as the maritime adventure ... the psychological novel ... the short story and the detective story, not to mention various scientific genres' (214). According to this view, the eighteenth-century Gothic, a highly 'unstable genre' (Hogle 2002: 1) and hybrid, eventually transcended its circumstantial limitations (the Enlightenment, the sedimentation of middle-class taste, terrorist fears about Europe) and became a literary mode of Victorian literature. This phase is not spelled out by Fowler, but the Gothic could be seen to have then further fragmented into abstract formulations that may be more readily understood as independent themes or motifs, such as female captivity, haunted buildings or distorted psychologies.

It has been claimed that the term 'mode' entails a liberation from any prescriptive set of 'themes, motifs and figures' (Hollinger 2014: 140). Yet the Gothic mode is very clearly marked by aesthetics, motifs and figures, more so than by affect or intended emotional outcomes. Is this not a contradiction in terms? Cuddon's *Dictionary of Literary Terms and Literary Theory* hesitantly refers to a mode 'as approximately synonymous with kind and form' and claims that it is 'associated with method, manner and style' (2013: 441), a meaning that resonates with those studies of the Gothic that have centred on imagery and artistic allegiances (Grunenberg 1997; Williams 2007; Gavin 2008). This gains significance when one considers that the Gothic novel was largely shaped and defined by its use of architecture and spaces – the Gothic was/is visual and identifiable at the level of surface – and that the apparently 'decorative effect' (Napier 1987: 29) of its buildings became imbricated in debates about identity, history and nationality (Townshend 2019). There is some critical consensus that an interpretation of the Gothic that does justice to the complexity of its appearance and that identifies it as deliberately formulaic is positive. Elaborating on the work of Robert Miles, Michael Gamer has referred to the Gothic as a 'shifting "aesthetic"' able 'to transplant itself *across* forms and media' (2000: 4); Fred Botting has further refined this notion by showing how it constitutes a 'negative aesthetics', its texts characterised by 'an absence of the light associated with sense, security and knowledge' (2013: 1–2); and Catherine Spooner has remarked on how a Gothic 'look' is increasingly targeted in the marketing of some subcultural products (2014: 184). If we are to move beyond the reduction of Gothic cinema to horror and avoid the intertextual pit that renders Gothic cinema redundant in its derivation, a new understanding of the mode as a transhistorical aesthetic becomes imperative.

Thus far the Gothic has been recuperated differently. It has been re-theorised as a type of artistic expression that continues to perform a cultural function, a specifically subversive or radical one. Undoubtedly, the reason for this alternative meaning of the term 'mode' is connected to the need to find an explanation for its steady commercial success as well as to its establishment as a high form of popular art that is ideologically significant. For Sue Chaplin, the Gothic is a mode because it 'responds in certain diverse yet recognisable ways to the conflicts and anxieties of its historical moment' (2011: 4). For her, what defines the mode is 'its capacity to represent individual and societal traumas' so that

> even works that lack an overt element of supernaturalism or monstrosity thus deserve the designation 'Gothic' by virtue of their narration of trauma through instances of psychological 'hauntings', or the depiction of extreme mental states productive of a certain kind of existential 'monstrosity.' (4–5)

Such a focus is not tantamount to suggesting that the Gothic is inherently political, rather that it is less concerned with 'particular conventions of content and/or style' (4) than it is with exploring the dark side of culture and human psychology. Whilst this understanding of the Gothic mode looks appealing, it lacks aesthetic precision. Let me, by illuminating on this question, propose how the Gothic may be usefully recast as an aesthetic mode for the purposes of tracing its cinematic history.

Monstrosity and psychological disturbance cannot, in and of themselves, be markers of the Gothic mode; they are simply not specific enough and they manifest in other genres. For example, monsters appear in epic fantasy and psychological hauntings have long been the source of legends and ballads.[25] More importantly, a question that quickly emerges is what separates the Gothic from even broader genre categories, such as the fantastic. After all, fantasy has also been described as a series of 'structural features underlying various works in different periods of time' (Jackson 1981: 7) that are inherently subversive at the artistic (if not always social) level. Chaplin is careful to point out that the supernatural is a requirement for the Gothic, but a similar point was made by Tzvetan Todorov (1975: 41–57) in his subdivision of the fantastic into various categories, some of which (the uncanny and the fantastic-uncanny) do not entail a break with the laws of reason and of reality as the reader understands them. The Gothic must therefore avoid the unproductive pitting together of different genres and modes of which theorisations of the supernatural and the fantastic have been susceptible. These loose terms work best as a means to think through non-mimetic genres and/or modes and their relation to reality, but the Gothic is not always supernatural or fantastic and it most definitely is not synonymous with high fantasy (the marvellous, in the Todorovian sense), despite initially borrowing elements from the chivalric romance. Palpably, the shift towards the Gothic in such instances has been motivated both by its cultural momentum, especially the establishment in academia of Gothic Studies throughout the 1990s and 2000s, and the fact that the term, through its architectural and historical connotations with national identity, has more intellectual cachet than horror.[26]

Furthermore, Gothic cinema is not just a horror subgenre because it can, and often does, manifest in other genres like melodrama or comedy (not necessarily just in parodies) and because, in cases like that of Gothic romance, the term 'Gothic' inflects meaning at a superficial level. It follows that the Gothic is an aesthetic mode: the predominant element for viewers, its main recognisable traits, remain visual or iconographic and, by association, thematic. A castle or mansion on a promontory on a stormy night or a dark dungeon – for example, in the posters for William Castle's *House on Haunted Hill* (1959) or for Roger Corman's *The Pit and the Pendulum* (1961) – can be connotative enough.[27] The Gothic may, of course, manifest interstitially, as disenfranchised motifs like that of the captive woman in thrillers like *Gone Girl* (2014) or *The Girl with the Dragon Tattoo* (2011), but this will not ultimately Gothicise a film at the level of aesthetics or setting. Similarly, hybrid films exist, like those that have fallen under the 'Gothic science fiction' rubric (Wasson and Alder 2011;

MacArthur 2015), but again, in these cases the Gothic is likely to work less as a genre marker than as an aesthetic or thematic determiner circumscribing a type of science fiction. This is why 'Gothic' becomes the qualifier, rather than the qualified.

The Gothic's intended narrative effects are not necessarily contiguous or comparable to social or cultural meaning. A monster, like that of Frankenstein, or a situation, like the incarceration of a defenceless heroine, might horrify us despite the fact that they explore the injustices of 'othering' and social exclusion or the wrongs of patriarchy. Although the Gothic's images and characters are not monolithic or employed homogeneously in every film, they tend to evoke certain ideas and elicit specific emotions. This is not tantamount to suggesting that every iteration of a vampire works according to the same patterns or indeed that the presence of that monster is what ultimately defines a Gothic film. Instead, there are three levels to the Gothic as an aesthetic mode: the surface level, that is, a film's use of a recognisable set of characters, settings, associated motifs and themes; the affective, or the consequences these images have on viewers – generally a set of negative emotional states we could usefully group as 'fear' and 'suspense'; and finally, the cultural, or the type of work carried out by a particular implementation, combination or subversion of the Gothic's main aesthetic elements. My contention is that the mode is identified primarily by its look, not by our reading of its social work as filtered through given national or psychological lenses, a process which is nevertheless manifest and of relevance.[28] The images, themes and effects that recur in Gothic cinema rarely appear in isolation, and they normally function by accumulation, conjuring up certain atmospheres and pervasive moods.

THE AESTHETICS OF GOTHIC CINEMA

Landscapes and buildings, especially when temporally remote, are arguably the most essential markers of the Gothic. The virtual synonymy between 'Gothic' and 'medieval' during the development of the Gothic romance, as well as the predication of this relationship on a feeling of 'loss' and an 'antiquarian' fascination (Miles 2002: 29), manifested in what Baldick calls 'a fearful sense of inheritance in time' (2009: xix). The past is an unfair, brutal place, one that is defined by threat and the possibility of return: of secrets, of curses, of the supposedly dead and of the actually dead (spectres). Pervading danger, occult or otherwise, is one of the elements that separates the Gothic film from the period drama. Ruins abound, as do mysterious subterranean passages, abandoned or derelict abbeys, imposing castles with many a locked door, monasteries full of hidden passages (these are as important as their Gothic style), inquisitorial dungeons (and chthonic chambers, more generally), dangerous mountainscapes and moors and, in the American Gothic, the wilderness of the forest.[29] In modern Gothic films, from *The Black Sleep* (1956) and *Mr. Sardonicus* (1961) to *The Legend of Hell House* (1973) and *The Woman in Black* (2012), the (Victorian) haunted house supersedes some of the older settings, especially as the nineteenth and early twentieth centuries become the modern equivalents of what medieval times represented to Enlightenment Gothic writers – suitably distant, superstitious and barbaric by today's standards (Spooner 2007: 44). Although the Gothic is a Western mode typically associated with Protestantism and Catholicism, it can also be seen to manifest in other countries with different religious beliefs. Japanese films like *Kaidan semushi otoko* (*House of Terrors*, 1965) and *Noroi no yakata: Chi o sû me* (*Lake of Dracula*, 1971) show an obvious debt to Western Gothic films, but others, such as *Tôkaidô Yotsuya kaidan* (*The Ghost of Yotsuya*, 1959), the anthology film *Kaidan* (*Kwaidan*, 1964) and *Onibaba* (1964), retroject the narrative action to their country's feudal past and depict unique folkloric ghosts.[30] Similarly, Kim Newman sees in martial arts and comedy horror films such as *Die bian* (*The Butterfly Murders*, 1979), *Geung si sin sang* (*Mr. Vampire*, 1985) and *Sien nui yau wan* (*A Chinese Ghost Story*, 1987) a distinctly Chinese cycle of Gothic cinema (2011: 52). Their settings (haunted temples and the occasional castle) and monsters (ghosts, revenants) can be analogous to the spaces and characters of the Western Gothic, even when, in cases like the 'jiangshi' (a hopping vampire) and the 'Huli jing' (a fox spirit), they stem from very different mythical traditions.[31]

A strong sense of decay and putrefaction (damp or mould, leaks, collapsing ceilings or stairs) as well as of overwhelming architectonic scope (labyrinthine buildings, wings of mansions kept closed, sombre gardens and forests) are also habitual elements in the cinematography. Gothic places are unknown spaces: characters inherit forgotten estates whose dark past they feel compelled to explore; they are locked in catacombs they escape only to find themselves just as disoriented; they are taken to foreign, savage lands. As regards the weather, the Gothic is much more evidently signalled by the autumn and winter seasons and by meteorological disturbances that may pose a risk to characters, reflect their state of mind or aid villains in their schemes by providing cover or an opportunity to attack. Gothic films tend to be windy and stormy during key dramatic moments, as the game of shadows and sounds encouraged by the pyrotechnics of lightning and thunder help to underscore a sense of danger. Filmmakers may also resort to plumes of concealing fog for suspenseful moods.

Gothic landscapes of any type are further enhanced by a generous helping of darkness. Darkness has negative connotations in a number of cultures and is suggestive of death, cold, occlusion, mystery and uncertainty. A dark castle becomes much scarier and a poorly lit Victorian street can shelter and camouflage its perils more expediently. The dark can also serve to insinuate and tease, when bursts of light halo a threatening and unknown silhouette, or to impair vision. As Dani Cavallaro (2002: 21) notes, Gothic narratives tend to also take place during 'times of transition, from day into night, from summer into winter'.[32] Despite this bias towards liminality, night still reigns supreme: it is the time of nightmares, when our connection with the beyond is at its strongest, when murderers and monsters take advantage of defenceless sleeping heroines, when the world rests and there is no one to come to the rescue. Darkness can permeate the aesthetics of a film to the point where it ends up being the main Gothic element, as in *Dark City* (1998). Similarly, the Gothic struggles to unfold in broad daylight, when people are about and aid is at hand. The dark can act as a filtering lens too. Gothic films may make extensive use of chiaroscuro lighting, bathing their characters in shadows that highlight their emotional disposition or vulnerability. They may also, by the same token, prefer black and white to colour. But Gothic cinema also tends to create tonal tensions between dark and bright colours, as *Dracula* (1958) does by pitting signifiers of purity and innocence (the white gown of the Gothic heroine) against those of evil and corruption (Dracula's black cape). The labyrinthine, excessive prose of the Gothic novel translates into syncopated editing, baroqueness and charged atmospheres.

Structurally, the Gothic film tends to be as torturous, untrustworthy and deceitful as its architectural backgrounds. Eve Kosofsky Sedgwick suggests that 'the difficulty the story has in getting itself told' is the most structurally significant '[o]f all the Gothic conventions dealing with the sudden, mysterious, seemingly arbitrary, but massive inaccessibility of those things that should normally be accessible' (1980: 13). The trapdoors, hinges and hidden chambers of Gothic buildings find their narrative correlates in plots that involve half-told, repressed or duplicitous stories, or else stage the return of repressed and silenced events. These, in turn, may find correspondences at the psychological level in characters who discover aspects about themselves they were not previously aware of, would rather forget or have actively repressed. Flashbacks, either in the form of confessions, as in *The Curse of Frankenstein* (1957) and *Interview with the Vampire* (1994), or of exposition scenes that fill the viewer in on necessary details, as in *La llorona* (*The Crying Woman*, 1960), can constitute considerable parts, even the bulk, of some Gothic films. Identities can be mistaken, with external doubling of characters or dual personalities being key to the action and denouement in *The Woman in White* (1948), *Mary Reilly* (1996) and *Los otros* (*The Others*, 2001). Gothic films may even possess Chinese box structures, like *Rękopis znaleziony w Saragossie* (*The Saragossa Manuscript*, 1965), and contain interconnected stories. The most narratively conventional of Gothic films will involve a journey of discovery, whether personal or familial (ancestral curses, buried murders and experiments, supernatural happenings), that is in consonance with the characters' physical trips: the arrival in an uncannily familiar place or into a regressive and inhospitable community with a buried secret. Renfield's (Dwight Frye) entrance into the count's dilapidated castle in 1931's *Dracula* and the Pastor's (Edmund Fetting) acceptance of an invitation to stay in a remote Lithuanian village in *Lokis: Rękopis profesora Wittembacha* (*Lokis: A Manuscript of Professor Wittembach*, 1970) both anticipate dramatic happenings. In those stories where the villain is the main character, as in *Amanti d'oltretomba* (*Nightmare Castle*, 1965), vengeful visitations from the past (real or counterfeit) set the record straight.

Gothic films, like any other form of narrative entertainment, need a minimum of crisis resolution. If a gloomy landscape, populated by archaic buildings is left empty, no dangers roaming the shadows, there will be little chance for such developments.[33] A source of threat is normally necessary for the Gothic to generate feelings of suspense and dread, even if it may be ultimately explained away as mere superstition or a trick of the mind. Before the development of the aristocratic vampire and the 'living' dead came into being in the 1810s, three main supernatural figures dominated the Gothic novel: the spectre, the devil and the witch/wizard. All had long been a part of popular culture in legends, fairy tales and religion, and in established texts like *Hamlet* (1599–1602), *Macbeth* (1606) and *Paradise Lost* (1667). Aside from their obvious connection to fear and threat, these monsters became entrenched in the Gothic aesthetic precisely because the mode's medieval retrojection allowed for explorations of superstitious belief. Their appearance in canonical texts such as *The Castle of Otranto, The Mysteries of Udolpho* or *The Monk* in the guise of pacts with the devil, occult cults and ghostly visitations cemented them in the Gothic imagination. In fact, as E. J. Clery argues, it is possible to think of the year 1800 as the time of the birth of supernatural fiction; its success 'announc[ing] the end of one particular struggle over the boundaries of fictional representation and the beginning of an era of acceptance' (1995: 2). Naturally, the supernatural had a history before the Gothic, not least in the chivalric romances that influenced the mode, and this is why it is crucial that the one is not collapsed into the other. It is perfectly feasible to think of supernatural films where ghosts, witches/wizards or Faustian pacts predominate but which are nevertheless not

Gothic. *Ghostbusters* (1984), *Ghost* (1990), *Bedazzled* (2000), *Shortcut to Happiness* (2003) and *Bewitched* (2005), to name a few, all utilise these motifs but are normally catalogued as romances, action films or comedies. Yet supernatural beings, when a source of threat and in a period setting, almost automatically denote 'Gothic'. For example, in *Viy* (*Spirit of Evil*, 1967), witchcraft and demonology are rendered Gothic through the mise-en-scène: a lugubrious, candle-lit chapel in medieval Ukraine.[34]

It was with the vampire and, eventually, the undead (first as mummies, then as zombies), the repressed self and the werewolf in the late nineteenth and early twentieth centuries, with their depictions in early German cinema and then Universal Studios' horror films of the 1930s and 1940s, that monsters became strongly linked to the Gothic (see Chapters 2 and 3). Although these materialised after the 'boom' of the Gothic novel in the 1790s and 1800s, they have, in cinema, been the most readily associated with the mode, partly because of the tendency,

Figure I.3 Supernatural elements combine with a period setting and a dark aesthetic to denote the Gothic in *Viy* (*Spirit of Evil*, 1967).

during key periods of horror production, to set films featuring these monsters in the past. Their prevalence as the main Gothic villains in modern times over evil monks or licentious abbesses has meant that we now use them to close the loop in a species of 'hermeneutically circular process' (Howard 1994: 1). This has its disadvantages. As I have argued, monsters have not been the exclusive province of the Gothic literary tradition or of Britain. Thus, while it is useful to read a number of them, such as the vampire or the reanimated corpse, as potential Gothic markers, the mise-en-scène is just as crucial. As supernatural creatures have grown more comforting, even lovable, films have, in turn, switched gears to embrace hybridity, romance and adventure. Surely, the repression model whereby monstrosity becomes a conceptual category through which we channel anxieties regarding 'normality' (Wright 2013) is ripe for unpicking in an age where vampires, read as expressive of repressed queer desire, can be explicitly queer.

The Female Gothic is a subgenre of the Gothic that stands out in its configuration of monstrosity, as the main villain tends to be a man who embodies the oppression of patriarchal systems. These narratives in fact develop an even older archetype, that of Bluebeard, the wife-murderer popularised by Charles Perrault in his 1697 folk tale of the same name.[35] Although the Female Gothic is as tricky to define as the Gothic and just as heterogeneous (Wallace and Smith 2009: 10–11), the type of blueprint that has thrived in cinema, especially during the 1940s cycle of women films, very much derives from a model that replaces the crazed monk or aristocrat with a paternalistic husband figure who will imprison, inhibit and, in some cases, attempt to kill his wife for her inheritance or insurance money. If one considers that property is largely the reason Montoni keeps Emily St. Aubert captive in *The Mysteries of Udolpho* and that money is once again the catalyst for crime in *Crimson Peak*, it is easy to trace a line between the late eighteenth-century Female Gothic of Radcliffe and more recent twenty-first-century interpretations.[36] This is one of the few areas where psychological monstrosity prevails over grotesque physiognomy. Although not every Bluebeard story is a Gothic film, the majority of Female Gothic films follow the examples of heroinism put forward in

Radcliffe and the novels *Jane Eyre* (1847) and *Rebecca* (1938): they feature endangered, initially fragile heroines who must overcome their situations and learn from the mistakes of other victimised women in order to survive the hostilities and attacks of non-supernatural male 'monsters'.

Monstrosity, however inextricable it may have once been from 'abnormal' physiology, also manifested in aberrant or deviant behaviours, for example in the indulgence on vices (Botting 1995: 7). Since a lot of villains in early Gothic novels tend to be tyrannical men, it is tempting to read troubled minds, especially those of the serial killer, as Gothic. Gothic criticism has actually traced the origin of crime fiction and of the psychotic killer to the Gothic (Spooner 2010; Simpson 2000: 26–69), and serial killers continue to feature in compendia to the contemporary Gothic. It is true that, where the setting and visual style is funereal and macabre, as in *À meia-noite levarei sua alma* (*At Midnight I'll Take Your Soul*, 1964), or the nineteenth century, the Gothic may be easily evoked. The latter is the case in Tod Slaughter's period melodramas, especially *Maria Marten, or The Murder in the Red Barn* (1935), *Sweeney Todd: The Demon Barber of Fleet Street* (1936), *The Crimes of Stephen Hawke* (1936) and *Crimes at the Dark House* (1940); in Jack the Ripper dramas like *The Lodger: A Story of the London Fog* (1927), its 1944 remake *The Lodger*, *Hands of the Ripper* (1971) and *From Hell* (2001); and in dark period thrillers like *The Limehouse Golem* (2016). Yet films about robbers and sociopaths like *Bonnie and Clyde* (1967) and *Natural Born Killers* (1994) show no signs of adherence to a Gothic aesthetic, either in their tone, atmospheres or temporality. The collapse of serial killers into Gothic cinema therefore needs to be resisted and qualified. Rather than suggest that all films about mass murderers, as explorations of psychological monstrosity, are Gothic, it is more productive to argue that perturbed mindstates that may include paranoia, obsessions, delusions or madness recur in the Gothic. I would go even further in suggesting that films like *M – Eine Stadt sucht einen Mörder* (*M*, 1931) are more readily understood as thrillers by general audiences. It also would not be correct to term surreal films concerned with repressed desires and sexual or morbid manias, such as *La Coquille et le Clergyman* (*The Seashell and the Clergyman*, 1928) and *Un chien andalou* (*An*

Andalusian Dog, 1929), Gothic. Although their thematic explorations may not be too removed from those of Tim Burton's *Sweeney Todd: The Demon Barber of Fleet Street* (2007), their aesthetic, artistic aspirations and intended effects differ greatly.[37]

To recapitulate, the Gothic is an aesthetic mode that is different from horror because, although both share atmospheric primers (effective lighting, unsettling sound and music, a framing that often aligns the camera with the victim), horror is a genre premised on emotion and not bound by time or setting. The Gothic, on the contrary, is a mode that cannot be reduced to the engendering of fear and which can be neatly fenced in aesthetically. Although medieval fantasies may have been superseded by Victorian and Edwardian ones, a strong sense of claustrophobic encroachment is required for the Gothic to manifest unambiguously. This anachronistic sense of temporality, associated with barbarism, superstition, revenge and tyranny, habitually takes place at the chronological level, through a retrojected narrative set in primitive or less tolerant times. Films like *Black Narcissus* (1947), *The Devils* (1971) and *L'arcano incantatore* (*Arcane Sorcerer*, 1996), set in remote periods and concerned with witchcraft, the occult and excesses that test conventional religious behaviour, can thus be read as Gothic despite their overall lack of explicit horror elements and sequences. As I show in Chapters 3 and 4, films set in modern times can also be Gothic in cases where buildings or spaces act as modern renditions of the two basic chronotopes of the Gothic novel: the medieval castle (later the Victorian/Edwardian mansion or estate) and the secretive abbey.[38] This is most patently the case in the Female Gothic, where ancestral homes become literal and figurative traps for the female heroines or else the backdrop for hauntings. My distinction does not preclude the Gothic from manifesting in horror films. In fact, many of the films studied in this book could indeed be classed as 'Gothic horror'. The reasons for this are that the period Gothic film was, until the 1970s, one of the most popular subgenres of horror cinema and that a great number of classical horror films are adaptations of stories from the Gothic canon. Horror's modernisation in films like *The Exorcist* (1973), where the supernatural surfaces in modern times, eventually extricated the horror genre from its traditional Gothic aesthetic.[39] As I argue in Chapter 7, the postmodern fragmentation of the Gothic has made it evident just how pervasive and adaptable this aesthetic is.

THIS BOOK

Since I am interested in the evolution of the Gothic, *Gothic Cinema* takes a roughly chronological approach that centres on the particular industry changes and market mores that have fashioned specific series or types of Gothic films. My intention is to identify its evolution through what I read as Gothic cinema's most significant transformations, rather than pay particular attention to individual films or masterpieces. Thus, while I devote some space to trendsetters, I privilege cycles and periods of intense activity over auteurs or case studies. I begin by tracing the origins of Gothic cinema to the magic lantern and phantasmagoria shows that eventually travelled into the work of cinema's first 'magicians', especially of Georges Méliès and Segundo de Chomón. Chapter 1, 'Transitional origins', also considers the first narrative films, which took the shape of 'féeries' (or fairy plays) and of quality literary adaptations of Gothic novels, such as *Frankenstein* (1910) or Poe's short stories. It argues that these prestige productions and the general direction of commercial cinema led to Gothic films eventually becoming story-driven. Chapter 2, 'Monstrous shadows', considers the long-lasting legacy of early German cinema, especially its development of supernatural narrative cinema and of shooting techniques that would become staples of the Gothic on screen, such as chiaroscuro lighting and the framing of the monster, in films like *Der Student von Prag* (The Student of Prague, 1913), *Das Cabinet des Dr. Caligari* (The Cabinet of Dr. Caligari, 1920), *Der Golem, wie er in die Welt kam* (The Golem: How He Came into the World, 1920) and *Nosferatu, eine Symphonie des Grauens* (Nosferatu, 1922). It also traces the influence of expressionism on other films from Europe and America. Chapter 3, 'Franchise gothic', turns to the establishment of the horror formula, with a special focus on *Dracula* and *Frankenstein*. I show how decisive these films were in cementing a visual style for horror cinema and its monsters, in transplanting Gothic motifs into present times and in creating a franchise model that would be copied by Mexican, British, Italian and Spanish filmmakers decades later. Chapter 4, 'The explained supernatural', explores the realist aesthetics of the subgenre of the old dark house film, which developed in the 1910s and culminated in *The Bat* (1926) and *The Cat and the Canary* (1927). These mysteries, often female-led, also provided a blueprint for the Female Gothics of the 1940s, where confrontations between heroines and tyrannical men served to question musty notions of gender roles. Concentrating on Hammer's period films and Roger Corman's Poe cycle, chapter 5, 'Gothic in technicolour', explores the gradual application of colour to the Gothic, as well as the connections between its widespread cinematic implementation and other forms of visual stimulation, from gore to eroticism. The chapter also explores the impact of Hammer on the films from rival British studios Amicus and Tigon. Chapter 6, 'Exploitation gothic', traces the ripples caused by Hammer and Corman's successful reinvigorations of Gothic cinema in continental Europe, where first the Italian and then the Spanish cinema industries underwent notable periods of national production. In this chapter, I contend that Gothic cinema's repressed undercurrents were gradually rendered explicit in films that conflated horror with latent desire, violence, nudity and sex. Chapter 7, 'Late dispersions', traces the fragmentation of the Gothic following its decoupling from the horror genre, which largely left behind the former's medieval accoutrements. My main argument is that, since the 1980s, the Gothic has been opened up and mainstreamed. While the Gothic has, architectonically, continued to symbolise barbarism and isolation, especially in regards to outdated beliefs or ideological systems, its images and tropes have more actively blossomed through the figure of the sympathetic monster and in other genres like animated films for children and the superhero action adventure.

Even fragmented, the Gothic continues to create meaning indexically, that is, by virtue of its stock images, and to be tied up with 'fear'. This is not the same as claiming that the Gothic has lost meaning beyond the superficial, beyond its images and affects. Gothic cinema, its characters and settings, meant and mean specific things to specific audiences at specific times (superstition and magic at one point, patriarchal oppression at another, eroticism at yet another) and these have had to adapt to stay relevant. The Gothic aesthetic still negotiates anxieties around power and its abuse, the tension between modern and outmoded structures of thinking and between the normative and the abjected Other. Nevertheless, the taxonomy advanced in this book has the significant advantage of being a lot more precise and of making a distinction between this mode and the horror genre. Through a model that is intuitive and transhistorically aware, readers may best recognise deviations and innovations from existing formulas as well as the introduction of new ones. My understanding of Gothic cinema does not negate the value of intertextuality or of adaptation either, but simultaneously does not impose these as syllogistic indicators of the Gothic. Chiefly, a tighter emphasis on aesthetics proves crucial when attempting to prioritise the purpose of Gothic cinema or its capacity to operate as a mediator of national or personal (artistic) anxieties. The social and cultural value of a mode cannot begin to be articulated unless its boundaries are first delimited, or else its integrity is sacrificed in favour of specific critical agendas.

NOTES ON FILMOGRAPHIES

Where directors used pseudonyms, I have reverted to their actual name for consistency unless the alias recurred throughout their careers or else separated their various acting, directing and scriptwriting personas. Due to spatial constraints, I have only provided the main export titles for films. I have alphabetised films in all languages word-by-word, including determiners.

FILMOGRAPHY

À meia-noite levarei sua alma (*At Midnight I'll Take Your Soul*, José Mojica Marins, 1964, Brazil)

Alien (Ridley Scott, 1979, UK/USA)
Amanti d'oltretomba (*Nightmare Castle*, Mario Caiano, 1965, Italy)
Bedazzled (Harold Ramis, 2000, USA/Germany)
Bewitched (Nora Ephron, 2005, USA)
Black Narcissus (Michael Powell and Emeric Pressburger, 1947, UK)
Blood from the Mummy's Tomb (Seth Holt, 1971, UK)
Bonnie and Clyde (Arthur Penn, 1967, USA)
Crimes at the Dark House (George King, 1940, UK)
Crimson Peak (Guillermo del Toro, 2015, USA/Canada)
Dark City (Alex Proyas, 1998, Australia/USA)
Das Cabinet des Dr. Caligari (*The Cabinet of Dr. Caligari*, Robert Wiene, 1920, Germany)
Der Dibuk (*The Dybbuk*, Michał Waszyński, 1937, Poland)
Der Golem, wie er in die Welt kam (*The Golem: How He Came into the World*, Carl Bose and Paul Wegener, 1920, Germany)
Der Student von Prag (*The Student of Prague*, Paul Wegener and Stellan Rye, 1913, Germany)
Die bian (*The Butterfly Murders*, Hark Tsui, 1979, Hong Kong)
Dracula (Tod Browning, 1931, USA)
Dracula (Terence Fisher, 1958, UK)
Ercole al centro della Terra (*Hercules in the Haunted World*, Mario Bava, 1961, Italy/West Germany)
Frankenstein (J. Searle Dawley, 1910, USA)
Frankenstein (James Whale, 1931, USA)
Freaks (Tod Browning, 1932, USA)
From Hell (The Hughes Brothers, 2001, USA)
Geung si sin sang (*Mr. Vampire*, Ricky Lau, 1985, Hong Kong)
Ghost (Jerry Zucker, 1990, USA)
Ghostbusters (Ivan Reitman, 1984, USA)
Gone Girl (David Fincher, 2014, USA)
Hands of the Ripper (Peter Sasdy, 1971, UK)
Hostel (Eli Roth, 2005, USA/Germany/Czech Republic/Slovakia/Iceland)
House (Ben Rivers, 2007, UK)
House on Haunted Hill (William Castle, 1959, USA)

Interview with the Vampire (Neil Jordan, 1994, USA)
Kaidan (Kwaidan, Masaki Kobayashi, 1964, Japan)
Kaidan semushi otoko (House of Terrors, Hajime Satô, 1965, Japan)
King Kong (Merian C. Cooper and Ernest B. Schoedsack, 1933, USA)
L'arcano incantatore (Arcane Sorcerer, Pupi Avati, 1996, Italy)
La Belle et la Bête (Beauty and the Beast, Jean Cocteau, 1946, France)
La Coquille et le Clergyman (The Seashell and the Clergyman, Germaine Dulac, 1928, France)
La llorona (The Crying Woman, René Cardona, 1960, Mexico)
La momia azteca (The Aztec Mummy, Rafael Portillo, 1957, Mexico)
Le Moine (The Monk, Adonis Kyrou, 1972, France/Italy/West Germany)
Le Moine (The Monk, Dominik Moll, 2011, Spain/France)
Lokis: Rękopis profesora Wittembacha (Lokis: A Manuscript of Professor Wittembach, Janusz Majewski, 1970, Poland)
Los otros (The Others, Alejandro Amenábar, 2001, Spain/USA/France/Italy)
M – Eine Stadt sucht einen Mörder (M, Fritz Lang, 1931, Germany)
Maciste all'inferno (The Witch's Curse, Riccardo Freda, 1962, Italy)
Maciste contro il vampiro (Samson vs. the Vampires, Sergio Corbucci and Giacomo Gentilomo, 1961, Italy)
Maria Marten, or The Murder in the Red Barn (Milton Rosmer, 1935, UK)
Mary Reilly (Stephen Frears, 1996, USA/UK)
Mr. Sardonicus (William Castle, 1961, USA)
Natural Born Killers (Oliver Stone, 1994, USA)
Noroi no yakata: Chi o sû me (Lake of Dracula, Michio Yamamoto, 1971, Japan)
Nosferatu, eine Symphonie des Grauens (Nosferatu, F. W. Murnau, 1922, Germany)
Old Dark House (Ben Rivers, 2003, UK)
Onibaba (Kaneto Shindô, 1964, Japan)
Otrantský zámek (Castle of Otranto, Jan Švankmajer, 1977, Czechoslovakia)
Peeping Tom (Michael Powell, 1960, UK)
Rebecca (Alfred Hitchcock, 1940, USA)
Rękopis znaleziony w Saragossie (The Saragossa Manuscript, Wojciech Has, 1965, Poland)
Shortcut to Happiness (Alec Baldwin, 2003, USA)
Sien nui yau wan (A Chinese Ghost Story, Siu-Tung Ching, 1987, Hong Kong)

Sweeney Todd: The Demon Barber of Fleet Street (George King, 1936, UK)
Sweeney Todd: The Demon Barber of Fleet Street (Tim Burton, 2007, USA/UK)
The Bat (Roland West, 1926, USA)
The Black Sleep (Reginald Le Borg, 1956, USA)
The Cat and the Canary (Paul Leni, 1927, USA)
The Crimes of Stephen Hawke (George King, 1936, UK)
The Curse of Frankenstein (Terence Fisher, 1957, UK)
The Devils (Ken Russell, 1971, UK)
The Exorcist (William Friedkin, 1973, USA)
The Girl with the Dragon Tattoo (David Fincher, 2011, USA/Sweden/Norway)
The Haunting (Robert Wise, 1963, UK)
The Innocents (Jack Clayton, 1961, UK)
The Legend of Hell House (John Hough, 1973, UK)
The Limehouse Golem (Juan Carlos Medina, 2016, UK)
The Lodger (John Brahm, 1944, USA)
The Lodger: A Story of the London Fog (Alfred Hitchcock, 1927, UK)
The Monk (Francisco Lara Polop, 1990, Spain/UK)
The Pit and the Pendulum (Roger Corman, 1961, USA)
The Woman in Black (James Watkins, 2012, UK/Canada/Sweden)
The Woman in White (Peter Godfrey, 1948, USA)
Tôkaidô Yotsuya kaidan (*The Ghost of Yotsuya*, Nobuo Nakagawa, 1959, Japan)
Un chien andalou (*An Andalusian Dog*, Luis Buñuel, 1929, France)
Vampir – Cuadecuc (Vampire – Cuadecuc, Pere Portabella, 1971, Spain)
Viy (Spirit of Evil, Konstantin Ershov and Georgiy Kropachyov, 1967, Soviet Union)

NOTES

1 See Brown (2013), Anon. (2013), Ivan-Zadeh (2013) and Masters (2013), respectively.
2 First wave Gothic is normally bookended in histories of the Gothic by the publication of Horace Walpole's *The Castle of Otranto* in 1764 and that of Charles Maturin's *Melmoth the Wanderer* in 1820.

3 The main exceptions are *The Castle of Otranto*, adapted as *Otrantský zámek* (*Castle of Otranto*, 1977) by director and animator Jan Švankmajer; Ann Radcliffe's *The Italian* (1797), made into the six-episode French miniseries *Le Confessionnal des pénitents noirs* (*The Confessional of the Black Penitents* in 1977); and Lewis's *The Monk* (1796), which has been filmed three times, in 1972 (*Le Moine*), 1990 (*The Monk*) and 2011 (*Le Moine*), although often with the Gothic elements played down or excised. None of these adaptations have had much cultural repercussion. Punter speculates that the original novels' 'inflated rhetoric', specific anxiety over religious excess and rambling structures may lie at the heart of their cinematic neglect (2013: 103). The lack of continued and profitable stage adaptations may be just as responsible.
4 This is also noted by Kaye (2000: 191).
5 A cursory browse of *The Sickly Taper*'s page for Gothic Film Criticism, a bibliographic source for academics, reveals most entries to be chapters in books or articles. See www.thesicklytaper.com/bibliographies/gothic-film-criticism (accessed 12 December 2016).
6 The tribute article was published in 1957, before the premiere that year of Terence Fisher's *The Curse of Frankenstein*. The term 'Gothick' is used as synonymous with the 'grotesque' (Edwards 1957: 96) and with 'macabre … humour' (98) and appears in its archaic spelling.
7 This soubriquet is the book's subtitle.
8 Pirie goes as far as to suggest that 'the horror genre, as it has been developed in this country by Hammer and its rivals, remains the only staple cinematic myth which Britain can properly claim as its own' (1973: 9).
9 Romanticism was an artistic and intellectual movement concerned with subjectivity, emotion, the past and nature that developed towards the end of the eighteenth century and the beginning of the nineteenth.
10 In fact, the selections mirror those of broad horror surveys – see Newman (1984; 2011) – and of studies of national horrors – see Hutchings (1993), Boot (1999), Chibnall and Petley (2001), Rose (2009), Walker (2015), Baschiera and Hunter (2016).
11 See Kavka (2002: 209) and Carver (2013: 236).

12 Cueto, for example, uses this dichotomy to separate the horror film (make-up heavy and driven by special effects) from the Gothic melodrama (focused on psychology and performance-led) (2010: 49–50).
13 See Townshend (2016).
14 The Gothic's inherent concern with subconscious and libidinal desires is also the reason one of the preferred methods adopted in its analytical enquiries has been psychoanalysis. See Aldana Reyes (2012; 2016).
15 I am borrowing the term from Freeland, who refers to 'numbers' as 'sequences of heightened spectacle and emotion', normally '[v]isions of monsters and their behavior or scenes of exaggerated violence' (2000: 256).
16 To push this argument to its logical extreme, we could end up in a situation where any horror film deemed to be of quality instantly becomes Gothic upon gaining recognition. My contention is that aesthetics have a greater role to play in our understanding of the Gothic.
17 Many studies have read the film as Gothic. For an example, see Botting (2013: 195–196).
18 The latter, especially when plays were written by the capable André de Lorde, often took inspiration from Gothic classics like Poe's stories.
19 As James Watt argues, the Gothic label was not used by the majority of those we now term Gothic writers ('terror/ist writing' began to be used in the 1790s) and the idea of the Gothic as 'a unitary genre' is 'a twentieth century creation' (1999: 1–2, 3).
20 Interestingly, its bloodiness did jar with the rest of the film for some critics (Bradshaw 2015; Debruge 2015), a clear indication that the combination of explicit horror and a Gothic mise-en-scène is still perceived as contradictory.
21 I first made this point in *Body Gothic* (Aldana Reyes 2014: 3–8).
22 Roberto Curti has even written of the 'Gothic peplum', or sword and sandal adventures. He lists films like *Maciste contro il vampiro* (*Samson vs. the Vampires*, 1961), *Ercole al centro della Terra* (*Hercules in the Haunted World*, 1961) and *Maciste all'inferno* (*The Witch's Curse*, 1962) as examples of this subgenre (2010: 248).
23 The view that horror is defined by a key character, the monster (Carroll 1990), has been contested and alternatives proposed. I, for example, have suggested that sources of direct, mainly physical, threat – rather than monsters *per se* – lie at the heart of horror film (Aldana Reyes 2016: 90–105).

24 Vieira seems to use the Gothic label to indicate that these early horror films take place in some barbaric European past, rather than to acknowledge specific sources. But even this more general definition seems hard to justify, since he also includes in his discussion films set in contemporary times, like *Freaks* (1932) or *King Kong* (1933).

25 See Cohen (1996), Asma (2011), Mittman and Dendle (2013) and Weinstock (2014).

26 Such a proposition cannot be underestimated in an age when external funding has the power to define areas of interest and even the direction of entire disciplines. The Gothic simply presents a much less morally objectionable field; it is still seen as pursuing higher intellectual aims than horror.

27 For some, the mad scientist's laboratory may be equally connotative because, as I show in Chapter 3, *Frankenstein*'s mingling of the medieval and the modern was very influential. I do not see all mad scientist films or settings as necessarily Gothic and, due to spatial constraints, largely sidestep them in this book. The interested reader should consult Skal (1998) and Frayling (2004).

28 I have elsewhere referred to this as the 'cathartic-traumatic' approach to the Gothic, as it seems to suggest that the Gothic is identified, and matters, through its relation to the role it plays in the psyche of individual viewers and for different nations (Aldana Reyes 2015).

29 It is possible to add pyramids to this list. The ancient and threatening chambers in films such as *La momia azteca* (*The Aztec Mummy*, 1957) and *Blood from the Mummy's Tomb* (1971) operate in similar ways to medieval castles and dungeons.

30 These films have been called 'Edo Gothic' (Balmain 2008: 50–69).

31 Whether it is productive or appropriate to apply the term 'Gothic' to Eastern traditions is a debate that falls outside the scope of this book, but see Ancuta (2019). Mostly, I limit my case studies to Western forms of the Gothic, but, allowing for production and generic differences, some of my conclusions about the development of Gothic cinema can certainly apply to its Eastern manifestations.

32 Not coincidentally, one of the most famous cinematic Gothic franchises of the twenty-first century is titled *Twilight* (2008–12).

33 This is not necessarily the case in the art-horror Gothic films of Ben Rivers, whose *Old Dark House* (2003) and *House* (2007) extract similar moods from non-narrative uncanny explorations of empty, dark and eerie spaces.
34 A film like *Der Dibuk* (*The Dybbuk*, 1937), which rarely veers into horrific territory, presents an interesting conundrum. To my mind, it would be best understood as a supernatural love story or a folkloric fantasy.
35 This archetype, especially after its crystallisation outside of the folk tale in Charlotte Brontë's *Jane Eyre* (1847), is so foundational to the Female Gothic that it has even been seen to develop its own subgenre, 'Bluebeard Gothic' (Pyrhönen 2010).
36 See Horner and Zlosnik (2016).
37 This is not to say that Gothic surrealism does not exist in, for example, *La Belle et la Bête* (*Beauty and the Beast*, 1946) and *Vampir – Cuadecuc* (*Vampire – Cuadecuc*, 1971).
38 It is crucial that the building is portrayed as anachronistic and overwhelming. This is what sometimes differentiates Gothic films from other ghost films.
39 I am not suggesting that classical horror film only manifested through the Gothic mode, rather that the Gothic aesthetic predominated during periods of intense production now seen as seminal to its history.

BIBLIOGRAPHY

Aldana Reyes, X. (2012) 'Beyond Psychoanalysis: Post-Millennial Horror Film and Affect Theory', *Horror Studies*, 3.2: 243–261.

Aldana Reyes, X. (2014) *Body Gothic: Corporeal Transgression in Contemporary Literature and Horror Film*, Cardiff: University of Wales Press.

Aldana Reyes, X. (2015) 'Gothic Affect: An Alternative Approach to Critical Models of the Contemporary Gothic', in L. Piatti-Farnell and D. Lee Brien (eds) *New Directions in 21st Century Gothic*, Abingdon and New York: Routledge.

Aldana Reyes, X. (2016) *Horror Film and Affect: Towards a Corporeal Model of Viewership*, Abingdon and New York: Routledge.

Ancuta, K. (2019) 'Asian Gothic', in M. Wester and X. Aldana Reyes (eds) *Twenty-First-Century Gothic: An Edinburgh Companion*, Edinburgh: Edinburgh University Press.

Anonymous (2013) 'BFI's Film Gothic Season Is Just a Scream', *Evening Standard*, 30 August. Available at: www.standard.co.uk/news/bfis-gothic-film-season-is-just-a-scream-8791610.html (accessed 6 December 2016).

Asma, S. T. (2011) *On Monsters: An Unnatural History of Our Worst Fears*, Oxford: Oxford University Press.

Baldick, C. (2009) 'Introduction', in C. Baldick (ed.) *The Oxford Book of Gothic Tales*, Oxford: Oxford University Press.

Balmain, C. (2008) *Introduction to Japanese Horror Film*, Edinburgh: Edinburgh University Press.

Baschiera, S. and R. Hunter (eds) (2016) *Italian Horror Cinema*, Edinburgh: Edinburgh University Press.

Bell, J. (2013) *Gothic: The Dark Heart of Film*, London: BFI.

Birkhead, E. (1921) *The Tale of Terror: A Study of the Gothic Romance*, London: Constable and Co.

Blake, L. (2008) *The Wounds of Nations: Horror Cinema, Historical Trauma and National Identity*, Manchester: Manchester University Press.

Boot, A. (1999) *Fragments of Fear: An Illustrated History of British Horror Movies*, London: Creation Books.

Bordwell, D. and K. Thompson (2016), *Film Art: An Introduction*, 11th edn, Berkeley, CA: University of California Press.

Botting, F. (1995) 'Introduction', in F. Botting (ed.) *Frankenstein: Contemporary Critical Essays*, London and Basingstoke: Macmillan.

Botting, F. (2013) *Gothic*, 2nd edn, London and New York: Routledge.

Bradshaw, P. (2015) 'Crimson Peak Review: Evil Springs from a Psychosexually Rich Soil of Horror', *The Guardian*. Available at: www.theguardian.com/film/2015/oct/14/crimson-peak-review-psychosexually-rich-soil-of-horror-guillermo-del-toro-mia-wasikowska (accessed 2 December 2016).

Brown, M. (2013) 'BFI's Mammoth Gothic Season Gets Its Teeth into Dark Heart of Film', *The Guardian*, 27 June. Available at: www.theguardian.com/film/2013/jun/27/bfi-gothic-season-dark-heart-film (accessed 6 December 2016).

Bruhm, S. (2002) 'The Contemporary Gothic: Why We Need It', in J. E. Hogle (ed.) *The Cambridge Companion to Gothic Fiction*, Cambridge: Cambridge University Press.

Carroll, N. (1990) *The Philosophy of Horror: Or, Paradoxes of the Heart*, London and New York: Routledge.

Carver, S. (2013) 'Film', in W. Hughes, D. Punter and A. Smith (eds) *The Encyclopedia of the Gothic*, Oxford and Malden, MA: Wiley-Blackwell.

Cavallaro, D. (2002) *The Gothic Vision: Three Centuries of Horror, Terror and Fear*, London and New York: Continuum.

Chaplin, S. (2011) *Gothic Literature: Texts, Contexts, Connections*, London: York Press.

Chibnall, S. and J. Petley (eds) (2001) *British Horror Cinema*, London and New York: Routledge.

Clemens, V. (1999) *The Return of the Repressed: Gothic Horror from The Castle of Otranto to Alien*, New York: SUNY Press.

Clery, E. J. (1995) *The Rise of Supernatural Fiction 1762–1800*, Cambridge: Cambridge University Press.

Cohen, J. J. (ed.) (1996) *Monster Theory: Reading Culture*, Minneapolis: University of Minnesota Press.

Conrich, I. (1998) 'Gothic Film', in M. Mulvey-Roberts (ed.) *The Handbook of Gothic Literature*, London and Basingstoke: Macmillan.

Cuddon, J. A. (ed.) (2013) *Dictionary of Literary Terms and Literary Theory*, 5th edn, Oxford and Malden, MA: Wiley-Blackwell.

Cueto, R. (2010) '¿Qué es "lo gótico"?: El adjetivo que se convirtió en un género', in A. J. Navarro (ed.) *Pesadillas en la oscuridad: El cine de terror gótico*, Madrid: Valdemar.

Curti, R. (2010) 'Fantasmas de amor: El gótico italiano entre literatura, cine y televisión', in A. J. Navarro (ed.) *Pesadillas en la oscuridad: El cine de terror gótico*, Madrid: Valdemar.

Davis, R. (2013) 'Shadowlands', *Sight and Sound*, 23.11: 24–30.

Debruge, P. (2015) 'Film Review: Crimson Peak', *Variety*. Available at: http://variety.com/2015/film/reviews/crimson-peak-film-review-1201613988 (accessed 2 December 2016).

Edwards, R. (1957) 'Movie Gothick: A Tribute to James Whale', *Sight and Sound*, 27.2: 95–98.

Elliott, K. (2007) 'Gothic – Film – Parody', in C. Spooner and E. McEvoy (eds) *The Routledge Companion to Gothic*, London and New York: Routledge.

Forshaw, B. (2013) *British Gothic Cinema*, Basingstoke: Palgrave Macmillan.

Fowler, A. (1971) 'The Life and Death of Literary Forms', *New Literary History*, 2.2: 199–216.

Frayling, C. (2004) *Mad, Bad and Dangerous?: The Scientist and the Cinema*, London: Reaktion.

Frayling, C. (2013) 'Foreword', in J. Bell (ed.) *Gothic: The Dark Heart of Film*, London: BFI.

Freeland, C. (2000) *The Naked and the Undead: Evil and the Appeal of Horror*, Oxford and Boulder, CO: Westview Press.

Gamer, M. (2000) *Romanticism and the Gothic: Genre, Reception and Canon Formation*, Cambridge: Cambridge University Press.

Gavin, F. (2008) *Hell Bound: New Gothic Art*, London: Laurence King Publishing.

Grant, B. K. (2007) *Film Genre: From Iconography to Ideology*, London and New York: Wallflower.

Grunenberg, C. (1997) *Gothic: Transmutations of Horror in Late-Twentieth-Century Art*, London and Cambridge, MA: MIT Press.

Hanich, J. (2010) *Cinematic Emotion in Horror Films and Thrillers: The Aesthetic Paradox of Pleasurable Fear*, Abingdon and New York: Routledge.

Hanson, H. (2007) *Hollywood Heroines: Women in Film Noir and the Female Gothic Film*, London and New York: I.B.Tauris.

Hills, M. (2005) *The Pleasures of Horror*, London and New York: Continuum.

Hogle, J. E. (2002) 'Introduction: The Gothic in Western Culture,' in J. E. Hogle (ed.) *The Cambridge Companion to Gothic Fiction*, Cambridge: Cambridge University Press.

Hollinger, V. (2014) 'Genre vs. Mode', in Rob Latham (ed.) *The Oxford Handbook of Science Fiction*, Oxford: Oxford University Press.

Hopkins, L. (2005) *Screening the Gothic*, Austin: University of Texas Press.

Horner, A. and S. Zlosnik (eds) (2016) *Women and the Gothic: An Edinburgh Companion*, Edinburgh: Edinburgh University Press.

Howard, J. (1994) *Reading Gothic Fiction: A Bakhtinian Approach*, Oxford: Clarendon Press.

Hutchings, P. (1993) *Hammer and Beyond: British Horror Film*, Manchester: Manchester University Press.

Hutchings, P. (1996) 'Tearing Your Soul Apart: Horror's New Monsters', in V. Sage and A. Lloyd Smith (eds) *Modern Gothic: A Reader*, Manchester: Manchester University Press.

Ivan-Zadeh, L. (2013) 'The BFI Celebrates Gothic Film – Where Sexy Meets Dangerous', *Metro*, 29 August. Available at: http://metro.co.uk/2013/08/29/the-bfi-celebrates-gothic-film-where-sexy-meets-dangerous-3940484/ (accessed 6 December 2016).

Jackson, R. (1981) *Fantasy: The Literature of Subversion*, London and New York: Routledge.

Jameson, F. (1975) 'Magical Narratives: Romance as Genre', *New Literary History*, 7.1: 135–163.

Jones, E. M. (1999) *Monsters from the Id: The Rise of Horror in Fiction and Film*, Dallas, TX: Spence Publishing Co.

Kavka, M. (2002) 'The Gothic on Screen', in J. E. Hogle (ed.) *The Cambridge Companion to Gothic Fiction*, Cambridge: Cambridge University Press.

Kaye, H. (2000) 'Gothic Film', in D. Punter (ed.) *A Companion to the Gothic*, Oxford and Malden, MA: Blackwell.

Kilgour, M. (1995) *The Rise of the Gothic Novel*, London and New York: Routledge.

Kosofsky Sedgwick, E. (1980) *The Coherence of Gothic Conventions*, London and New York: Methuen.

Langford, B. (2005) *Film Genre: Hollywood and Beyond*, Edinburgh: Edinburgh University Press.

MacArthur, S. (2015) *Gothic Science Fiction: 1818 to the Present*, Basingstoke and New York: Palgrave Macmillan.

Masters, T. (2013) 'BFI Gothic Season Explores "Dark Heart of Film"', *BBC News*, 28 June. Available at: www.bbc.co.uk/news/entertainment-arts-23095437 (accessed 6 December 2016).

Miles, R. (2002) *Gothic Writing 1750–1820: A Genealogy*, 2nd edn, Manchester and New York: Manchester University Press.

Mishra, V. (1994) *The Gothic Sublime*, New York: SUNY Press.

Mittman, A. S. and P. J. Dendle (eds) (2013) *The Ashgate Research Companion to Monsters and the Monstrous*, Farnham and Burlington, VT: Ashgate.

Napier, E. R. (1987) *The Failure of Gothic: Problems of Disjunction in an Eighteenth-Century Literary Form*, Oxford: Clarendon Press.

Neale, S. (2000) *Genre and Hollywood*, London and New York: Routledge.

Newman, K. (1984) *Nightmare Movies: Wide Screen Horror since 1968*, New York: Proteus.

Newman, K. (2011) *Nightmare Movies: Horror on Screen since the 1960s*, London: Bloomsbury Publishing.

Palmer, P. (2012) *The Queer Uncanny: New Perspectives on the Gothic*, Cardiff: University of Wales Press.

Peirse, A. (2013) *After Dracula: The 1930s Horror Film*, London and New York: I.B. Tauris.

Pirie, D. (1973) *A Heritage of Horror: The English Gothic Cinema 1946–1972*, London: The Gordon Fraser Gallery.

Praz, M. (1933) [1930] *The Romantic Agony* (trans. Angus Davidson), London: Humphrey Milford.

Punter, D. (1980) *The Literature of Terror: A History of Gothic Fictions from 1765 to the Present Day*, London and New York: Longman.

Punter, D. (2013) 'The Original Gothics', in J. Bell (ed.) *Gothic: The Dark Heart of Film*, London: BFI.

Pyrhönen, H. (2010) *Bluebeard Gothic: Jane Eyre and Its Progeny*, Toronto: University of Toronto Press.

Radcliffe, A. (2000) [1826] 'On the Supernatural in Poetry', in E. J. Clery and R. Miles (eds) *Gothic Documents: A Sourcebook, 1700–1820*, Manchester and New York: Manchester University Press.

Radcliffe, A. (2008) [1794] *The Mysteries of Udolpho*, Oxford: Oxford University Press.

Railo, E. (1927) *The Haunted Castle: A Study of the Elements of English Romanticism*, London: E. P. Dutton and Co.

Rhodes, G. D. (2018) '"Horror Film": How the Term Came to Be', *Monstrum*, 1.1: 90–115.

Rigby, J. (2000) *English Gothic: A Century of Horror Cinema*, Richmond: Reynolds and Hearn.

Rigby, J. (2007) *American Gothic: Sixty Years of Horror Cinema*, Richmond: Reynolds and Hearn.

Rigby, J. (2015) *English Gothic: Classic Horror Cinema 1897–2015*, London: Signum Books.

Rigby, J. (2016) *Euro Gothic: Classics of Continental Horror Cinema*, London: Signum Books.

Rigby, J. (2017) *American Gothic: Six Decades of Classic Horror Cinema*, London: Signum Books.

Rose, J. (2009) *Beyond Hammer: British Horror Cinema since 1970*, Leighton Buzzard: Auteur.

Simpson, P. L. (2000) *Psycho Paths: Tracking the Serial Killer through Contemporary American Film and Fiction*, Carbondale and Edwardsville, IL: Southern Illinois University Press.

Skal, D. J. (1998) *Screams of Reason: Mad Science and Modern Culture*, New York: W. W. Norton and Co.

Spooner, C. (2006) *Contemporary Gothic*, London: Reaktion.

Spooner, C. (2007) 'Gothic in the Twentieth Century', in C. Spooner and E. McEvoy (eds) *The Routledge Companion to Gothic*, London and New York: Routledge.

Spooner, C. (2010) 'Crime and the Gothic', in C. J. Rzepka and L. Horsley (eds) *A Companion to Crime Fiction*, Oxford and Malden, MA: Wiley-Blackwell.

Spooner, C. (2014) 'Twenty-First-Century Gothic', in D. Townshend (ed.) *Terror and Wonder: The Gothic Imagination*, London: British Library Publishing.

Summers, M. (1938) *The Gothic Quest: A History of the Gothic Novel*, London: The Fortune Press.

Todorov, T. (1975) [1970] *The Fantastic: A Structural Approach to a Literary Genre* (trans. Richard Howard), Ithaca, NY: Cornell University Press.

Tompkins, J. M. S. (1932) *The Popular Novel in England, 1770–1800*, London: Constable and Co.

Townshend, D. (ed.) (2014) *Terror and Wonder: The Gothic Imagination*, London: British Library Publishing.

Townshend, D. (2016) 'Gothic and the Cultural Sources of Horror, 1740–1820', in X. Aldana Reyes (ed.) *Horror: A Literary History*, London: British Library Publishing.

Townshend, D. (2019) *Gothic Antiquity: History, Romance, and the Architectural Imagination, 1760–1840*, Oxford: Oxford University Press.

Twitchell, J. B. (1985) *Dreadful Pleasures: An Anatomy of Modern Horror*, Oxford: Oxford University Press.

van Elferen, I. (2012) *Gothic Music: The Sounds of the Uncanny*, Cardiff: University of Wales Press.

Varma, D. P. (1957) *The Gothic Flame: Being a History of the Gothic Novel in England; Its Origins, Efflorescence, and Residuary Influences*, London: Arthur Barker.

Vieira, M. A. (2003) *Hollywood Horror: From Gothic to Cosmic*, New York: Harry N. Abrams.

Walker, J. (2015) *Contemporary British Horror Cinema: Industry, Genre and Society*, Edinburgh: Edinburgh University Press.

Wallace, D. and A. Smith (2009) 'Introduction: Defining the Female Gothic', in D. Wallace and A. Smith (eds) *The Female Gothic: New Directions*, Basingstoke: Palgrave Macmillan.

Warwick, A. (2007) 'Feeling Gothicky?', *Gothic Studies*, 9.1: 5–15.

Wasson, S. and E. Alder (eds) (2011) *Gothic Science Fiction 1980–2010*, Liverpool: Liverpool University Press.

Watt, J. (1999) *Contesting the Gothic: Fiction, Genre and Cultural Conflict, 1764–1832*, Cambridge: Cambridge University Press.

Weinstock, J. A. (ed.) (2014) *The Ashgate Encyclopedia to Literary and Cinematic Monsters*, Farnham and Burlington, VT: Ashgate.

Williams, G. (ed.) (2007) *The Gothic*, London: Whitechapel Art Gallery.

Wood, R. (1978) 'Return of the Repressed', *Film Comment*, 14.4: 25–32.

Wood, R. (1979) 'An Introduction to the American Horror Film', in R. Wood and R. Lippe (eds) *American Nightmare: Essays on the Horror Film*, Toronto: Festival of Festivals.

Wright, A. (2013) *Monstrosity: The Human Monster in Visual Culture*, London and New York: I.B.Tauris.

1

TRANSITIONAL ORIGINS

It is tempting to suggest that Gothic cinema begins with Georges Méliès's *Le Manoir du diable* (*The Haunted Castle*, 1896), a very early three-minute film that boasts various transformations (from a bat to a demon and vice versa) and the appearance of a skeleton and a group of spectres, all set against a painted backdrop that reproduces the entrance to an ancient castle.[1] In it, at least two of the three traditional meanings of the term 'Gothic', namely 'medieval' and 'supernatural' (Longueil 1923: 454), are in interplay, explored inventively through cinema's unique visual language. Stop-motion photography and substitution splices are used to create the illusion that figures become something other than they initially were, that they disappear or that they are fantastically summoned. Appropriately, the setting is archaic and intended to evoke ideas of alchemical magic: there is a cauldron from which a fully formed woman springs forth, and the evil character is Mephistopheles, a supernatural being of German folklore associated with the Faust legend and its source, the German astrologer Johann Georg Faust. Although the film is not, strictly speaking, narrative, driven as it is by the visual spectacle that derives from incantations rather than by plot, it stages one of the first battles between good and evil. The ending sees Mephistopheles vanished by a cavalier brandishing a crucifix, a scene that would recur time and again throughout the history of vampire cinema. *Le Manoir du diable* certainly displays, aesthetically and cinematically, what could, in hindsight, be called a Gothic aesthetic.

If we take the Gothic's third meaning, 'barbarous' (Longueil 1923: 454), as a significant one for the manifestation of the mode, Alfred Clark's film *Execution of Mary, Queen of Scots* (1895) becomes another potential contender for earliest Gothic cinematic example of the mode. Running to a mere fifteen seconds, it simulates the beheading of Mary Stuart (Mrs Robert L. Thomas), shown kneeling down and placing her neck on a chopping block. After the executioner brings down his axe, her head rolls away, an effect achieved via dummy substitution. The edit is so subtle that the film accomplishes its verisimilitudinous intention, to simulate spatiotemporal unity between the two frames. Importantly, the film retrojects this moment of savagery. No date is offered to the viewer, but we know from history that Mary's execution took place on 8 February 1587 and the actress is surrounded by onlookers dressed as knights. The film is not at all supernatural and hinges entirely on the optical illusions made possible by cinema as a photographic medium that incorporates movement and is susceptible to manipulation in postproduction. For some, *Execution of Mary, Queen of Scots* can even be considered an early example of horror exploitation that gruesomely transforms a serious historical event into pure decontextualised thrill.[2] There is, after all, no build-up and no morale to the story.

And yet, to identify *Le Manoir du diable* or *Execution of Mary, Queen of Scots* as distinct points of origin for Gothic cinema would be somewhat disingenuous if what is meant by this is not first thoroughly qualified. These films were not created in isolation and neither do they betray a specific desire to fashion a unique Gothic product in the 1890s. Instead, they must be understood as part of a wider contemporary engagement with discoveries in cinematic technology and as the culmination of much older developments in photographic optical illusions and theatrical magic shows. The latter had, in the nineteenth century, already employed the machinery typical of theatre (which would be taken to scary extremes in the theatre of the Grand Guignol), as well as lighting effects and mirrors.[3] In short, these efforts were much more dependent on the birth of cinema and its strong ties to various configurations of the magic lantern, to stagecraft (pantomimes, ballet and music hall shows) and to early forms of motion picture exhibition, such as the kinetoscope and the kinetograph, than on a particular contemporary preoccupation with the Gothic.[4]

Gothic cinema, like all cinema shot before the establishment of story-led films, was very varied, encompassing scenarios of different narrative complexities and lengths.[5] Films made during this period, sometimes called the 'cinema of attractions' (Gunning 1986), do not align well with our current fascination with genre.[6] Even within the oeuvre of one director, Méliès, sketches depicting current and historic events, such as *Visite sous-marine du 'Maine'* (*Divers at Work on the Wreck of the Maine*, 1898) and *Jeanne d'Arc* (*Joan of Arc*, 1900), happily co-existed with fictional comedic ones, such as *Le Savant et le Chimpanzé* (*The Doctor and the Monkey*, 1900), and even erotica, in *Après le bal* (*After the Ball*, 1897).[7] The vast majority of films that were not documentary utilised special effects to surprise audiences. These have been called 'trick films' ('films à trucs'), as they showcased at least one trick each, often more, and they typically included magicians. Their debt to stage magic is evident in the direct address to the camera, the final bow and the general reliance on techniques of prestidigitation and circus performances (acrobats, dancers, pyrotechnics).[8] Trick films revolved around a number of optical effects that could be achieved through use of matte shots and negative masking, dioramas, superimpositions, reverse motion, silhouette animation, multiple exposures and lap dissolves, as well as the aforementioned substitution splices and stop-motion photography, to accomplish illusions like transformations, objects moving of their own accord, portraits coming to life and ghostly visitations. For this reason, characters popularly associated with magic, such as wizards, sorcerers, alchemists, witches and devils (mostly Satan and Mephistopheles), and hellish scenarios and oneiric visions (in the form of dreams and nightmares) were likely to feature in them. Some of these nightmare films, such as *Le Cauchemar* (*The Nightmare*, 1896) or the later *Superstition andalouse* (*Andalusian Superstition*, 1912), show how difficult it is to separate trick films from narrative films which made heavy use of special effects.[9] Because optical illusions were such an important part of early cinema, their subjects, especially for the longer ones, would often draw on the fantastic traditions of fairy tales, as in *Cendrillon* (*Cinderella*, 1899) and *Le Petit Poucet* (*Tom Thumb*, 1909), and folk tales, as in *La Damnation de Faust* (*The Damnation of Faust*, 1903) and *Le Palais des mille et une nuits* (*The Palace of the Arabian Nights*, 1905).[10] Alternatively, they would explore the creative possibilities offered by science fiction, especially in the ambitious *Le Voyage dans la lune* (*A Trip to the Moon*, 1903) and *À la conquête du pôle* (*The Conquest of the Pole*, 1912). Genre and subject matter were inextricable from visual spectacle and surprise, but trick films were not beholden to a specific time and setting. Instead, they were largely coloured by a focus on the visual appeal of supernatural happenings.

It is therefore necessary to understand early Gothic cinema as an accidental affair. The work of early filmmakers does not reveal a predilection for the medieval past, rather Gothic iconography was built into trick films because of its connection to illusionism. Contemporary times were as likely to be haunted as the Middles Ages, and thematic trends were usually the result of previous successes with particular tricks, such as the many 'haunted hotel' scenarios that followed Méliès's *L'Auberge ensorcelée* (*The Bewitched Inn*, 1897). The medieval settings in films such as *The Magic Sword* (1901), *Les Sept Châteaux du diable* (*The Devil's Seven Castles*, 1904), *La Légende du fantôme* (*The Black Pearl*, 1908), *Le Château hanté* (*Haunted Castle*, 1908), *Il fantasma del castello* (*The Castle Ghosts*, 1908), *Des Sängers Fluch* (*The Curse of the Wandering Minstrel*, 1910), *La Mariée du château maudit* (*The Bride of the Haunted Castle*, 1910) and *Beneath the Tower Ruins* (1911) offered more barbaric and exotic locales idiosyncratically linked to manifestations of superstition (ghosts and hauntings) and magic, especially witchcraft, alchemical sorcery and Faustian pacts.[11] The actual effects on display, and even the roster of fantastic characters (imps and demons, apparitions, witches, magical objects), were not exclusive to these archaic times. Their iconography was already familiar and thus easy to interpret and digest. It is possible, in this light, to think of early Gothic cinema as involving several media, as originating at a juncture in the history of optical technology for ludic purposes when various traditions, theatrical and photographic, were meaningfully interconnected.[12]

Gothic cinema is not just indebted to the Gothic tradition in prose, even if it cannot be extricated from it. The coterie of monsters in early trick films did not evolve from Gothic novels but rather from common superstition, folklore, fairy tales and legends as they had manifested in other visual forms.[13] In particular, the many demons, apparitions and witches of early Gothic cinema derive from the early eighteenth-century phantasmagoria show.[14] Although initially presented as real witchcraft

Figure 1.1 The setting of La Légende du fantôme (The Black Pearl, 1908) is suggestive of archaism and superstitious magic, key elements of the early Gothic film.

and pretend séances (Heard 2006: 41–55), ghost raising for didactic and ludic purposes became a popular form of horror theatre during the nineteenth century. In phantasmagoria shows, images of skeletons, ghosts and demons would be projected onto walls, and sometimes smoke, with the aid of moving magic lanterns to create spooky effects.[15] They would be made to appear to lunge towards audiences and then to recede, and even to feign transformations, effects all achieved through the manipulation of slides and camera lenses. These shows were not exclusively macabre in their themes, although apparitions, witches and Satan were regular subjects of the shows and the distribution materials for phantasmagorias unequivocally emphasised their occult and marvellous aspects, as well as their capacity to induce terror and dread.[16] In some cases, phantasmagorias were directly influenced by the Gothic. For example, the bleeding nun in Matthew Lewis's The Monk may have appeared in one of Étienne Gaspard-Robertson's shows as early as 1798 and would, like the witches in Shakespeare's Macbeth (1606), become a typical subject in later repertoires.[17] As Marina Warner suggests, it is possible to read the phantasmagoria as a modern form of 'secular entertainment' that adapted the conventional spiritual imaginary and 'occupie[d] a transitional zone between the sublime and the Gothic, between the solemn and the comic, and between seriously intended fears and sly mockery of such beliefs' (2006: 150, 152). In this respect, Gothic cinema and, before it, the phantasmagoria show, can be seen to extend into the early twentieth century the ambiguous relationship between the Gothic and religious icons and figures in literature (Long Hoeveler 2010). Early Gothic cinema only partly aimed to scare; it was more concerned with demonstrating the potential the medium had to alter reality and, by indulging in the fantastic, with parading new forms of mystification. The Gothic was essentially reconceptualised and reformulated for a new public through changes in duration (the embrace of the multiple-reel film in 1912), technical novelty (filming and postproduction craftsmanship) and exhibition (itinerant amusement, such as vaudeville shows and fairground bioscopes and cinematographs).

The phantasmagoria show also provides a good example of how iconography that is now perceived as decidedly Gothic (hauntings, demonic visitations, witchcraft) developed alongside the Gothic literary tradition, instead of strictly from it. In turn, cinema drew inspiration from its tricks, from its themes and engagement with the supernatural. A good example of this cross-fertilisation of ideas through different media is the Lumière brothers' *Le Squelette joyeux* (*Happy Skeleton*, 1898), a 40-second film in which a skeleton is seen dancing and, in the process, accidentally dropping some of its bones, even its skull. This film makes the most of a simple marionette, but its visual antics, like the stop-motion tricks in *The X Rays* (1897), go back to at least the 'dancing skeleton' of the choreutoscope, an 1866 pre-cinema device in which sequential images running through a viewing pane would appear to move.[18] The slide show itself developed, at least partially, from the *danse macabre*, an iconic dance of death and *memento mori* motif already in circulation in fifteenth-century European morality plays, sixteenth-century engravings and the nineteenth-century magic lantern. Similarly, apparitions were common in old folk tales, lantern slides and the stage, where Pepper's famed ghost made it possible to merge the optical basis of the phantasmagoria with theatre as early as 1862. Later films, such as D. W. Griffith's *The Avenging Conscience* (1914), Victor Sjöström's *Körkarlen* (*The Phantom Carriage*, 1921) and Benjamin Christensen's *Häxan* (*Witchcraft Through the Ages*, 1922) would be as thematically indebted to their literary sources (Edgar Allan Poe, Selma Lagerlöf and Heinrich Kramer, respectively) as they would be visually determined by the photographic slide of the 1880s and spiritualist photography.[19]

From the vast world of existing trick films, one director stands out as particular innovator and developer of a Gothic aesthetic in his cinema: Méliès.[20] Méliès was a magician and inventor of spectacular theatrical compositions based around illusions before he became a director, and this experience is one he was able to easily translate into film. In fact, the three-dimensional props, two-dimensional cut-outs, painted black cloth and grisaille (a method of painting in grey monochrome) and humour that characterise his numerous films were all attributes of his 'stage spectaculars' (Hammond 1974: 22, 47, 91). His Gothic films, which are a minority among the surviving ones, were naturally influenced by the world of prestidigitation. Some of them are Gothic in setting only. In *Le Chevalier mystère* (*The Mysterious Knight*, 1899), the background for the film is that of a medieval castle with a big sword and shield hanging from the wall, but the dynamics and tricks played by the cavalier (the animation of a painted head and its eventual transformation into a full-bodied person) are not significantly different from those in other films set in contemporary times. Others, especially the alchemical workshop and witch's den, clearly have an esoteric value.[21] This is the case in *L'Hallucination de l'alchimiste* (*An Hallucinated Alchemist*, 1897), *Le Magicien* (*The Magician*, 1898), *Chez la sorcière* (*The Bachelor's Paradise*, 1901), *Le Sorcier, le Prince et le Bon Génie* (*The Wizard, The Prince and the Good Fairy*, 1900), *Les Quatre Cents Farces du diable* (*The Merry Frolics of Satan*, 1906) and *L'Alchimiste Parafaragaramus, ou La Cornue infernale* (*The Mysterious Retort*, 1906), where their respective mises-en-scène include the obligatory cauldrons, model skeletons, retorts and Gothic arches. In yet other films, there is little temporal context, only an insinuation of archaism and danger. For example, all the tricks in *L'Antre des esprits* (*The Magician's Cavern*, 1901) take place under a huge dark gate decorated with the shadow-laden statues of a gigantic animal skull, a rapacious bird, a dragon and a demon. The set clearly evokes danger and antiquity, notions befitting an uncanny metamorphosis from skeleton to woman (and vice versa) or the manifestation of floating chairs, both of which are, it is assumed, phenomena caused by black magic. Although caverns sometimes simply signify Biblical remoteness, as in *Tentation de Saint Antoine* (*The Temptation of Saint Anthony*, 1898), they are strongly Gothicised, rendered infernal in their chthonic evocations in *L'Enchanteur Alcofribas* (*Alcofribas, The Master Magician*, 1903), the aforementioned *La Damnation de Faust, La Cascade de feu* (*The Firefall*, 1904), *La Cuisine de l'ogre* (*In the Bogie Man's Cave*, 1907), *Le Nouveau Seigneur du village* (*The New Lord of the Village*, 1908) and *Hallucinations pharmaceutiques, ou Le Truc du potard* (*Pharmaceutical Hallucinations*, 1908).

Churches are also Gothicised in *Le Diable au couvent* (*The Devil in a Convent*, 1899), where the devil summons imps and wreaks havoc until vanquished by nuns and priests, and in *Un miracle sous l'inquisition* (*A Miracle Under the Inquisition*, 1904), where a victim of the stake returns to take revenge on her executioner. Most of these films are so short that there is barely any time for a complex relationship between setting, plot and characters to develop. The Gothic or Gothicised buildings and places portrayed are connotative; they complement or enhance the supernatural quality of the major events.

For all that Europe, France in particular, led the trick film race, America did not lag far behind.[22] Comedian Carl Stewart, in his role as country bumpkin Uncle Josh, appeared in films such as *Uncle Josh in a Spooky Hotel* (1900) and *Uncle Josh's Nightmare* (1900), where he is assailed by a ghost and a playful devil. Similar impish forces play mischief in other short trick films like *The Cavalier's Dream* (1898), *The Prince of Darkness* (1900) and *Ballet of the Ghosts* (1900), and in haunted building films such as *The Haunted House* (1899), *The Haunted Curiosity Shop* (1901), *The Haunted Hotel* (1907) and *'Tis Now the Very Witching Time of Night* (1909), in which naughty apparitions terrorise unsuspecting lodgers. Some of these trick films situated their dark magical scenarios in the present, codifying superstition at a regional level. If the medieval setting in Europe connoted alchemical magic and remoteness, credulity could be projected onto rural ingenuity in America. These films certainly engaged with the supernatural and, in some of them, the background indicated archaism or dereliction, but their contemporary times and spaces prevented them from being straightforwardly 'Gothic'. Where, in later films like *The Imp of the Bottle* (1909), based on Robert Louis Stevenson's story 'The Bottle Imp' (1891), and *In the Days of Witchcraft* (1909), American cinema did resort to Europe's architectonic past, the reason for this scenographic choice may have been more than a simple case of copycat. Kendall R. Phillips has, in fact, made a compelling case for the construction of the myth of the rational, incredulous American hero (and his country) set in opposition to 'Old World beliefs and customs' (2018: 104) at this point in history. This scenario played out in films like *The Ghost Breaker* (1914), where the American Jarvis (H. B. Warren) helps dispel the superstitious rumours around an old haunted castle in Spain.

Between 1903 and 1904, story films began to be actively pushed by urban theatres and were met with enthusiasm by audiences (Musser 1990: 337). This resulted in further investment in them. Although many short trick films continued to be made during this period and up until the beginning of their decline in 1912, longer pieces were also produced that, if in many cases were still driven by effects, relied on a narrative continuum holding different tableaux together. Ever-expanding films required the development of newer methods to maintain interest and focus attention. These characteristics would also be influenced by the serial format, whose reliance on cliffhangers and mysterious situations in the darkest of the detective offerings, such as *Fantômas* (1913–14), *Les vampires* (*The Vampires*, 1915), *The Crimson Stain Mystery* (1916), *The Mysteries of Myra* (1916), *The Voice on the Wire* (1917), *The Phantom Foe* (1920) and *The Mystery Mind* (1920), would prove influential.[23] Master shots unbroken by montage (typical of early films and of the stage) continued to dominate, but different points of view and close-ups began to be used to provide emphasis and allow for closer inspection of certain aspects of the action or the mise-en-scène. Subjects also evolved to embrace stories drawn from folk tales and from different artistic forms – mainly from operas, theatre and literature. Many of these included strange phenomena and retrojected European and medieval settings.

For his longer films, Méliès drew inspiration from the French genre of the late eighteenth-century 'féerie' play. This was 'a type of melodrama in which acrobatics, music and mime were the main elements', usually adapted from plays and revolving around the struggle between good and evil, 'forces incarnated onstage by gnomes and witches' (Singer Kovács 1976: 1).[24] The irruption of supernatural creatures into the real world and the use of talismans to effect transformations in the characters or the settings were also common to the genre (Singer Kovács 1976: 2). Their magical mechanics and Manichean principles made féeries attractive to cinema, as the latter could enhance the visual spectacle of costumed players, elaborate sets and stagecraft (trapdoors, use of props and lights, pyrotechnics) with additional optical illusions. Méliès adapted various fairy tales, such as the aforementioned Cinderella (readapted in 1912), some of them with darker themes and moods, notably *Barbe-bleue* (*Bluebeard*, 1901); *Le Royaume des fées* (*The Kingdom of the Fairies*, 1903), after the popular 1845 féerie *La Biche au bois*; *La Fée Carabosse, ou Le Poignard fatal* (*The Witch*, 1906), after the Breton legend; and *Le Chevalier des neiges* (*The Knight of the Snows*, 1912).[25] These films featured medieval castles with Gothic towers and captive women, rescue squads that, with one exception, took the shape of knights or princes, evil monsters (Bluebeard, witches and wizards, a baron who makes a pact with the devil) and fantastic happenings (a witch flies with her broomstick, demons magically burn down a building, a key grows and shrinks in size, characters witness spectral visions or meet weird animals). One of these féeries, *Bluebeard*, is perhaps the oldest Female Gothic film and contains one of the first scenes of Gothic horror in the history of cinema. When the new wife (Jeanne d'Alcy) enters a room forbidden to her, a half-light renders the contents diffuse. Upon opening the window, a scene of slaughter is revealed: the room is actually a secret death chamber. Inside it, the corpses of Bluebeard's seven wives have been left hanging, their blood dripping onto the floor. The new wife is so shocked by this scene that she screams in fear. The image is not easily dispelled either: she is later haunted by the spirits of the seven wives, who perform a ghostly dance over her sleeping body. In its build-up and delivery, the scene plays like an early experiment on the type of horrific reaction shot that would be perfected a few years later in *The Phantom of the Opera* (1925) (see Chapter 3).

It is important to contextualise these films, as well as any other made before horror became a generic category. These films were not intended as Gothic pieces that would horrify audiences but as féeries, a genre for which Méliès became well-known.[26] In fact, in 1907 the director used this term to refer to some of the most aesthetically Gothic of his films, such as the

Figure 1.2 The tricks, set and formulae of a film like *La Fée Carabosse, ou Le Poignard fatal* (*The Witch*, 1906) evince the intermedia origins of Gothic cinema.

aforementioned *Le Manoir du diable* and *Le Diable au couvent*, and emphasised the importance of the substitution trick to their development (quoted in Robinson 1993: 17). The Gothic elements in these films are, if not accidental, then certainly minor and part of a number of tableaux intended to elicit various emotions connected to surprise, wonder and amusement. They are a great example of how early Gothic cinema can be read as existing interstitially, in the gaps between different traditions and media. The monsters in these films, as Gary D. Rhodes has shown, do not appear uniquely in Gothicised settings but in a plurality of them, including Native American narratives, historical films about the Salem witch trials or comedy films informed by the 'diableries' stereoscopic cards of the 1860s (2018: 125–186). A significant reminder of the distance between these productions and the Gothic fictional tradition is the relative dearth of werewolves, vampires and mummies and the fact that, when these creatures did appear, they did so in very different contexts: the werewolf in that of the Native American Other in films such as *The Werewolf* (1913) and *The White Wolf* (1914); the vampire as a modern serpentine dancer in *Loïe Fuller* (1905), titled after the performer; and the mummy as a comedic subject (Rhodes 2018: 194–208).[27] The monsters in these films only display some of the fictional traits horror cinema would furnish them with a few years later. The Gothic, where it manifested architectonically, betrayed the tradition's debt to the chivalric romance. Its chronotopic functions, above all its evocation of remote and magical pasts, is evident in some films, but its supernatural scenarios were not exclusive to the mode, appearing in more modern 'bewitched' settings in other of Méliès's trick films and in the work of other early directors. Segundo de Chomón's *La Maison ensorcelée* (*The Haunted House*, 1906) and *Une excursion incohérente* (*Traveller's Nightmare*, 1909) operate like horror films insofar as their narrative arches involve groups of people scared witless by supernatural forces, yet take place in contemporary times.

Finally, in the era before synchronised sound recording, colour was incredibly important in the evocation of certain moods. Although we associate colour with more modern cinema (see Chapter 5), selected films were manually stencilled or hand-coloured frame by frame during the silent period. This technique generally achieved the effect of singling out individual objects or characters, making them stand out, but it could also be merged with the plot in more symbolically complex ways. *Le Spectre rouge* (*The Red Spectre*, 1907) is a great example of a film coloured with more ambitious intent. It features a skeletal devil amusing himself with various conjuring tricks, including turning women into fireballs. The use of red tinting in the first few moments, which mark the devil's emergence from a coffin amid flames, serves to reinforce the infernal aspect of the grotto. Attention is thus drawn to the background, which aims to be simultaneously threatening and captivating. Red, as suggestive of fire, was often used alongside other colours that carried supplementary meanings: yellow signalled candlelight or daytime, blue was utilised in night-time scenes and green or lavender indicated eeriness. These colours would be popular throughout the silent period, especially in early German cinema, and be used decisively in films such as *Der Golem, wie er in die Welt kam*. De Chomón's film is also interesting for what it says about the supernatural implications of colour, its capacity 'to intensify the make-believe nature of such characters as fairies, wizards, shape-changers, clowns, acrobats, demons and so on' (Minguet Batllori 2009: 97–98). As far as early photographic enhancers go, tinting could infuse a scene with affective charge.

The period between 1908 and 1917 has been called the 'transitional era' (Keil and Stamp 2004) because it accommodated the gradual establishment of what has come to be known as 'classical Hollywood cinema', marked by industrialised film production processes (with the concomitant end of the artisan director in the style of Méliès) and the emergence of the studio system, the prevalence of the narrative film over the trick film (and thus an increase in intertitles before sound arrived in 1927), the sedimentation of continuity editing as de facto narrative technique and the origins of the star system. This period also saw the rise and fall of nickelodeons, the first type of theatres dedicated to projecting selections of short films for entertainment. As a result of these shifts in the production, marketing and exhibition of films, innovative visual techniques became subsumed into cinema's wider narrative machinery and were put to the service of enhancing emotional, rather than simply visual, impact. Still sometimes the *pièce de résistance*, supernatural happenings would punctuate moments of dread, awe or suspense in service of wider overarching plots and stock motifs. For example, the majority of *Superstition andalouse* is actually a fantasy dream that acts as a cautionary tale for the female character, with all the supernatural elements confined to her imagination. Later films, such as *Spellbound* (1945), would make more extensive use of this type of narrative technique. As storytelling blended with, and even overtook, demonstration, the Gothic was able to move away from magical curio and carry out the type of reflective cultural work it has grown to embody.

After 1910, films also started to look to theatre for the longer, more complex stories demanded by the public. This happened in at least two ways. Firstly, as Ben Brewster and Leah Jacobs have argued, films 'became much more like plays in the kind of narratives they related' (1997: 213), borrowing theatrical tableaux, acting styles and staging techniques from the pictorial tradition and taking a 'situational approach to narrative' (14). Secondly, films began to adapt successful plays with more regularity. Their length, acting and structure brought them experientially closer to cinema than to novels and their popularity offered some guarantee of audience interest. Even the later *Dracula* and *Frankenstein*, covered in detail in Chapter 3, were largely adapted from the plays by Hamilton Deane (and revised by John L. Balderston) and Peggy Webling.[28] John S. Robertson's celebrated *Dr. Jekyll and Mr. Hyde* (1920), which featured classically trained actor John Barrymore, is illustrative of the synergies between stage and cinema, notably because Barrymore created the illusion of a personality change without recourse to make-up or embellishing special effects. Literary adaptations also became a way of investing cinema, then a novel form, with high artistic intentions. The reliance on nineteenth-century Gothic novels and stories must be read within the context of an industry vying for respectability through its reaching out to a 'high literary tradition' (Phillips 2018: 113). *Lord Feathertop* (1908) adapted an 1852 short story by Nathaniel Hawthorne about a witch who brings a scarecrow to life in order to teach someone a lesson, and *The House of the Seven Gables* (1910), also based on a Hawthorne text, told the story of the Pyncheon family, victims of a devastating ancestral curse. There were many others: Charlotte Brontë's *Jane Eyre* was adapted in 1910, Victor Hugo's *Notre-Dame de Paris* (*The Hunchback of Notre Dame*, 1833) in 1911, Wilkie Collins's *The Woman in White* (1860) in 1912, Nikolai Gogol's 'Strashnaya mest' ('A Terrible Vengeance', 1832) in 1913 and Charles Dickens's *The Mystery of Edwin Drood* (1870) in 1914. The most adapted Gothic writer during this period was, without a doubt, Edgar Allan Poe, whose name became synonymous with horror and mystery themes, and whose stories would continue to be made into increasingly longer films. The list of adaptations is significant, but the most Gothic of these were *Le Puits et le Pendule* (*The Pit and the Pendulum*, 1909), *Le Château de la peur* (*The Plague-Stricken City*, 1912) and *The Pit and the Pendulum* (1912), based on 'The Pit and the Pendulum' (1842), which follows the torture of a victim of the Inquisition, and 'The Masque of the Red Death' (1842). Elements of 'The Cask of Amontillado' (1846), a story about live immurement, were also used in D. W. Griffith's *The Sealed Room* (1909), which takes place in an indeterminate courtly past.

Perhaps the most significant of these transitional films is J. Searle Dawley's *Frankenstein*, a self-professed 'liberal' adaptation of Mary Shelley's novel that is as narrative as it is spectacular.[29] The film is story-driven: Frankenstein (Augustus Phillips) intends to create a perfect man, but due to the 'evil' in his mind, he instead gives life to a grotesque monster. The being vanishes into a mirror after Frankenstein accepts marital love, an indication that, to a certain extent, he operates as the dark side of his psyche. The film is structured so as to tell this story in just over 12 minutes in as clear a fashion as possible: Frankenstein conceives of the monster; Frankenstein makes him; Frankenstein is horrified and 'haunted' by his creation; the terror is overcome and normal (married) life resumes.[30] In this respect, Searle Dawley's *Frankenstein* is linear and coherent. Yet the legacy of cinema's previous fifteen years in it is also observable. The mise-en-scène of Frankenstein's laboratory and bedroom is strongly reminiscent of Méliès's alchemical workshops, complete with skulls, a distiller flask, fossils, a stuffed raven, dusty tomes and a Gothic chair that resembles a tombstone. Crucially, the creation scene is its most memorable moment. In it, the monster is created out of chemical reactions in a cauldron, a magical feat mimicked visually through a reverse-motion sequence in which a papier-mâché figure with a mobile arm gradually recomposes (rather than burns down) into the shape of the monster. The figure is then replaced by actor Charles Stanton Ogle, who is coded as monstrous: an intertitle explains that Frankenstein is 'appalled at the sight of his evil creation'.[31] The monster then hovers over a bereft Frankenstein lying on his bed, a scene that, at one point, recalls Henry Fuseli's painting 'The Nightmare' (1781).

For Richard J. Hand, the creation sequence is a lot more than a mere optical 'trick'. The fact that it is the 'dominant' one, 'the focus of the narrative and the set-piece of the film', and that it completely reverses the original by explaining what the novel only glosses over, signals its interest in making audiences '*see* the monster come into being' (2007: 12, italics in original). In so doing, Hand argues, Searle Dawley's *Frankenstein* may be seen as having 'create[d] the horror genre' (12). The film's preoccupation with generating fear, instead of mere curiosity or amusement, can be identified from other characteristics. For one thing, neither the monster nor the story provide any comic relief or acknowledge their artificiality. For another, as Kendall R. Phillips, working from archival materials, has been able to demonstrate, the initial incidental music recommendations

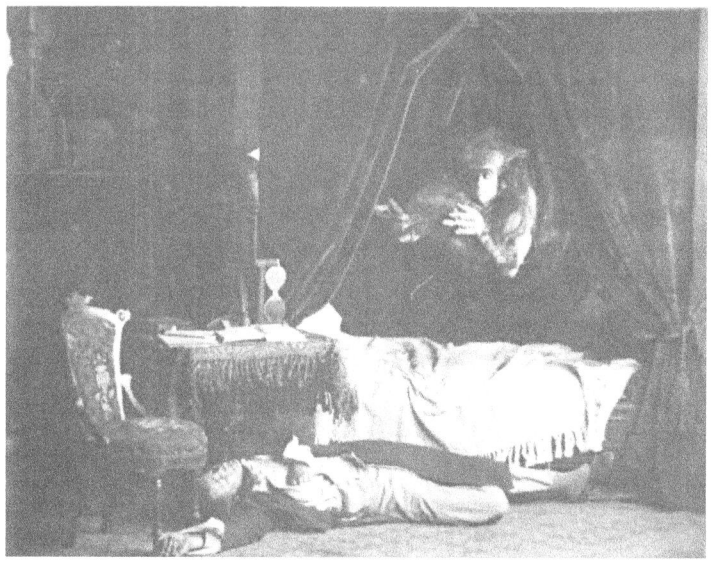

Figure 1.3 *Frankenstein* (1910) is the first cinematic adaptation of Mary Shelley's classic and one of many transitional narrative films of the period.

were '"dramatic" passages' from Carl Maria von Weber's ghost story opera *Der Freischütz* (1821), a decision that seems incontrovertible evidence 'that the Edison studio sought to evoke feelings of fear in its audiences' (2018: 118). Regardless of our specific position in relation to this assessment, *Frankenstein* offers a treatment of the story that marries Gothic settings (the views from the windows are of a medieval town with castles, and period props crop up throughout) and a Gothic monster (the creature's dishevelled appearance and old-fashioned rag-like burlap garments and bandages mark him as archaic Other and as part mummy) with the chemical magic of the mad scientist tradition.

Another film that deserves a special mention is Nino Oxilia's *Rapsodia satanica* (*Satan's Rhapsody*, 1917), based on the poem 'Rapsodia satanica: Poema cinema-musicale' (1915) by Fausto Maria Martini. It follows the misadventures of one Countess Alba d'Otrevita (Lyda Borelli) as she makes a deal with Mephisto (Ugo Bazzini) in order to regain her lost youth. The deal does not go according to plan after she fails to comply with her promise to resist falling in love. Apart from being notable for its gendered approach to the Faust legend, *Rapsodia satanica* is also the first concerted exploration of the 'regained beauty' motif that would become the subject of such later horror films as *The Corpse Vanishes* (1942) and the brilliant *I vampiri* (*The Vampires*, 1957).[32] Its 'Castle of Illusions', a Gothic neverwhere in which the devil is capable of jumping out of a painting at any moment, is also, naturally, a symbol for Alba's current state: like her, the building is old and suggestive of past glories. The imagery also emphasises the passing of time, with the interplay and 'fusion of funerary and nuptial rite[s]' (Jones 2018: 59) played out in the dance scenes and the final wedding. Alba's marital veil becomes a species of shroud as her beloved is revealed to be Mephisto. His embrace returns Alba to her old age, seemingly killing her, and her white garments are replaced by Alba's original black dress, now indicative of her proximity to the grave. Like other Gothic characters who attempt to bend the rules of nature, Alba and her lovers are doomed to failure. Her reverse transformation proves not just a moralistic tale about accepting one's lot in life but an allegorical *memento mori*. Broadly,

Rapsodia satanica is a good illustration of the points raised in this chapter regarding early cinema. The film was not made as a deliberate Gothic piece, even if its setting and themes render it one, but as a piece of 'high' art that brought together opera, literature and theatre (Paulicelli 2016: 56). At the same time, its cultural pretensions did not preclude it from utilising the optical techniques and tricks specific to cinema to create spatial effects halfway between the fearful and the amusing. Crucially, these effects were put to the larger service of its story. Clocking up at 55 minutes (45 in its restored version), *Rapsodia satanica* was preoccupied with the melodramatic development of its narrative.

The period that runs from the late 1890s to the popular reception of early German supernatural films, especially during the early 1920s, is defined by the impulse to exploit the unique opportunities granted by cinema as a visual mode that, while photorealistic, could be altered and edited in awe-inducing ways to generate specific affective and emotional reactions. This playfulness, not so much a novelty as the continuation of an earlier fascination with the possibilities of animated photography and optical illusions, was maintained even when cinema made the jump from short scenarios and vignettes to multi-reelers. Early films, although stylistically and narratively disparate, started to experiment with the Gothic aesthetically because of its associations with wonderment and fear. Lightning and storms became expected atmospheric cues for moments of terror, and past times could be presented as suitably remote, archaic and superstitious. Crucially, the boundary between the supernatural past and the secular present began to be blurred in ways that point towards Universal's more concerted efforts to migrate the horrific echoes of past times and their grandiose, austere settings to the present. If this period did not produce anything remotely close to a self-avowed Gothic strand of cinema, it did further develop images that would return in Robert Wiene's *Das Cabinet des Dr. Caligari* and James Whale's *Frankenstein*. Scenarios mixed fantasy, the fairy tale and mystery with Romantic motifs, and a long trail of witches, alchemists, demons and ghosts ebbed forth from a desire to experiment with cinematic magic. Phantasmagorical lenses and shadow play, as well as ghostly superimpositions and double-exposures, would eventually become an intrinsic part of the Gothic on screen.

FILMOGRAPHY

À la conquête du pôle (The Conquest of the Pole, Georges Méliès, 1912, France)
Après le bal (After the Ball, Méliès, 1897, France)
Barbe-bleue (Bluebeard, Méliès, 1901, France)
  Beneath the Tower Ruins (Charles Urban (producer), 1911, UK)
Cendrillon (Cinderella, Méliès, 1899, France)
Cendrillon (Cinderella, Méliès, 1912, France)
Cendrillon, ou la Pantoufle merveilleuse (Cinderella, Albert Capellani, 1907, France)
Chez la sorcière (The Bachelor's Paradise, Méliès, 1901, France)
Das Cabinet des Dr. Caligari (The Cabinet of Dr. Caligari, Robert Wiene, 1920, Germany)
Der Golem, wie er in die Welt kam (The Golem: How He Came into the World, Paul Wegener and Carl Boese, 1920, Germany)
Des Sängers Fluch (The Curse of the Wandering Minstrel, Messter-Film (producer), 1910, Germany)
Dr. Jekyll and Mr. Hyde (John S. Robertson, 1920, USA)
Dracula (Tod Browning, 1931, USA)
Execution of Mary, Queen of Scots (Alfred Clark, 1895, USA)
Fantômas (Louis Feuillade, 1913–14, serial, France)
Frankenstein (J. Searle Dawley, 1910, USA)
Frankenstein (James Whale, 1931, USA)
Hallucinations pharmaceutiques, ou Le Truc du potard (Pharmaceutical Hallucinations, Méliès, 1908, France)
Häxan (Witchcraft Through the Ages, Benjamin Christensen, 1922, Sweden/Denmark)
I vampiri (The Vampires, Riccardo Freda, 1957, Italy)
Il fantasma del castello (The Castle Ghosts, Aquila Films (producer), 1908, Italy)

In the Days of Witchcraft (Edison Manufacturing Company (producer), 1909, USA)

Jane Eyre (Thanhouser Film Corporation (producer), 1910, USA)

Jeanne d'Arc (Joan of Arc, Méliès, 1900, France)

Körkarlen (The Phantom Carriage, Victor Sjöström, 1921, Sweden)

L'Alchimiste Parafaragaramus, ou La Cornue infernale (The Mysterious Retort, Méliès, 1906, France)

L'Antre des esprits (The Magician's Cavern, Méliès, 1901, France)

L'Auberge ensorcelée (The Bewitched Inn, Méliès, 1897, France)

L'Enchanteur Alcofribas (Alcofribas, The Master Magician, Méliès, 1903, France)

L'Hallucination de l'alchimiste (An Hallucinated Alchemist, Méliès, 1897, France)

La Belle au bois dormant (Sleeping Beauty, Albert Capinelli and Lucien Nonguet, 1908, France)

La Cascade de feu (The Firefall, Méliès, 1904, France)

La Cuisine de l'ogre (In the Bogie Man's Cave, Méliès, 1907, France)

La Damnation de Faust (The Damnation of Faust, Méliès, 1903, France)

Le Fakir de Singapour (The Indian Sorcerer, Méliès, 1908, France)

La Fée Carabosse, ou Le Poignard fatal (The Witch, Méliès, 1906, France)

La Légende du fantôme (The Black Pearl, Segundo de Chomón, 1908, France)

La Maison ensorcelée (The Haunted House, Segundo de Chomón, 1906, France)

La Mariée du château maudit (The Bride of the Haunted Castle, Albert Capellani, 1910, France)

La Poule aux œufs d'or (The Hen That Laid the Golden Eggs, Gaston Velle, 1905, France)

La torre dei vampiri (The Vampire's Tower, Gino Zaccaria, 1913, Italy)

Le Cauchemar (The Nightmare, Méliès, 1896, France)

Le Château de la peur (The Plague-Stricken City, Louis Feuillade, 1912, France)

Le Chevalier des neiges (The Knight of the Snows, Méliès, 1912, France)

Le Chevalier mystère (The Mysterious Knight, Méliès, 1899, France)

Le Diable au couvent (The Devil in a Convent, Méliès, 1899, France)

Le Magicien (The Magician, Méliès, 1898, France)

Le Manoir du diable (The Haunted Castle, Georges Méliès, 1896, France)

Le Monstre (The Monster, Méliès, 1903, France)

Le Nouveau Seigneur du village (The New Lord of the Village, Méliès, 1908, France)

Le Palais des mille et une nuits (*The Palace of the Arabian Nights*, Méliès, 1905, France)
Le Petit Chaperon rouge (*Little Red Riding Hood*, Méliès, 1901, France)
Le Petit Poucet (*Tom Thumb*, Segundo de Chomón, 1909, France)
Le Pied de mouton (*The Talisman*, Albert Capellani, 1907, France)
Le Puits et le Pendule (*The Pit and the Pendulum*, Henri Desfontaines, 1909, France)
Le Royaume des fées (*The Kingdom of the Fairies*, Méliès, 1903, France)
Le Savant et le Chimpanzé (*The Doctor and the Monkey*, Méliès, 1900, France)
Le Sorcier, le Prince et le Bon Génie (*The Wizard, the Prince and the Good Fairy*, Méliès, 1900, France)
Le Spectre rouge (*The Red Spectre*, Segundo de Chomón, 1907, France)
Le Squelette joyeux (*Happy Skeleton*, Louis Lumière, 1898, France)
Le Voyage dans la lune (*A Trip to the Moon*, Méliès, 1903, France)
Les Aventures du Baron de Münchhausen (*Baron Munchausen's Dream*, Méliès, 1911, France)
Les Quatre Cents Farces du diable (*The Merry Frolics of Satan*, Méliès, 1906, France)
Les Sept Châteaux du diable (*The Devil's Seven Castles*, Ferdinand Zecca, France, 1904)
Les Vampires (*The Vampires*, Louis Feuillade, 1915, serial, France)
Les Vampires de la côte (*Vampires of the Coast*, Pathé Frères (producer), 1908, France)
Loïe Fuller (Segundo de Chomón, 1905, France)
Lord Feathertop (Edison Manufacturing Company (producer), 1908, USA)
Miss Jekyll and Madame Hyde (Charles L. Gaskill, 1915, USA)
Notre-Dame de Paris (*The Hunchback of Notre Dame*, Albert Capellani, 1911, France)
Pan Twardowski (Wiktor Biegański, 1921, Poland)
Pan Twardowski (Henryk Szaro, 1936, Poland)
Rapsodia satanica (*Satan's Rhapsody*, Nino Oxilia, 1917, Italy)
Spellbound (Alfred Hitchcock, 1945, USA)
Strashnaya mest (*The Terrible Vengeance*, Wladyslaw Starewicz, 1913, Russia)
Superstition andalouse (*Andalusian Superstition*, Segundo de Chomón, 1912, France/Spain)
Tentation de Saint Antoine (*The Temptation of Saint Anthony*, Méliès, 1898, France)
The Avenging Conscience (D. W. Griffith, 1914, USA)
The Cavalier's Dream (Edwin S. Porter, 1898, USA)

The Corpse Vanishes (Wallace Fox, 1942, USA)
The Crimson Stain Mystery (T. Hayes Hunter, 1916, serial, USA)
The Ghost Breaker (Cecil B. Demille and Oscar Apfel, 1914, USA)
The Haunted Curiosity Shop (Walter R. Booth, 1901, USA)
The Haunted Hotel (J. Stuart Blackton, 1907, USA)
The Haunted House (Siegmund Lubin (producer), 1899, USA)
The House of the Seven Gables (J. Searle Dawley, 1910, USA)
The Imp of the Bottle (Edison Manufacturing Company (producer), USA, 1909)
The Magic Sword (Walter R. Booth, 1901, UK)
The Mysteries of Myra (Leopold and Theodore Wharton, 1916, serial, USA)
The Mystery Mind (Will S. Davis and Fred Sittenham, 1920, serial, USA)
The Mystery of Edwin Drood (Herbert Blaché and Tom Terriss, 1914, USA)
The Phantom Foe (Bertram Millhauser, 1920, serial, USA)
The Phantom of the Opera (Rupert Julian, 1925, USA)
The Pit and the Pendulum (Alice Guy Blaché, 1912, USA)
The Prince of Darkness (American Mutoscope and Biograph (producer), 1900, USA)
The Sealed Room (D. W. Griffith, 1909, USA)
The Vampire (Robert G. Vignola, 1913, USA)
The Village Vampire (Edwin Frazee, 1916, USA)
The Voice on the Wire (Stuart Paton, 1917, serial, USA)
The Werewolf (Henry MacRae, 1913, USA)
The White Wolf (Nestor Film Company, 1914, USA)
The Woman in White (George Nichols, 1912, USA)
The X Rays (George Albert Smith, 1897, UK)
'Tis Now the Very Witching Time of Night (Edison Manufacturing Company (producer), 1909, USA)
Un miracle sous l'inquisition (*A Miracle Under the Inquisition*, Méliès, 1904, France)
Uncle Josh in a Spooky Hotel (Edwin S. Porter, 1900, USA)
Uncle Josh's Nightmare (Edwin S. Porter, 1900, USA)
Une excursion incohérente (*Traveller's Nightmare*, Segundo de Chomón, 1909, France)
Vampires of the Night (Aquila Films, 1914, Italy)

Vampyren (*The Vampire*, Mauritz Stiller's, 1913, Sweden)

Visite sous-marine du 'Maine' (*Divers at Work on the Wreck of the Maine*, Méliès, 1898, France)

NOTES

1 The term 'trick film' refers to short films made during the early days of cinema which usually showcased one or more innovative optical illusions or special effects.

2 The film is the first to receive attention in Gary D. Rhodes's encyclopaedic study of horror film up to 1915, where he argues that it was received as horrific by the press (2018: 2).

3 The Grand Guignol Theatre opened its doors in 1897 and specialised in realistic, often gory and macabre, horror plays.

4 The kinetoscope was a device for film exhibition designed to be viewed through a peephole by one individual at a time. It created the illusion of movement through the sequential conveyance of a strip of film. The kinetograph was the first camera to take pictures on a moving strip of film. For more on them and their connection to early Gothic and horror cinema, see Jones (2011: 1–17) and Leeder (2017: 2–3).

5 Filmed theatre and filmed magic shows were also popular at the time.

6 Genre categories did exist, but these were very different from the ones we use today. Pathé's catalogue for 1905 distinguished between 'scènes de plain air' (open air scenes), 'scènes comiques' (comical scenes), 'scènes à trucs' (trick films), 'sports et acrobaties' (sports and acrobatics), 'scènes historiques' (historical scenes), 'scenes grivoises d'un caractère piquant' (loose scenes of a provocative nature), 'danses et ballets' (dancing and ballet), 'scènes dramatiques et realistes' (realistic and dramatic scenes), 'féeries et contes' (féeries and fantastic tales), 'scènes religieuses et bibliques' (religious and biblical scenes) 'scènes ciné-phonographiques' (cinematic-phonographic scenes) and 'scènes diverses' (diverse scenes) (Minguet Batllori 2010: 85, my translation).

7 I am not providing my personal taxonomy based on subject matter but following the genre categories in the booklet to *Georges Méliès: Le Premier Magicien du Cinéma* (1896–1913), released by Lobster Films in 2009, the most thorough DVD collection on Méliès's surviving work.

8 In some cases, the correspondences were quite direct, with magic tricks reused or adapted to film. Such is the case of the 'vanishing lady' trick, first performed in 1886 and filmed three times between 1896 and 1898. Méliès even said at one point that the reason he stopped innovating in prestidigitation was that all his inventions had been applied to cinema (Solomon 2010: 3, 48). Many early directors were initially magicians too. For a list of them, see Barnouw (1981: 45–83).

9 In fact, it could be argued that most trick films are, to a point, narrative films, since they tell stories, however basic and simple, and present a series of actions. The point normally made by film historians is that trick films are less interested in telling stories than in producing fantastic spectacles.

10 Méliès adapted the Faust legend on several occasions, although *La damnation de Faust* was directly inspired by the musical composition of the same name by Hector Berlioz. Similarly, *Le Palais des mille et une nuits* was influenced by the Arabic collection *Alf Layla wa-Layla* (*One Thousand and One Nights*). My point is that, when it comes to general intellectual properties, such as folk tales and legends, which have received other artistic treatments, direct correspondences between text and source are hard to determine with absolute precision.

11 The ghost is not real in *Il fantasma del castello*.

12 The synergy between stage magic and film carried on into the 1930s, when midnight 'spook shows' combining a live magic show and a B-movie horror became popular in America (Walker 1994). It is, of course, also possible to read William Castle's many cinema gimmicks in the late 1950s and early 1960s as a continuation of such practices (Heard 2006: 263).

13 Some of these legends would continue to be the subject of longer narrative Gothic films. A good example is the Polish folkloric legend of Pan Twardowski, a man who sells his soul to the devil in exchange for special powers. It was adapted in 1921 and 1936, both as *Pan Twardowski*.

14 In fact, the 'darker' trick films of director Segundo de Chomón were categorised as 'phantasmagorias' in the 2010 DVD release of his work by

the Filmoteca de Catalunya, *Segundo de Chomón, 1903–1912: El cine de la fantasía*, a decision that betrays the currency of the term in cinematic discourse on early film.

15 The phantasmagoria show is defined by the use of back projection, the projection of opaque objects, a special apparatus to manipulate size, lantern images (painted on black backgrounds) and other additional elements borrowed from the theatre tradition (mirrors, smoke, actors, shadows) (Heard 2006: 148). Dissolving views, which allowed for transitions from one object/state to another, would replace phantasmagoria shows in the 1820s.

16 Robertson's repertoire drew on a wide range of topics drawn from Greek mythology, romantic poetry and the lives of the Saints (Heard 2006: 107). He would conduct his phantasmagorias in an abandoned Gothic convent, dressed up for the occasion. These are important indicators of the mood the phantasmagoria aimed to elicit.

17 Heard sees this as a crucial moment in which there is, for the magic lantern, 'the first point of divergence into the realms of fictional fantasy' (2006: 93).

18 The skeleton detaches the skull from its body and then replaces it.

19 *The Avenging Conscience* adapts Edgar Allan Poe's short story 'The Tell-Tale Heart' (1843) and the poem 'Annabel Lee' (1849). *The Phantom Carriage* adapts Lagerlöf's novel *Körkarlen* (1912), published in English as *Thy Soul Shall Bear Witness!* in 1921. *Witchcraft Through the Ages* was partly based on Kramer's *Malleus Maleficarum*, the influential witchcraft treatise first published in 1487.

20 Equally significant in terms of cinematic innovation were the English George Albert Smith and the American Edwin S. Porter.

21 Magicians also appear in other settings and countries. See, for example, the dervish in *Le Monstre* (*The Monster*, 1903), set in ancient Egypt, or the Singaporean fakir in *Le Fakir de Singapour* (*The Indian Sorcerer*, 1908).

22 There were early cinema directors in other countries – the British Walter R. Booth, the Danish Viggo Larsen, the Japanese Asana Shiro and Shozo Makino, the Mexican Salvador Toscano, the Russian Vasilii Goncharov – who made occasional Gothic-inflected trick films. Given that most of their work is lost, and for the sake of conciseness, I am not including them in this chapter. The interested reader should consult Workman and Howarth (2016).

23 Serials, or serialised films, began in the early 1910s and involved consecutive screenings, typically one a week. The cliff-hanger was their defining aspect and enabled an understanding of film as offering partial views of the overall action (Brasch 2018: 19–22).

24 Jack Zipes argues, via Paul Ginisty, that féerie plays originated in the Italian court ballets of the sixteenth and seventeenth centuries (2011: 36).

25 Méliès also filmed Little Red Riding Hood as *Le Petit Chaperon rouge* (1901). *Les Aventures du Baron de Münchhausen* (*Baron Munchausen's Dream*, 1911) includes elements of the féerie, but can be more adequately classed as a nightmare film.

26 Other major féeries by other directors include Gaston Velle's *La Poule aux œufs d'or* (*The Hen That Laid the Golden Eggs*, 1905) and Albert Capellani's *Cendrillon, ou la Pantoufle merveilleuse* (*Cinderella*, 1907), *Le Pied de mouton* (*The Talisman*, 1907) and, with Lucien Nonguet, *La Belle au bois dormant* (*Sleeping Beauty*, 1908).

27 There were a significant number of films made in the early twentieth century with 'vampire' in their title, such as *Les vampires de la côte* (*Vampires of the Coast*, 1908), *Vampyren* (*The Vampire*, 1913), *La torre dei vampiri* (*The Vampire's Tower*, 1913), *The Vampire* (1913), *Vampires of the Night* (1914) and *The Village Vampire* (1916). In these, however, the term 'vampire' is used either to describe ruffians or, more often, the parasitic 'vamp' seductress popularised by actresses like Theda Bara, a proto-femme fatale.

28 The popular Thomas R. Sullivan 1887 dramatisation was revived in 1906, and a rival adaptation appeared in 1897 that was performed in 1908 and was filmed by William Selig (Rigby 2017: 12). This one became the first of at least four adaptations of the classic made before Robertson's, the others appearing in 1910, 1912 and 1913 (Rhodes 2018: 318–322).

29 I use, and cite intertitles from, the newly restored version available from the Library Congress website: https://blogs.loc.gov/now-see-hear/2018/10/frankenstein-post/ (accessed 29 October 2018).

30 The monster is said to be 'haunting' Frankenstein in one of the intertitles.

31 The synopsis printed in the original catalogue supports this when it describes the creature as an *'awful, ghastly and abhorrent monster'* (quoted in Wiebel 2010: 60, italics in original).

32 The film was shot the same year as *Miss Jekyll and Madame Hyde*, which trod the same ground, but was released two years later.

BIBLIOGRAPHY

Barnouw, E. (1981) *The Magician and the Cinema*, Oxford and New York: Oxford University Press.

Brasch, I. (2018) *Film Serials and the American Cinema, 1910–1940: Operational Detection*, Amsterdam: Amsterdam University Press.

Brewster, B. and L. Jacobs (1997) *Theatre to Cinema: Stage Pictorialism and the Early Feature Film*, Oxford and New York: Oxford University Press.

Gunning, T. (1986) 'The Cinema of Attraction: Early Cinema, Its Spectator and the Avant-Garde', *Wide Angle*, 8.3: 63–70.

Hammond, P. (1974) *Marvellous Méliès*, London: Gordon Fraser.

Hand, R. J. (2007) 'Paradigms of Metamorphosis and Transmutation: Thomas Edison's *Frankenstein* and John Barrymore's *Dr Jekyll and Mr Hyde*', in R. J. Hand and J. McRoy (eds) *Monstrous Adaptations: Generic and Thematic Mutations in Horror Film*, Manchester: Manchester University Press.

Heard, M. (2006) *Phantasmagoria: The Secret Life of the Magic Lantern*, Hastings: The Projection Box.

Jones, D. J. (2011) *Gothic Machine: Textualities, Pre-cinematic Media and Film in Popular Visual Culture, 1670–1910*, Cardiff: University of Wales Press.

Jones, D. J. (2018) *Re-Envisaging the First Age of Cinematic Horror, 1896–1934: Quanta of Fear*, Cardiff: University of Wales Press.

Keil, C. and S. Stamp (2004) *American Cinema's Transitional Era: Audiences, Institutions, Practices*, Berkeley: University of California Press.

Leeder, M. (2017) *The Modern Supernatural and the Beginnings of Cinema*, Basingstoke: Palgrave Macmillan.

Long Hoeveler, D. (2010) *Gothic Riffs: Secularizing the Uncanny in the European Imaginary 1780–1820*, Columbus: Ohio State University Press.

Longueil, A. E. (1923) 'The Word "Gothic" in Eighteenth Century Criticism', *Modern Language Notes*, 38.8: 453–460.

Minguet Batllori, J. M. (2009) 'Segundo de Chomón and the Fascination for Colour', *Film History*, 21.1: 94–103.

Minguet Batllori, J. M. (2010) 'Segundo de Chomón: Beyond the Cinema of Attractions', in *Segundo de Chomón, 1903–12: El cine de la fantasía*, Barcelona: Filmoteca de Catalunya.

Musser, C. (1990) *The Emergence of Cinema: The American Screen to 1907*, Oxford and New York: Charles Scribner's Sons.

Paulicelli, E. (2016) *Italian Style: Fashion and Film from Early Film to the Digital Age*, London and New York: Bloomsbury.

Phillips, K. R. (2018) *A Place of Darkness: The Rhetoric of Horror in Early American Cinema*, Austin: University of Texas Press.

Rhodes, G. D. (2018) *The Birth of the American Horror Film*, Edinburgh: Edinburgh University Press.

Rigby, J. (2017) *American Gothic: Six Decades of Classic Horror Cinema*, 2nd rev. edn, Cambridge: Signum Books.

Robinson, D. (1993) *Georges Méliès: Father of Film Fantasy*, London: BFI.

Singer Kovács, K. (1976) 'Georges Méliès and the Féerie', *Cinema Journal*, 16.1: 1–13.

Solomon, M. (2010) *Disappearing Tricks: Silent Film, Houdini, and the New Magic of the Twentieth Century*, Urbana and Chicago: University of Illinois Press.

Walker, M. (1994) *Ghostmasters: A Look Back at America's Spooks Shows*, rev. edn, Boca Raton, FL: Cool Hand Communications.

Warner, M. (2006) *Phantasmagoria: Spirit Visions, Metaphors, and Media into the Twenty-first Century*, Oxford: Oxford University Press.

Wiebel, F. C. (2010) *Edison's Frankenstein*, Albany: BearManor Media.

Workman, C. and T. Howarth (2016) *Tome of Terror: Horror Films of the Silent Era*, London and Baltimore, MD: Midnight Marquee Press.

Zipes, J. (2011) *The Enchanted Screen: The Unknown History of Fairy-Tale Films*, Abingdon and New York: Routledge.

2

MONSTROUS SHADOWS

In the 1910s and 1920s, the exploitation of cinema's visual possibilities encompassed a concomitant interest in polishing what would become a transgressive aesthetic of fear. A medium-specific way of shooting the Gothic monster that would have a significant effect on horror cinema from 1923 to 1935 crystallised around a number of supernaturally themed, sometimes adaptational, films made in Germany that drew inspiration from the country's Romantic tradition in literature. The work of some of the best directors would be truly transformative and have transnational consequences. Most famously, Paul Leni, director of *Wachsfigurenkabinett* (*Waxworks*, 1924), would eventually put his suggestive shadows and discombobulating angles to excellent use in *The Cat and the Canary*, after Carl Laemmle asked him to join the Universal Studios team, and Fritz Lang would go on to direct *Secret Beyond the Door* (1947), one of the many American Female Gothics of the 1940s.

The Gothic films of Germany emerged from a historical and political period of upheaval marked by the First World War (1914–18) and the establishment of the democratic but unstable Weimar Republic (1918–33). The war against France, the country that had dominated early cinema, meant that their film imports were banned and that Germany was free to grow its own industry. Further stimulation came from the perceived need to fight competition from the Danish production and distribution company Nordisk and from governmental intervention designed to support the centralisation of the industry (Brockmann 2010: 23–24). By 1918, Germany had lost the war, but its cinema had become a veritable monopoly and its audiences grown fivefold (Saunders 1994: 21). Indeed, the films made in Germany between then and Hitler's ascent to power in 1933 are still its best-remembered today. This is understandable, given that these years yielded landmark films such as Fritz Lang's science-fiction epic *Metropolis* (1927) and the serial killer narrative *M – Eine Stadt sucht einen Mörder*, to name only two. They also saw the development of expressionist cinema, which may be taken as an extension of expressionism as an artistic movement in painting and poetry, and is so called because its aesthetics favour subjective and distorted perspectives. Peaking before its application to film in the work of artists like Ersnt Ludwig Kircher, Erich Heckel and Wassily Kandinsky, its emotional perception of the world travelled into cinema in the form of sharp-angled and geometrically improbable settings. Shadows and streaks of light painted directly onto buildings or exaggerated acting have been taken as other tell-tale signs of this cinematic movement, even though their deliberateness has been put into question.[1] Regardless of their specific or voluntary origin, the aesthetic of these films conveys a pervasive sense of the uncanny (Coates 1991: 1–17), and the villains of films like Robert Wiene's *Das Cabinet des Dr. Caligari* (henceforth *Caligari*), Paul Wegener and Carl Boese's *Der Golem, wie er in die Welt kam* and F. W. Murnau's *Nosferatu, eine Symphonie des Grauens* (henceforth *Nosferatu*) were foundational to the development of Gothic cinema.

It is important to note that a lot has been written about the need to de-essentialise German cinema from the early twentieth century on the grounds that a number of the films that are normally studied as expressionist do not actually display expressionistic characteristics and that this term does not do justice to the wider spectrum of films made during the Wilhelmine period (1890–1918) and the Weimar Republic (Elsaesser 2000: 18–60). The reading of apparently proto-fascist figures in films such as *Caligari* as artistic anticipations of Adolf Hitler and Nazism, a psychosocial argument developed by Siegfried Kracauer in his 1947 landmark study of German cinema, has also been actively challenged by film critics over the years (Scheunemann 2003a: x). In my discussion of key early German Gothic films, I am also keen to refute the myth of origins that positions *Caligari*, a film about a mad hypnotist who uses a somnambulist to commit his murders, as an urtext of sorts.[2] In fact, as Dietrich Scheunemann (2003b: 130–134) has perceptively argued, *Caligari* is better understood as the culmination of the Mephistophelian doppelgänger typical of German Romanticism. This motif found its best expression in the literature of Johan Wolfgang von Goethe, Friedrich Schiller and E. T. A. Hoffmann, and was revived by early twentieth-century writers like Gustav Meyrink, in his novel *Der Golem* (*The Golem*, 1913–14), and by Hanns Heinz Ewers.[3] It is, in fact, more accurate to think of early German cinema as 'a development of German Romanticism', the medium's modern techniques merely 'lend[ing] visible form to Romantic fancies' (Eisner 1965: 113).

Ewers was himself responsible for the script of *Der Student von Prag*, a self-professed Romantic drama ('Romantisches Drama') and melange of tales of shadow-selling, Satanic pacts and unruly doubles drawn from sources such as Adelbert von Chamisso's novella *Peter Schlemihl* (1814), Hoffmann's 'Die Abenteuer der Sylvester-Nacht' ('A New Year's Eve Adventure', 1814), Edgar Allan Poe's 'William Wilson' (1839) and the Faust legend.[4] Set in the early nineteenth century, it tells the story of a disillusioned, impoverished man, Balduin (Paul Wegener), who sells his reflection to Scapinelli (John Gottowt), an eccentric adventurer ('ein Abenteurer'), in exchange for wealth. Although the utilisation of double exposure to conjure up a harrowing doppelgänger was not new, in this film it received its most extensive and 'large-scale application' (Guido Seeber, quoted in Elsaesser 2000: 48). The most memorable scenes to exploit the technique include the moment when Balduin's shadow-bathed reflection steps out of the mirror and the one where a split screen creates the illusion that a game of cards is being played between the man and his double. The latter also employs overhead lighting to add a touch of eeriness to what is already an extremely uncanny encounter. Undoubtedly, *Der Student von Prag* is important because it constitutes one of the first determined attempts to produce a work of art (hence Ewers's involvement as a popular, published writer) comparable to theatre at a time when cinema was struggling for intellectual recognition. But it is the film's investment in the medium and its optical effects that made it stand out and proved most influential. *Der Student von Prag* was one of the first narrative films (the first in Germany) to emphasise and visualise the fantastic: the threat the double poses pervades a narrative interested in making the strange and invisible, if not palpable, then certainly imaginable; it blurs the boundaries between reality and dreams. This aim, the exploitation of cinema's distinct own technical possibilities, is not one retroactively impinged upon the filmmakers either. As Casper Tybjerg points out, the publicist for *Der Student von Prag* suggested as much in his booklet for the film when he wrote that '[Ewers] ha[d] forced fantastic images into reality' (2004: 32). Importantly, the film picked up where Edison's *Frankenstein*'s early experiments had left off and gave them a longer treatment. Gothic cinema had begun to travel beyond the purely optical and spectacular and into the world of psychologically rich narrative.[5]

Der Student von Prag was also a resounding commercial success, and this had two connected effects. Firstly, at a national level, it paved the way for more doppelgänger films. Some focused on mirror images, such as the 1926 remake of *Der Student von Prag*; others on stolen shadows, in *Der verlorene Schatten* (*The Lost Shadow*, 1921); or else on repressed human desires that take over the rational self. A number of films made subsequently, such as *Die Augen des Ole Brandis* (*The Eyes of Ole Brandis*, 1914) and Murnau's *Faust: Eine deutsche Volkssage* (*Faust*, 1926), would also explore the myth by expanding on the trope of the Faustian bargain.[6] Filmmakers also mined foreign works for repressed selves, doubles and rebellious

Figure 2.1 Double exposure was used in *Der Student von Prag* (*The Student of Prague*, 1913) to give the illusion that Balduin (Wegener) is playing a game of cards against his doppelgänger.

body parts. There were two direct adaptations of Robert Louis Stevenson's *Strange Case of Dr Jekyll and Mr Hyde*, *Ein seltsamer Fall* (*A Strange Case*, 1914) and Murnau's lost *Der Januskopf* (*The Head of Janus*, 1920); Richard Oswald made *Das Bildnis des Dorian Gray* (*The Picture of Dorian Gray*) in 1917, after the 1890 novel by Oscar Wilde; Conrad Veidt starred in Robert Wiene's atmospheric *Orlacs Hände* (1924), adapted from Maurice Renard's novel *Les Mains d'Orlac* (*The Hands of Orlac*, 1920); and an atmospheric version of the Sherlock Holmes novel *The Hound of the Baskervilles* (1902), *Der Hund von Baskerville*, premiered in 1929.[7] These were not the only foreign Gothic adaptations, as Germany, like other countries during this period, turned to literature for ideas and artistic legitimacy. Gaston Leroux's *Le Fantôme de l'Opéra* (*The Phantom of the Opera*, 1909–10) was adapted for the first time by Ernst Matray in 1916 as *Das Phantom der Oper*, and Alexander Pushkin's 'Pikovaya dama' ('The Queen of Spades', 1834) in 1918 as *Pique Dame*. At the international level, *Der Student von Prag* facilitated the exportation of German cinema, especially to America, where it would eventually be perceived as a threat to Hollywood. Rye and Wegener's film already contained all the ingredients that would make Weimar directors popular: effective use of light and camera techniques, characters developed from the country's Romantic tradition in a bid to establish 'a truce between highbrow culture and a lowbrow medium' (Elsaesser 2000: 50) and a desire to transport the eerie effects of literature to the visual realm.

Made shortly after *Der Student von Prag*, *Der Golem* (*The Golem*, 1915) was an attempt to exploit the success of the former by continuing to use the captivating scenery of Prague, although this time not by shooting on location, and by developing the fantastic without renouncing artistic pretensions. To this end, Wegener worked with co-director and co-screenwriter Henrik Galeen, who would eventually become responsible for penning some of the most important of Gothic German films, the already mentioned *Nosferatu* and *Wachsfigurenkabinett* and, with Ewers, the 1926 remake of *Der Student von Prag*. Wegener, who was by this point a theatre and cinema celebrity, also helped with the script. Both men were interested in finding a monster comparable to the doppelgänger in *Der Student von Prag*. The mythical golem, a figure of traditional Jewish folklore associated with power and strength and whose Hebrew name translates into 'shapeless thing', offered plenty of cinematic and dramatic scope.[8] Although Wegener's original idea was for the film to be a period piece, financial constraints meant *Der Golem* would end up being set in the present. For this reason, the golem would become a Gothic remnant of the past set in modern times. Sadly, only fragments of the film have survived, but the extant script reveals that the planned story is not wildly different from that of its 1920 remake: the tomb of the golem is found, the monster is awakened by a rabbi, who subsequently asks him to look after his daughter, and the creature's increasingly violent behaviour leads to its demise. Not many promotional and journalistic materials exist, but we know that Cliese's design for the monster was a hit and that *Der Golem* was enough of a success to grant it an English-language print for distribution in America, where it was retitled *The Monster of Fate*.

As important as the monster was Wegener's performance. The actor's imposing, lumbering body and glacial expression made him a good choice for the role of the golem. His acting was definitely on point: threatening yet gentle, able to channel both fear and pity. A review from 1915 extolled Wegener's 'haunting and consistent portrayal', which 'grippingly capture[d] the ghostly and the supernatural nature of the apparition' (quoted in Nicolella and Soister 2012: 100). Wegener's combination of carefully modulated gestures with more sudden jerky, robotic movements suggests a potentially unstable entity. The application of pasty, lead-like make-up enhanced the actor's attributes and made them more threatening. More importantly, the film's finale, in which the golem relentlessly stalks the lead actress, marks the beginning of what we could call 'monster-framing'. The short scene shows the golem walking up the stairs of a tower-like structure and towards the camera, its silhouette rendered menacing against a bright window. Its eyes and wooden expression appear to glow as threads of light hit them. The moment is brief and perhaps not all that scary, but it is a significant one nonetheless. Wegener's work was so iconic, and the film so successful, that there was a parodic follow-up, *Der Golem und die Tänzerin* (*The Golem and the Dancing Girl*, 1917), also lost, where Wegener, playing himself, pretends to be the golem brought back to life to attract the attention of a young dancer. The golem did not simply descend into parody. A fully fledged remake would be shot in 1920 in which Wegener would reprise this creature as a source of horror and pity. By the time *Caligari* arrived in 1920, German cinema had already birthed its share of Gothic figures, but expressionism would breathe new life into them.

Caligari, hailed as 'the birth of horror', has also been seen as a milestone in Gothic cinema (Carver 2013: 238; Groom 2012: 124). Taking place in the fictional, misshapen town of Holstenwall and potentially the nightmare of a madman, the film appears to be a natural repository of social anxieties, its title hypnotist (Werner Krauss) a tyrant who uses somnambulist Cesare (Conrad Veidt) to sublimate his repressed desires and to rule despotically. The unhinged sets, which may or may not reflect the psychology of the characters or the nature of the film as a hallucination, are not architectonically Gothic, but are an obviously 'medieval fantasy' (Robinson 2013: 35) that serves to displace the action onto a distant past full of the magic of fairground attractions and dark, concave back alleys.[9] The film's 'painted landscapes' offer 'some of the most haunting images of Gothic cinema' (Robinson 2013: 8), and the motif of the double and the theme of oppression may seem enough to 'most certainly qualify the film generically as Gothic horror' (Morgart 2014: 380).[10] There are other elements in the film that draw from this tradition: the wax figure that replaces Cesare in his coffin is reminiscent of that found by heroine Emily St. Aubert in Ann Radcliffe's *The Mysteries of Udolpho*, which she takes to be the corpse of one Signora Laurentini; the kidnapping scene in Jane's (Lil Dagover) bedroom quotes Henry Fuseli's 'The Nightmare' (1781) and the murder of Elizabeth in Mary Shelley's *Frankenstein*; Francis's (Friedrich Fehér) unearthing of both a book and diary that shed light on the identity of the asylum director and the 'real' Caligari plays out as an update of the partial found manuscripts in Radcliffe's *The Romance of the Forest* (1791) and *The Italian*.

The unearthing of the documents supporting Caligari's madness is worth discussing in more detail, as it challenges our preconceptions of the main character. The book Francis digs out is titled *Somnambulism: A Collected Edition by the University of Upsala* [sic], and contains the tale of 'The Cabinet of Dr. Caligari', tellingly written in Gothic typeface.[11] In its pages, it is revealed that Caligari was a 1793 mystic who 'toured the fairs of numerous villages in northern Italy, accompanied by a somnambulist named Cesare' and that he 'sowed panic amongst villager folks through a series of foul murders'. Aside from the relocation of the root of evil to a remote Europe, a trick typical of English Gothic romance projections of villainy onto the Continent, this moment implies that we can no longer safely refer to the hypnotist as Caligari. The sketchy entries in the suspect's diary show the man's immense joy at the admission of a new somnambulist to his asylum, for this will enable him to 'satisfy [his] life's unwavering wish ... to unravel the psychiatrist secrets of this Caligari!' The obsession is taken to impersonating extremes. His adoption of the mystic's name and introduction of his victim as Cesare points towards more than an experiment: 'Caligari' has either adopted a new identity or, as the film seems to emphasise in the subsequent scene, has been possessed. As the director walks home, the sentence 'You must become Caligari!' flashes in front of him various times. This moment either suggests the return of a murderer across time via body snatching or, more likely given the story's setting, the delusions brought about by excessive academic zeal. It also resonates with the tales of the repressed 'id' common in early German cinema. Even the film's safe ending, in which Caligari is apparently absolved by a return to the framing story that exposes Francis's narration as a fabrication, does little to resolve the action and is arguably even more disturbing for its ambiguity (Scheunemann 2003b: 148).

Caligari is best known for its innovative use of painted settings, for its hallucinatory, intoxicating 'mise-en-scène of fear and desire' (Hake 2008: 31), which has more generally been retroactively applied to a variety of films released after it. For all its novelty, *Caligari* was not overtly experimental in its use of shooting techniques, especially when compared to other roughly contemporaneous films attempting to reflect madness – the deforming mirrors in Abel Gance's *La Folie du Docteur Tube* (*The Madness of Dr. Tube*, 1915) are a good example. *Caligari*'s use of, sometimes diamond-shaped, iris lenses does nevertheless highlight expressions to bring a certain degree of ambiguity to specific sequences, especially when the camera lingers over the doctor's face in the closing shot, seemingly asking if he really is who he appears to be. Expressionism's distinct interplay between light and shadow, the exploitation of chiaroscuro for affective purposes, only apparent in the painted settings in *Caligari*, would become far more pronounced in later films exploring obsessive and traumatised psychologies, such as *Von morgens bis mitternachts* (*From Morn to Midnight*, 1920), *Phantom* (1922), Wiene's own Fyodor Dostoevsky adaptation *Raskolnikow* (*Crime and Punishment*, 1923) and the Jack the Ripper sequence in *Wachsfigurenkabinett*. It would also be used to suggest visions and the powers of hypnotism in *Dr. Mabuse, der Spieler* (Dr. Mabuse, The Gambler, 1922) and *Schatten – Eine nächtliche Halluzination* (Warning Shadows, 1923). It would, however, be the supernatural *Der Golem, wie er in die Welt kam* (henceforth *Der Golem*) and the oddly naturalistic *Nosferatu* that would perfect this defining trait of early German cinema, its aesthetics, by combining it with Gothic plots, monsters and emotional correlates.

The visually arresting remake of *Der Golem* acts as a species of prequel tracing the creature's origins. The story, set in medieval Prague, centres on Rabbi Löw's (Albert Steinrück) efforts to defend the Jewish community from the Roman Empire by giving life to the title clay creature (Wegener). Created in 'classical times by a Thessalonian sorcerer', as a book insert reveals, the creature will do the bidding of whoever brings him to life, something which may only be achieved by placing 'life-awakening words' into an amulet on his chest (the 'Shem').[12] Astaroth, a spirit, is invoked by Löw in his search for this word after consulting another book, *Necromancie: The Art of Bringing Dead Beings to Life*. It will be this very same spirit who will possess the golem once the constellations change and 'the dark powers' seek vengeance. Kabbalistic mysticism serves to revive a creature that then turns monstrous and rebels against its maker, a plot that belies the influence of the Frankenstein myth and which would influence Murnau's *Faust* only a few years later. In any case, the film's most significant contributions are more visual than narrative. The creature is a forerunner of Boris Karloff's monster in its muteness and mildly threatening air.[13] Rabbi Löw, himself an echo of Scapinelli in *Der Student von Prag*, would also provide a blueprint for future 'creationists', both in German cinema – Rotwang in *Metropolis* – and outside it – again, the Frankenstein in Whale's adaptation – demonstrating how alchemy found a home in the popular representation of science in the 1920s and 1930s (Skal 1998: 46–47; Frayling 2005: 53–54). *Der Golem* is also a key example of the German craze for artificially created humans, which would also include a man without a soul in the six-part serial *Homunculus* (1916–17), an evil woman made out of the semen of a hangman in the 1928 and 1930 *Alraune* adaptations and a robotic double in the Hoffmann-inspired Gothic romantic fantasy *Die Puppe* (*The Doll*, 1919).

The set design for *Der Golem* is one of the most archetypically Gothic found in German silent cinema and was designed by expressionist architect Hans Poelzig.[14] The medieval ghetto in which events take place is earthy and primordial, much like the title creature, and Gothic arches are evident in the buildings' windows. All of these, as well as the tower, the fountain and Löw's alchemical workshop were seen by contemporary critic Rudolf Kurtz, as early as 1926, to make Wegener's film 'everything of a Gothic dream' (quoted in Scheunemann 2003c: 18). As Lotte Eisner noted, the interiors enhance the exteriors, for in them there is 'a tracery of Gothic ribs and ogives transformed into oblique semi-ellipses' that 'compose ... a framework for the characters' (1965: 59). The set is combined with a very pronounced use of chiaroscuro, the film's other major contribution to a Gothic aesthetic, itself borrowed from the theatre of Max Reinhardt. The interplay between light and darkness serves to heighten facial expressions, especially those that show concern or fear, adds a strong sense of atmospherics (the golem is silhouetted against bright backgrounds, an effect that emphasises its menace and proportions) and helps focus attention on specific parts of the shot. Particularly memorable are the invocation scene, where a magical circle is rendered supernatural through a very bright light, and the moments when characters hold candles or lamps, where the glow of the burning wicks punctuate otherwise dark shots. This mood-enhancing trickery naturally borrows from the Gothic tradition (the candelabrum-wielding heroine), but is also a testament to cinema's evolving shooting techniques. *Der Golem* was incredibly innovative and created a Gothic ambiance not just by turning to architectural markers and claustrophobic spaces, but by making the most of cinema's capacity to adapt techniques previously pioneered in painting (low-key lighting, underlighting, high contrasts). Working on a studio, rather than on a stage, made it possible for foci of light to be placed where desired and for their effect to be minutely calculated.

The same precision, from a cinematographic point of view, is noticeable in the composition and cinematography of Murnau's Gothic masterpiece, *Nosferatu*. An unofficial adaptation of one of the most canonical of Victorian Gothic novels, Bram Stoker's *Dracula*, the film follows the machinations of Count Orlok (Max Schreck), a vampire who brings a plague to the fictional town of Wisborg. As with *Der Golem*, the film makes an incredible use of shadows, most notably when Orlok's hands and head loom dangerously over a sleeping Hutter (Gustav von Wangenheim); when his profile is shown going upstairs and opening the door to the bedroom in which Hutter's wife, Ellen (Greta Schröder), lies; and when, in the film's finale, Orlok clutches his fist over Ellen's heart in a symbolic moment of possession. As in *Der Golem*, chiaroscuro lighting accentuates the vampire's features: his pointed nose and ears, his rodent-like teeth and intense eyes and the distinct contrast between his pale face and the funereal darkness of his suit. *Nosferatu* also introduced interesting visual sequences that help connote the supernatural elements of its title creature: his carriage moves at a very fast pace, the result of speeded-up stock, and the use of negative film renders the woods surrounding the castle an uncanny white. All these instances, although iconic, are not as innovative as Murnau's use of depth of field photography, his reliance on low-angle shots for certain horrific scenes and his tension-building editing. These are brilliantly deployed to heighten Orlok's presence. His framing is, in fact, one of Gothic cinema's first concerted efforts to align victims and viewers in a bid for affective impact.

Orlok appears in scenes where the camera follows his victims, or else in sequences where his approach is cross-edited with the actions of a doomed character incapable of resisting his powers. One of these depicts in some detail one of his various attacks on Hutter, a clerk sent to Transylvania to liaise with him over the purchase of a house in Germany. At a key moment when the man dares look outside his room, he makes out the vampire at the far end of the room. Scared, Hutter closes the wooden arched door, but it is quickly thrown open, apparently by magic. The dark space beyond is only faintly illuminated and decidedly ominous. The film emphasises the anxiety of this moment by cutting to Hutter's concerned expression. It then cuts back to the dreaded door, where the profile of the vampire encroaches upon, and eventually fills, all available space. The vampire's gradual advance, made more effective by the extension of his left claw towards the camera, is halted. This allows Murnau to cut back to Hutter for a reaction shot but also for the image's subsequent lingering over the vampire's wooden expression and shape. The combination of Orlok's posture, which makes him look like he is resting horizontally, of back and forward lighting and of a masterful use of mise-en-scène manages to create the effect that the vampire is encased in a coffin. Even more crucially, the positioning of the camera at a slightly lower angle and the use of an iris lens that blurs the edges of the image situate the viewer in an experiential place close to that of Hutter. The film conjures up a similar illusion in the cargo scenes in the Empusa, when the vampire travels from Transylvania to Germany. After Orlok is awoken, he moves towards the last man standing. The camera is situated below deck so that the vampire, moving slowly but assuredly, can be felt to tower over it. A sense of threat is generated without the need to twist images or landscapes, simply through effective positioning and spatial arrangement.

Nosferatu is also an important piece of Gothic cinema for its vampiric iconography. Apart from starring the first bloodsucker to die of sunlight on film, Orlok's distinctive look would become iconic, copied in *Salem's Lot* (1979) and *Nosferatu a Venezia* (*Vampire in Venice*, 1988) and homaged in the made-for-television *Adivina quién soy* (*A Real Friend*, 2006) and in *What We Do in the Shadows* (2014). Some of the film's novelty factors at the thematic level have not been as powerful, perhaps because of their connection to the occult. What little we know about Orlok as a 'nosferatu' comes from information presented to the viewer via two of the documents that weave the story together and reflect Stoker's textual assemblages in *Dracula*. The first is the *Chronicle of the Great Death in Wisborg, Anno Domini 1838*, by † † † (an omniscient narrator who is never disclosed) and the second a book that Hutter

Figure 2.2 Gothic cinema began to frame monsters as dangerous and inextricable from the mise-en-scène in films like *Nosferatu, eine Symphonie des Grauens* (*Nosferatu*, 1922).

picks up in an inn the night before meeting Orlok, *Of Vampyres, Ghastly Spirits, Bewitchments and the Seven Deadlie Sins*.[15] The former warns readers to '[t]ake care in saying it, lest life's images fade into shadows, and ghostly dreams rise from your heart and nourish themselves on your blood', a poetic and proleptic passage that could certainly summarise *Nosferatu* as an aesthetic phantasmagorical experience. The second is more precise in delivering information about the monster's hellish origins and limitations: '[f]rom Belial's seed sprang the vampire Nosferatu, who doth live and feed on the bloode of humankind – Beyond deliverance he doth swell in ghastly caves, sepulchres and coffins, filled so with god-curst earth from the fields of the Black Death'. Later, the same archaic document serves to introduce the motif of the 'maiden wholly without sin' who can 'maketh the Vampyre forget the first crow of the cock' and who needs to, in a moment of self-sacrifice, 'give freely of her blood'. These explanatory pieces mingle indistinctively with superstitious belief (locals mention that werewolves are said to roam the forests of Transylvania), newspaper cut-outs reporting on the effects of the plague and Hutter's own handwritten observations. Interestingly, no overarching explanation for Orlok, his intentions or his history, is offered, and he only appears intermittently, in moments of tension, so that viewers' fears may be more freely projected onto the conglomerate of the uncanny, the contagious and the abject he represents.

It is important to highlight one last cinematic development, usually associated with Britain thanks to its *The Tempter* (1913) and *Dead of Night* (1945): the portmanteau or anthology film. Richard Oswald's *Hoffmanns Erzählungen* (*The Tales of Hoffmann*, 1916), based on Jacques Offenbach's very successful opera of the same title (1905), brought together three stories from the Romantic writer into a feature-length film. More interestingly, the film included a framing narrative where Hoffmann (Erich Kaiser-Titz) himself recounts the tragic stories of his dead lovers. A similar formula was developed in *Der müde Tod* (*Destiny*, 1921), where an unnamed young woman (Lil Dagover) challenges death, personified by a sombre, cape-wearing Bernhard Goetzke, after her fiancé (Walter Janssen) is suddenly snatched from her. Given the chance to prove that 'love is stronger than death', the woman is allowed to travel back to three periods in history (ancient Persia, Renaissance Venice and a largely mythical China), but her efforts to save her lover prove ineffective. In one of German cinema's most Gothic scenes, the young woman enters death's church (crammed with Gothic arches) to discover human lives represented by candles, a *memento mori* of sorts. The contrast between the starkly illuminated candles and the dark background, as the small figures move towards the centre of the camera, is designed to elicit sublime awe. Oswald himself would return to the anthology film in 1919 with *Unheimliche Geschichten* (*Eerie Tales*), which adapted Poe's 'The Black Cat' (1843) and Stevenson's 'The Suicide Club' (1878). Finally, Paul Leni's *Wachsfigurenkabinett* included three stories, those concerning three wax models exhibited in a museum.[16] The second of these, based on the life of Ivan the Terrible, is of particular interest for its use of Gothic architecture in its mise-en-scène, as well as for its composition. As Jürgen Kasten (2003: 178–179) has noted, its crowded arrangement of objects, the use of depth and low camera angles are conducive to an atmosphere of oppression.

The effect that German expressionism, and early German films more widely, had in the development of Gothic cinema was not one of direct equivalence, of thematic or mythic borrowing: there was no direct foreign adaptation of *Caligari* or *Der Golem*, and a film like Browning's *Dracula* would be more shaped by the 1927 American stage adaptation written by Hamilton Deane and revised by John L. Balderston (Skal 1993: 82–96) than by Murnau's *Nosferatu*. It is, however, possible to find visual echoes in the Soviet film *Medvezhya svadba* (*The Bear's Wedding*, 1925) and in Universal's horror films. Actually, it is not difficult to spot in James Whale's introduction of its Frankenstein monster traces of Cesare's awakening scene in *Caligari*, with its dramatic close-up of a traumatised face and his mute, slumberous stepping out of a coffin-shaped box, or to notice the resonance between the mob scene in Whale's film and that in Wiene's *Genuine* (*Genuine: The Tragedy of a Vampire*, 1920). Early German cinema, especially its expressionistic flourishes, resonated with other directors both in and outside Europe.

Before *Nosferatu* was released, Alexander Korda turned Baron Munchausen into a blood-drinking magician in the lost *Mágia* (*Magic*, 1917), one of the first representations of vampirism in cinema history.[17] Hungarian director Károly Lajthay had also shot what has come to be known as the first (very loose) adaptation of *Dracula*, the also lost *Drakula halála* (*Dracula's Death*, 1921).[18] Although little is known about the film's distribution and exhibition history, journalistic reviews, two film stills (publicity photographs) and a 1924 Hungarian novelisation have survived. Like *Caligari*, *Drakula halála* is partly set in an asylum and passes its Gothic nightmares off as potential deliriums (or as a long extended dream) from one Mary (Margit Lux) after she visits her ailing father. In the asylum, she meets Drakula (Paul Askonas), an old composer who taught her how to sing but who now appears to have gone mad, claiming to be immortal. The exchange with the patient is brief but intense, and Mary soon has a nightmare in which Drakula forces her to travel to his castle, where she is to become his eternal bride. If the novella is anything to go by, Drakula is eventually shot dead in a dare to test his supernatural powers and Mary is reunited with her beloved.[19] The two surviving stills 'include some evocative shadows', and one of them 'depicts an artistically painted flat depicting a building and dreary sky in the distance', an indication that the film may have been as aesthetically influenced by Caligari as its script (Rhodes 2010: 30). Vampires would be given at least one more avantgarde treatment in Carl Theodor Dreyer's *Vampyr* (1932), a loose and surreal adaptation of Sheridan Le Fanu's 'Carmilla' (1872).[20] The bare bones of the plot are recognisable from many a horror film: after what appears to be a vampire attack on a young woman, Léone (Sybille Schmitz), protagonist Allan (Nicolas de Gunzburg) learns more about the creature from an old book gifted to him. He eventually destroys the evil creature and escapes with Léone's sister, Gisèle (Rena Mandel). However, this story is complicated by a series of macabre events apparently imagined, among them Gray's own funeral. As Dreyer once put it, his aim was 'to create a daydream on film', 'to show that the sinister lies not in the things around us but in our subconscious' (quoted in Drum and Drum 2000: 153). Real horrors become virtually indistinguishable from their hallucinated counterparts in this subtle reflection on the human psyche.

Key to expressionism was the mapping out of repressed desires and altered psychologies onto the settings themselves. Given Edgar Allan Poe's penchant, and unique literary talent, for writing about warped minds and obsessive characters, it is not surprising that his stories would be given expressionistic treatments. *The Telltale Heart* (1928), based on the 1843 story of the same name about a murderer who succumbs to his sense of guilt, shows a direct debt to *Caligari*.[21] The room in which the majority of the action takes place foregrounds a distinctly angular and contorted door, and the use of chiaroscuro to accentuate facial expressions is particularly noticeable. This 24-minute short makes its intention clear from the start; an insert tells the viewer that '[t]his is a story, as related by an insane man, and presented thusly, as the events recorded themselves in his distorted mind'.[22] More patently Gothic were two adaptations of 'The Fall of the House of Usher' (1839), a story that follows the simultaneous mental disintegration of Roderick Usher and of his ancestral home. The first of these, *The Fall of the House of Usher* (1928), was a 13-minute largely experimental film where 'fact, story, character, and the themes of Poe finish a distant second to the visuals, which attempt not so much to tell a story as to create a mood through cinematic poetry' (Smith 1999: 34). The various scenes, dominated by the motif of the coffin and by the house's shadow-laden and disjointed spaces (vaults, arches, corridors and stairs), is full of suggestive prismatic effects, multiple exposures, dissolves and animated objects. The result is disorientating and deeply evocative; the film establishes a direct correspondence between the faltering minds of its characters, especially Madeline's (Hildegarde Watson), and the sombre, inhospitable architecture of a house out of joint. Jean Epstein's *La Chute de la maison Usher* (*The Fall of the House of Usher*, 1928), which he co-wrote with Luis Buñuel, was less evidently expressionistic than avant-garde, but its first scene, where Allan (Charles Lamy) arrives at an inn near the Ushers and is warned of the attendant danger by the locals, bears the hallmarks of *Nosferatu*'s influence. The film perhaps corrupts Poe's interest in stagnation and decay with its emphasis on regeneration (the copulating frogs at Madeleine's funeral; the 'happy' ending where Madeleine saves, rather than kills, Usher), but Epstein's suggestive imagery, full of billowing curtains in dimly lit corridors, barren interiors and foggy exterior shots, give *La Chute de la maison Usher* a strong dreamlike and melancholic feeling.[23] Another Poe story, 'The Masque of the Red Death', had also been previously adapted by Otto Rippert, from a script by Fritz Lang, into the Gothic melodrama *Die Pest in Florenz* (*The Plague in Florence*, 1919).

Expressionism also reached Mexico, where it most evidently manifested in the cinema of Juan Bustillo Oro. His *Dos monjes* (*Two Monks*, 1934) tells a dualistic tale of two men in love with the same woman. The framing story is located in a nineteenth-century Gothic monastery, where a monk, Javier (Carlos Villatoro), recognises in the face of another, Juan (Víctor Urruchúa), the murderer of his fiancée. After

Javier attempts to bludgeon him to death with a crucifix, the men are separated and they both relate their version of events to the Prior (Beltrán de Heredia). The melodramatic story uncovers that Ana (Magda Haller) had once been Juan's betrothed, but their rekindled love for each other was complicated by Javier's delicate health. In Javier's story, a dejected and molesting Juan ends up shooting Ana by mistake. In Juan's story, however, it is Javier who shoots Ana when she tries to protect him. No resolution is offered, even though Javier dies shortly after a hallucination scene in which the monks appear to him wearing white, surreal masks. Instead, the film seems to reflect on the subjective nature and ambiguity of all human experience. In fact, Juan speaks at one point of Javier's 'verdad parcial' (partial truth) and, in the murder scene, the characters are dressed in contrasting colours (black and white) that point to their polarities. As in the Poe adaptations, expressionism underscores the psychological lens through which events are filtered. As David J. Hogan argues, although the film's expressionistic techniques are not as obvious as those of German cinema, they are definitely noticeable and have a cumulative effect (2016: 277–278).[24] Bustillo Oro also co-wrote *El fantasma del convento* (*The Phantom of the Convent*, 1934), which is just as Gothic. In this film, the stranded protagonists find themselves forced to spend the night at a convent inhabited by strange monks. The brethren guard the body of brother Rodrigo, whose soul is damned to return periodically after he uses black magic to obtain the love of his friend's fiancée. Like *Dos monjes*, *El fantasma del convento* is largely a morality tale, as the end reveals that the monks do not exist and events may have been no more than a cautionary daydream.

France and America introduced the ghost, the witch and the devil to Gothic cinema, but Germany developed a type of supernatural film that would eventually change the way suspense and dread were filmed and begin to push the monster towards becoming the narrative axis. For the most part, the influence of German expressionism, the most striking of early German cinema's manifestations, would be an aesthetic and stylistic preoccupation with mood. As Misha Kavka has suggested, the stylistic techniques perfected by early German cinema

Figure 2.3 Expressionism's dramatic interplay between light and darkness is evident in this still from *Dos monjes* (*Two Monks*, 1934), which depicts a (hallucinated) masked monk.

that would have a more lasting impact on the development of a Gothic aesthetic include 'chiaroscuro lighting effects … distorted backdrops, claustrophobic spaces, extreme camera angles and shadows disproportionate to the objects that cast them' (2002: 215). All of these are evident in the Gothic films of Universal and in the old dark house mystery films that developed in the 1910s and 1920s. Expressionism in particular, with its abstracted, exaggerated, irrational and emotional style, would resonate with the Gothic's eminently visual preoccupations. At the same time, the Gothic had begun to turn inwards. Tortured spaces, especially the dramatic, angular architecture of the Gothic building, could now reflect traumatised and obsessive psyches.

FILMOGRAPHY

Adivina quién soy (*A Real Friend*, Enrique Urbizu and James Phillips, 2006, Spain)
Alraune (*A Daughter of Destiny*, Henrik Galeen, 1928, Germany)
Alraune (Richard Oswald, 1930, Germany)

Caligari – Wie der Horror ins Kino kam (*Caligari: The Birth of Horror in the First World War*, Rüdiger Suchsland, 2014, Germany/France)

Das Bildnis des Dorian Gray (*The Picture of Dorian Gray*, Richard Oswald, 1917, Germany)

Das Cabinet des Dr. Caligari (*The Cabinet of Dr. Caligari*, Robert Wiene, 1920, Germany)

Das Phantom der Oper (*The Phantom of the Opera*, Ernst Matray, 1916, Germany)

Dead of Night (Alberto Cavalcanti, Charles Crichton, Robert Hamer and Basil Dearden, 1945, UK)

Der Andere (*The Other*, Max Mack, 1913, Germany)

Der Golem (*The Golem*, Paul Wegener and Henrik Galeen, 1915, Germany)

Der Golem, wie er in die Welt kam (*The Golem: How He Came into the World*, Paul Wegener and Carl Boese, 1920, Germany)

Der Golem und die Tänzerin (*The Golem and the Dancing Girl*, Paul Wegener and Rochus Gliese, 1917, Germany)

Der Graf von Cagliostro (*The Count of Cagliostro*, Reinhold Schünzel, 1920, Austria)

Der Hund von Baskerville (*The Hound of the Baskervilles*, Richard Oswald, 1929, Germany)

Der Januskopf (*The Head of Janus*, F. W. Murnau, 1920, Germany)

Der müde Tod (*Destiny*, Fritz Lang, 1921, Germany)

Der Student von Prag (*The Student of Prague*, Stellan Rye and Paul Wegener, 1913, Germany)

Der Student von Prag (*The Student of Prague*, Henrik Galeen, 1926, Germany)

Der verlorene Schatten (*The Lost Shadow*, Rochus Gliese, 1921, Germany)

Die Augen des Ole Brandis (*The Eyes of Ole Brandis*, Stellan Rye, 1914, Germany)

Die Pest in Florenz (*The Plague in Florence*, Otto Rippert, 1919, Germany)

Die Puppe (*The Doll*, Ernst Lubitsch, 1919, Germany)

Dos monjes (*Two Monks*, Juan Bustillo Oro, 1934, Mexico)

Dr. Mabuse, der Spieler (*Dr. Mabuse, The Gambler*, Fritz Lang, 1922, Germany)

Dracula (Tod Browning, 1931, USA)

Drakula halála (*Draculas' Death*, Károly Lajthay, 1921, Hungary/Austria/France)

Ein seltsamer Fall (*A Strange Case*, Max Mack, 1914, Germany)

El fantasma del convento (*The Phantom of the Convent*, Fernando de Fuentes, 1934, Mexico)

Faust: Eine deutsche Volkssage (*Faust*, F. W. Murnau, 1926, Germany)
Genuine (*Genuine: The Tragedy of a Vampire*, Robert Wiene, 1920, Germany)
Hoffmanns Erzählungen (*The Tales of Hoffmann*, Richard Oswald, 1916, Germany)
Homunculus (Otto Rippert, 1916–17, serial, Germany)
Il cuore rivelatore (*The Tell-Tale Heart*, Alberto Mondadori, 1934, Italy)
La Chute de la maison Usher (*The Fall of the House of Usher*, Jean Epstein, 1928, France)
La Folie du Docteur Tube (*The Madness of Dr. Tube*, Abel Gance, 1915, France)
Le Golem (*The Legend of Prague*, Julien Duvivier, 1936, France/Czechoslovakia)
Lucrezia Borgia (Richard Oswald, 1922, Germany)
M – Eine Stadt sucht einen Mörder (*M*, Fritz Lang, 1931, Germany)
Mágia (*Magic*, Alexander Korda, 1917, Hungary)
Medvezhya svadba (*The Bear's Wedding*, Konstantin Eggert and Vladimir Gardin, 1925, Soviet Union)
Metropolis (Fritz Lang, 1927, Germany)
Nächte des Grauens (*A Night of Horror*, Richard Oswald and Arthur Robison, 1917, Germany)
Nosferatu, eine Symphonie des Grauens (*Nosferatu*, F. W. Murnau, 1922, Germany)
Nosferatu a Venezia (*Vampire in Venice*, Augusto Caminito, Mario Caiano, Luigi Cozzi, Claus Kinski and Maurizio Lucidi, 1988, Italy)
Phantom (F. W. Murnau, 1922, Germany)
Pique Dame (*The Queen of Spades*, Arthur Wellin, 1918, Germany)
Orlacs Hände (*The Hands of Orlac*, Robert Wiene, 1924, Austria)
Salem's Lot (Tobe Hooper, 1979, USA)
Schatten – Eine nächtliche Halluzination (*Warning Shadows*, Arthur Robison, 1923, Germany)
Secret Beyond the Door (Fritz Lang, 1947, USA)
The Cat and the Canary (Paul Leni, 1927, USA)
The Fall of the House of Usher (Melville Webber and James Sibley Watson, 1928, USA)
The Telltale Heart (Charles Klein, 1928, USA)
The Tempter (R. H. Callum and F. Martin Thornton, 1913, UK)
Unheimliche Geschichten (*Eerie Tales*, Richard Oswald, 1919, Germany)
Vampyr (Carl Theodor Dreyer, 1932, Germany and France)

Von morgens bis mitternachts (*From Morn to Midnight*, Karl Heinz Martin, 1920, Germany)

Wachsfigurenkabinett (*Waxworks*, Paul Leni, 1924, Germany)

What We Do in the Shadows (Jemaine Clement and Taika Waititi, 2014, New Zealand)

Zur Chronik von Grieshuus (*The Chronicles of the Gray House*, Arthur von Gerlach, 1925, Germany)

NOTES

1 Ian Roberts, for example, proposes that these traits could just as easily be 'a response to the acute shortages in power and materials which prevailed in the early days of the Weimar Republic' (2008: 17–18).

2 S. S. Prawer refers to horror films as 'Caligari's children' in the title of his 1980 study of the horror genre.

3 Ewers famously completed Schiller's fragmentary *Der Geisterseher* (*The Ghost-Seer*, 1787) in 1922.

4 Translations are taken from the 2016 DVD version released by Edition Filmmuseum.

5 *Der Student von Prag* was so influential in this regard that it even became the starting point for Otto Rank's *Der Doppelgänger: Eine psychoanalytische Studie*, the first monograph of the literary double (published in 1925, but written in 1914).

6 It is important to note that *Der Andere* (*The Other*, 1913), adapted from a play by Paul Lindau, preceded *Der Student von Prag*. In it, a horse fall leads to the awakening of a man's repressed self.

7 As Casper Tybjerg (2004: 20) notes, *A Strange Case* was also based on a stage adaptation of that same novel by E. Morton and J. F. Cunniver.

8 There are two possible reasons for the choice of story. The first is that Wegener visited the Old-New Synagogue while shooting in Prague and his curiosity was piqued upon learning that the place was allegedly the tomb of the medieval golem. The second is that Wegener was already set to be cast as the golem in an Arthur Holitscher play of 1908 ultimately rejected by Max Reinhardt (Nicolella and Soister 2012: 68–69).

9 As Robinson also notes (2013: 35), Caligari's costume suggests the Biedermeier era, but this style is not consistently used throughout. The film is not interested in historical verisimilitude.
10 The reference is to the title of the 2014 documentary *Caligari – Wie der Horror ins Kino kam* (*Caligari: The Birth of Horror in the First World War*, 2014).
11 The English translation from the original German text is taken from the Masters of Cinema special dual format edition released in 2014.
12 The origin of the creature in classical times seems to contradict a previous scene that shows Löw building the golem from scratch using clay. I cite the translations in the 2007 Eureka Entertainment DVD version of the film.
13 The creature would be played very similarly by Ferdinand Hart in the French *Le Golem* (*The Legend of Prague*, 1936).
14 *Der Graf von Cagliostro* (*The Count of Cagliostro*, 1920), *Lucrezia Borgia* (1922) and *Zur Chronik von Grieshuus* (*The Chronicles of the Gray House*, 1925), three historical melodramas set in Italy, are other early German films that include Gothic settings.
15 As Kevin Jackson (2013: 25) argues, the choice of 1838 is not accidental. There was an actual outbreak of the plague in Bremen that year. All translated titles and intertitles are taken from the 2013 Blu-ray Eureka Entertainment version of the film.
16 Four stories were originally planned, but problems with the budget meant the film could only develop two of the stories in full. The third, concerning Jack the Ripper and set in the present, feels more like an improvised scenario.
17 Kinnard mentions that in the German *Nächte des Grauens* (*A Night of Horror*, 1917), released the same year, '[v]ampire-like people are depicted' (1995: 85), but this has been challenged by Workman and Howarth (2016: 175).
18 The film was set to premiere in Budapest in 1921, but there is no record that it ever actually did. Gary D. Rhodes has only found evidence that it was shown to Hungarian audiences in April 1923 (2010: 19).
19 The novella, translated by Gary D. Rhodes and Péter Litván, is available in full in Rhodes (2010: 31–47).
20 The two main versions of the film discussed by critics had subtitles that gesture towards the dreamlike quality of the film. The English-titled

German-language version was subtitled *The Strange Adventure of David Gray* (the film's working title), while the English-titled German-language version was subtitled *Der Traum des Allan Gray*, or *The Dream of Allan Gray* (Rudkin 2005: 28–29, 77 n30).

21 There was another, less obviously expressionistic, Italian adaptation in 1934, *Il cuore rivelatore* (*The Tell-Tale Heart*) that nevertheless showcases similar aesthetic quirks.

22 I am quoting from the existing print in the National Film and Television Archive of the British Film Institute.

23 Epstein's film also adapts elements from 'The Oval Portrait' (1842).

24 Bustillo Oro described his intentions for the film as follows: 'I wanted to give the film a surreal atmosphere, entering an Expressionistic place' that would 'reflect the profound influence that the German masters sealed in my imagination' (quoted in Hogan 2016: 285).

BIBLIOGRAPHY

Brockmann, S. (2010) *A Critical History of German Film*, Rochester, NY: Camden House.

Carver, S. (2013) 'Film', in W. Hughes, D. Punter and A. Smith (eds) *The Encyclopedia of the Gothic*, Oxford and Malden, MA: Wiley-Blackwell.

Coates, P. (1991) *The Gorgon's Gaze: German Cinema, Expressionism, and the Image of Horror*, Cambridge: Cambridge University Press.

Drum, J. and D. D. Drum (2000) *My Only Great Passion: The Life and Films of Carl Th. Dreyer*, London and Lanham, MD: The Scarecrow Press.

Eisner, L. (1965) *The Haunted Screen: Expressionism in the German Cinema and the Influence of Max Reinhardt*, rev. edn, Berkeley and Los Angeles, CA: University of California Press.

Elsaesser, T. (2000) *Weimar Cinema and After: Germany's Historical Imaginary*, London and New York: Routledge.

Frayling, C. (2005) *Mad, Bad and Dangerous? The Scientist and the Cinema*, London: Reaktion.

Groom, N. (2012) *The Gothic: A Very Short Introduction*, Oxford: Oxford University Press.

Hake, S. (2008) *German National Cinema*, rev. edn, Abingdon and New York: Routledge.

Hogan, D. J. (2016) 'Dos Monjes and the Tortured Search for Truth', in O. Brill and G. D. Rhodes (eds) *Expressionism in the Cinema*, Edinburgh: Edinburgh University Press.

Jackson, K. (2013) *Nosferatu: Eine Symphonie des Grauens*, Basingstoke: Palgrave Macmillan.

Kasten, J. (2003) 'Episodic Patchwork: The Bric-à-Brac Principle in Paul Leni's *Waxworks*', in D. Scheunemann (ed.) *Expressionist Film: New Perspectives*, Rochester, NY: Camden House.

Kavka, M. (2002) 'The Gothic on Screen', in J. E. Hogle (ed.) *The Cambridge Companion to Gothic Fiction*, Cambridge: Cambridge University Press.

Kinnard, R. (1995) *Horror in Silent Films: A Filmography, 1896–1929*, London and Jefferson, NC: McFarland.

Kracauer, S. (1947) *From Caligari to Hitler: A Psychological History of the German Film*, Princeton, NJ: Princeton University Press.

Morgart, J. (2014) 'Gothic Horror Film from *The Haunted Castle* to *Psycho*', in G. Byron and D. Townshend (eds) *The Gothic World*, Abingdon and New York: Routledge.

Nicolella, H. and J. T. Soister (2012) *Many Selves: The Horror and Fantasy Films of Paul Wegener*, Duncan, OK: BearManor Media.

Prawer, S. S. (1980) *Caligari's Children: The Film as Tale of Terror*, Oxford: Oxford University Press.

Rank, O. (1925) *Der Doppelgänger: Eine psychoanalytische Studie*, Vienna: Internationaler Psychoanalytischer Verlag.

Rhodes, G. D. (2010) '*Drakula halála*: The Cinema's First Dracula', *Horror Studies*, 1.1: 25–47.

Roberts, I. (2008) *German Expressionist Cinema: The World of Light and Shadow*, London and New York: Wallflower.

Robinson, D. (2013) *Das Cabinet des Dr. Caligari*, Basingstoke: Palgrave Macmillan.

Rudkin, D. (2005) *Vampyr*, London: British Film Institute.

Saunders, T. J. (1994) *Hollywood in Berlin: American Cinema and Weimar Germany*, Berkeley, CA: University of California Press.

Scheunemann, D. (2003a) 'Preface', in D. Scheunemann (ed.) *Expressionist Film: New Perspectives*, Rochester, NY: Camden House.

Scheunemann, D. (2003b) 'The Double, the Décor, and the Framing Device: Once More on Robert Wiene's *The Cabinet of Dr. Caligari*', in D. Scheunemann (ed.) *Expressionist Film: New Perspectives*, Rochester, NY: Camden House.

Scheunemann, D. (2003c) 'Activating the Differences: Expressionist Film and Early Weimar Cinema', in D. Scheunemann (ed.) *Expressionist Film: New Perspectives*, Rochester, NY: Camden House.

Skal, D. J. (1993) *The Monster Show: A Cultural History of Horror*, London: Plexus.

Skal, D. J. (1998) *Screams of Reason: Mad Science and Modern Culture*, London and New York: W. W. Norton.

Smith, D. G. (1999) *The Poe Cinema: A Critical Filmography*, Jefferson, NC: McFarland.

Tybjerg, C. (2004) 'Shadow Souls and Strange Adventures: Horror and the Supernatural in European Silent Film', in S. Prince (ed.) *The Horror Film*, New Brunswick, NJ: Rutgers University Press.

Workman, C. and T. Howarth (2016) *Tome of Terror: Horror Films of the Silent Era*, London and Baltimore, MD: Midnight Marquee Press.

3

FRANCHISE GOTHIC

Films in the 1910s and 1920s, especially those made in Germany during the late years of the Wilhelmine period and during the Weimar Republic, began experimenting with longer narratives and emphasising feelings of apprehension. The advance publicity for *Nosferatu* underscored this point: '[y]ou want to see a symphony of horror? You may expect more. Be careful. Nosferatu is not just fun, not something to be taken lightly. Once more: beware' (quoted in Jackson 2013: 94). Yet it would be American films of the 1930s that would be most foundational in setting up a blueprint for the Gothic in cinema. The cautioning tone in *Nosferatu*'s publicity materials would later reappear in Edward Van Sloan's disclaimer during the opening credits for *Frankenstein*, where audiences were forewarned of the strain its viewing might put on their nerves. Films such as Whale's masterpiece were not just responsible for the gradual development of 'horror' as a cinematic label, a critical term that only solidified in journalistic discourse in the 1930s (Peirse 2013: 5–9), but for its establishment of a corporate strategy and eventual franchise logic driven by economic imperatives and the endless reanimation and repetition of given ideas, motifs and scenarios. The Gothic past would merge, sometimes problematically, with present times in a bid to make fearful tableaux timelier and more threatening, ultimately migrating into the mise-en-scène. The films of Universal Studios, in particular, would provide visual models for a number of monsters, such as the vampire, the Frankenstein creature, the mummy and the werewolf, that would have a tremendous impact on the history of the Gothic beyond the screen. In some cases, the cinematic monsters of the 1930s would become as significant, if not more so, than the literary sources that inspired them.

Two of the three Romantic melodramas made before *Dracula*, *The Hunchback of Notre Dame* (1923) and *The Man Who Laughs* (1928), both based on Victor Hugo novels, were envisaged primarily as historically accurate 'prestige' films that built on the reputation of a classic author.[1] The pressbook for the former emphasises Lon Chaney's participation, the numerous members of the cast and production team and the overall scope of the endeavour, but does not mention any horrific or suggestive elements.[2] *The Man Who Laughs* was intended as a Universal Jewel super-production, rather than a specifically Gothic film, and was discussed in periodicals of the time alongside mainstream films like *Show Boat* (1936).[3] *The Hunchback of Notre Dame* was also one of the first spectacle pictures, its projected cost exceeding well over a million dollars. Part of this money went into building what would come to be the largest American set for a picture of the time, covering nineteen acres of the studio and requiring the manpower of over 750 crew members (Blake 1993: 106–107). Its *pièce de résistance* was a partial recreation of the cathedral of Notre Dame. It is this medieval building (completed in 1345) and its interiors, as well as the film's fifteenth-century setting, more than Quasimodo, which make the film susceptible of a Gothic reading. If horror is not totally precluded in *The Hunchback of Notre Dame*, its titular character is, unlike future Gothic monsters, a deaf and visually impaired bell-ringer whose physique serves more readily to elicit pity and concern than fear. Similarly, Gwynplaine (Conrad Veidt), a man whose mouth has been maliciously carved into a perpetual grin, is an empathetic tragic hero.

Both films, with their emphasis on the past, the grotesque and period settings – *Variety* called them part of a string of '17th century movies' (Landry 1928: 14) – may be considered forerunners of Universal's Gothic monster films of the 1930s.

Chaney, well-known for his versatility and innovative use of make-up, also starred in *The Phantom of the Opera* (1925), a Gothic masterpiece based on the novel by Gaston Leroux that deserves attention for being the first silent cinema attempt to construct a screen monster according to the parameters Universal would perfect in the early 1930s. The reveal of Erik's contorted and grotesque face after a heedless Christine (Mary Philbin) defies his Bluebeard-style warning not to pry behind his mask is particularly important for its implementation of the shot-reverse shot dynamic that would become a staple of the gaze in horror.[4] In it, the monster is uncovered, his otherness rendered physical, and the heroine responds with a scream. Christine's reaction acts as an emotional cue, encouraging the same behaviour from the potential audience, who will be both empathetic and sympathetic towards her as a virtuous woman. The moment is not unproblematic, as it betrays the disablist relationship between exterior and interior deformity common to early horror films (Smith 2012: 121–128). Unlike Quasimodo or Gwynplaine, Erik's personal story is left unexplored so that his face can more seamlessly correlate evil deeds. Erik, who is not supernatural but haunts the Paris Opera House and is given the soubriquet 'the phantom', is also a vampiric prototype, inhabiting the shadows of a lonely castle, in this case the opera's abandoned neo-Gothic catacombs.

The phantom's netherworld, bathed in shadows, evokes barbarism in its echoes of medieval dungeons and torture chambers, yet is emptied of any specific episodes in French history. The ornate, hidden and underground locations in which Erik dwells reflect his condition as a social outcast and allow for a reading of his character as the embodiment of unconscious and repressed desires, both sexual and social. Sets are also important to this film for their grandiosity. The

Opera House auditorium was built especially for it and was the first to be 'constructed on a structural steel framework set in concrete foundations' (Turner 1982: 674). If not as enormous as that of *Hunchback*, it was still an expensive and much-touted affair that drew journalistic attention for its ambition and scope.[5] In fact, the opera house set would have a long Gothic afterlife, reappearing in films such as *The Last Warning* (1929), *Dracula*, *Svengali* (1931) and *The House of Fear* (1939), among others. The decision to shoot the masquerade ball in Technicolor is also noteworthy. At the time, the recording procedure for colour scenes was a lot more expensive than that for black and white, but the set was so accomplished a piece of mise-en-scène that it was felt it needed to be showcased in all its splendour. Importantly, given the great expense, *The Phantom of the Opera* did very well in theatres; it appealed both to the highly educated (in its operatic connections) and to the middle- and working-class audiences Universal had cultivated (thanks to its emphasis on action and humour) and thus ensured maximum interest (Hogle 2002: 146–147).

There was, however, no specific or self-avowed tradition of Gothic horror at the time, so *Phantom* and *Hunchback* were accidental precursors of films like *Dracula*. The latter was adapted to cinema partly because of the enthusiasm Carl Laemmle Jr. had for horror films, a passion his father did not share, and because the 1927 Liveright stage adaptation of Stoker's *Dracula* had performed so well that it had continued to run into 1929.[6] Most famously, the Hungarian actor Bela Lugosi, who had been playing the role of the count since he had replaced Raymond Huntley, ended up reprising it on screen. The year 1929 was also when an illicit print of *Nosferatu*, thought destroyed following Florence Stoker's winning lawsuits against the production company Prana Film, resurfaced in America. Concerned with the potential effects it could have on what had already proven an arduous pre-production process, *Nosferatu* was surveyed with care by Universal and eventually bought from Symon Gould, founder of the International Film Arts Guild. Despite such worries, *Dracula*, one of the first 'talkie' horrors, would outdo *Nosferatu* in its recasting of the vampire as a suave, yet deadly,

Figure 3.1 Grandiose and antiquated sets were a key component of early Universal melodramas like *The Phantom of the Opera* (1925).

500-year-old Carpathian nobleman who had more in common with Lord Ruthven from John Polidori's 'The Vampyre' (1819), than with Stoker's count. Lugosi's performance and attire, as innovative as they were palimpsestic, would be forever associated with this character.[7] Lugosi and Boris Karloff, in his role as Frankenstein's creature, would go down in the history of Gothic cinema as two of the most important genre actors, their looks memorable and copyrighted.[8]

Dracula opens with an impressive set and a painted glass background replicating the Carpathian landscapes Renfield (Dwight Frye) crosses by carriage; dramatic rugged peaks rise up against a downcast sky that signals trouble. Unlike *Nosferatu*, where vampire lore is introduced mostly through documents, Renfield is made aware of the dangers that lie ahead through his interactions with fellow passengers and locals. It is Walpurgisnacht ('the night of Evil! Nosferatu!', cries a superstitious man), and it is believed that vampires live in Castle Dracula. More importantly, especially for an audience who may have not been as familiar with vampire lore, it is established that the count and his wives can assume the shape of wolves and bats, live in coffins, drink the blood of the living and come out at night. These exposition scenes are complemented by another not present in the novel or the play. Before Renfield meets the count pretending to be his driver, the film abandons our hero and cuts to an establishing shot of the approach to a medieval castle perched over a cliff, an image that has become a Gothic standard.[9] After a dissolve, the camera roams the interior of its Gothic crypt. It gradually nears a coffin, which proceeds to open and reveal a squalid hand. Shots of two opossums and a bee are intercut with others of the female vampires rising from their slumber. The camera then dollies in on a rigid, face-lit male figure standing tall and staring into the camera (Dracula wrapped up on his cape), then cuts to a wider shot that emphasises the depth of space, height and cobweb-punctuated obscurity of the setting. Dracula exits through a staircase on the right, slowly and sombrely.

It is a brief, but very powerful, scene. The literal awakening of the children of the night is both uncanny and random, the intercutting syncopated and more suggestive and aesthetic than strictly narrative. The lack of music or dialogue and the very spare use of sound – the creaking of the opening coffins, the squeaking and scurrying around of the animals – give the scene an eerie quality. The same technique is used when a candle-wielding Dracula introduces himself in the parlour of his castle. The vastness of the towering set, which belittles an already apprehensive Renfield, is coupled with the sound and images of armadillos and bats and with a very careful use of window lighting that only intermittently falls on the characters. The effect is both chilling and thrilling; it raises anticipation and creates an atmosphere of threat and wonder further emphasised by the howling of a wolf and by Dracula's apparent immateriality (when he nonchalantly walks through a gigantic cobweb). The sublime grandiosity of the place is reinstated once the men reach the main dining area, with both shot from afar and a candelabrum on the foreground left-hand of the screen looking nearly twice their size. Further disquieting effects include a dramatic dolly in on the count's shadowy face after Renfield accidentally cuts his finger and the recurring focus on Lugosi's hypnotic stare through a strategically placed light beam. Other notable images are the high-angle shot of a crazed Renfield on the cargo of the ship, the motif of the flying bat and the moment a mirror does not reflect Dracula. The marketing of the vampire as undead lover prefigured the interspecies attachments of late twentieth and early twenty-first-century paranormal romances too. In this film, the vampire mirrors Gothic spaces: strange and full of awe, threatening and appealing all at once.

Dracula's best-remembered moments are beset by sometimes stagey constraints (acting, wide shooting), especially in the film's second half. For Robert Spadoni (2007: 92), the wooden theatricality of *Dracula* is not just a result of the film's genesis on the stage. The shortcomings of films made immediately after *The Jazz Singer* (1927), the first feature-length with synchronised sound, are signs of an industry in a state of transition. *Dracula* is as forward-looking as it is steeped in the past, halfway between the silent film and the talkie, both theatrical and cinematic. Aural effects had already been exploited with horrific intent in the Liveright play version of *Dracula*, in the part-talkie *The Last Warning* and the now lost *The Cat Creeps* (1930) and *La voluntad del muerto* (*The Will of the Dead Man*, 1930), Universal's own English- and Spanish-language sound remakes of *The Cat and the Canary*. The inclusion of loud and sudden noises or screams in *Dracula*, alongside more uncanny sounds like the count's hissing or maniacal laughing (Spadoni 2007: 54–60) also hinted at the future establishment of accompanying auditory cues. By the end of the Universal cycle the possibilities of sound technology began to merge with those of images in the building of atmospheres and moods: 'the distant howling of wolves, the sinister creaking of doors, and the eerie wind passing through some desolate landscape, all help[ed] to signify a mysterious world existing apart from everyday reality' (Hutchings 2004: 128). Dramatic scores would, in time, become intrinsic to the Gothic film.

Dracula was a resounding success and made horror worth further investment. Before the end of 1931, Universal had released an even more successful follow-up, another adaptation of a stage play based on a British Gothic novel, James Whale's *Frankenstein*. If Count Dracula had started the mainstream craze for Gothic castles and supernatural monsters, *Frankenstein* patented the formula: the creature (Boris Karloff), deprived of speech, was turned into an abject monster that generates fear by dint of his looks. Like the character in Shelley's novel, however, he was also eminently tragic and empathetic. The cut scene where he inadvertently drowns a little girl is as horrific as it is devastating, for viewers are aware that he has no understanding of the consequences of certain actions. Similarly, it is obvious that it is the treatment the creature receives from others – especially from Fritz (Dwight Frye), who sadistically torments him – that engenders aggressive responses. Physical otherness as extreme and irreconcilable alterity is one of *Frankenstein*'s most important additions to the Gothic canon. The scene where the creature is finally introduced, after much build-up, is a masterful moment of affect: a long shot shows a framing door, as in *Nosferatu*, through which a towering figure enters the room from behind. The creature then turns left, the light forming shadows over Karloff's gaunt face. This is followed by three quick sequential close-ups of his features that draw attention to the dead eyes and signature neck bolts. This Frankenstein monster is no alchemical nightmare but most definitely an aberrant composite come back from the dead.

The most interesting pieces of mise-en-scène in *Dracula* were the count's Transylvanian castle and its English counterpart, Carfax Abbey. The former's opulent and decaying magnificence and the latter's chthonian grandiosity and darkness inherently convey a number of emotions connected to fear. The architecture of Dracula's London home, with its groined arches, dramatic shadows and grand staircase, evokes the archaism of legend-ridden, folkloric central Europe. *Frankenstein*, which takes place in eighteenth-century Holdstadt if the references to phrenology (the abnormal brain), chemical galvanism and electrobiology are anything to go by, borrowed aesthetically from its predecessor's setting for its laboratory. The set, built specifically for the film, is a perfect combination of science fantasy, reminiscent of Rotwang's dwelling in *Metropolis*, and the cavernous, chiaroscuro remoteness of Dracula's castle as drawn by Giovanni Battista Piranesi.[10] In fact, when Henry's fiancée Elizabeth (Mae Clarke), Victor (John Boles) and Dr. Waldman (Edward Van Sloan) arrive at Frankenstein's old watchtower in the mountains, the building is also shown sitting atop a cliff. The interiors have impossibly high ceilings and the primitive stone stairway and walls contrast starkly with the high voltage Jacob's ladders, spark gaps and Tesla coil that reign over the refitted laboratory. The opening scene in the cemetery is equally impressive: a lateral pan that brushes past the dimly lit faces of the mourners and a life-sized decorative skeleton clothed in a monastic cloak eventually settles on the expectant, severe faces of graverobbing Frankenstein (Colin Clive) and his assistant Fritz (Dwight Frye). The film conjures up a very specific eerie atmosphere through its cinematography, use of lighting, camerawork and sounds.

There were other Gothic films in the wake of *Frankenstein* and *Dracula*, the vast majority of them sequels, but horror as a filmic product, freed from historical periodisation, would blossom more generally.[11] Monster features with creatures like the werewolf, such as *Werewolf of London* (1935) and *The Wolf Man* (1941), and the invisible man, such as *The Invisible Man* (1933) and *The Invisible Man Returns* (1940), would be set in contemporary times. Unlike *Dracula*, *Frankenstein* and, to a certain extent, *The Mummy* (1932), however, these would make do without the throwback medieval settings. Frankenstein's particular melange of Gothic and modern architecture returned in the opening scene of *The Invisible Ray* (1936), storm included, but would be gone, replaced by a more state-of-the-art set, by the time of *Man-Made Monster* (1941). Horror, as it gained a commercial foothold, could be suddenly located in the present and channel scientific, class-based or sexual anxieties. This means that the Gothic survived predominantly in some of the films that specifically harked back to a barbaric past, in ghost films (associated with

Figure 3.2 The cliff-perched medieval castle, with its signature ruined entrance, became as iconic as Bela Lugosi's interpretation of the count in *Dracula* (1931).

abandoned buildings) and in adaptations of works by specific writers. For example, the three pre-Code films inspired by Poe, *Murders in the Rue Morgue* (1932), *The Black Cat* (1934) and *The Raven* (1935), although not strictly Gothic in period or subject matter, utilise spaces that either look or feel Gothic: an expressionistic Frankensteinian laboratory appears in *Rue Morgue*, a Satanist chamber reigns over the last third of *The Black Cat* and a medieval torture chamber, complete with a swinging pendulum, is the main horrific locale in *The Raven*. The historical drama *Tower of London* (1939), a loose retelling of the story of Richard III, also made extensive use of a Gothic torture dungeon in its horrific moments. At the same time, the medieval castle aesthetic migrated to the Victorian mansion in the old dark house subgenre and the films that followed the success of *Rebecca* (see Chapter 4).

Of the Gothic sequels to *Dracula* and *Frankenstein*, the most notable are *Bride of Frankenstein* (1935), *Dracula's Daughter* (1936) and *Son of Frankenstein* (1939). The first of these essentially followed on from the events in *Frankenstein* and, to a certain extent, replayed them. It incorporated scenes from Shelley's novel that had been left out of the first film, such as one where the creature meets a blind man or another where he requests that Frankenstein build him a companion. The film also decided to acknowledge, in a curious case of metafictional framing, the Villa Diodati events that led to the genesis of Shelley's novel and which would eventually become the source of films like *Gothic* (1986). In the opening scene, Lord Byron (Gavin Gordon) and Percy Shelley (Douglas Walton) praise Mary Shelley, played by Elsa Lanchester, for the quality of her novel. Mary takes the chance to remind them of the moral message of the tale, in an echo of Van Sloan's warning at the beginning of *Frankenstein*, before she proposes there is more to the story. The film then switches to the ending of Frankenstein and never returns to the present. With a bigger budget than its predecessor and a legendary score by Franz Waxman, *Bride of Frankenstein* was able to re-stage more spectacularly its most well-remembered sequences (the creature's reanimation, the destruction of a building at the end), thus further canonising them. The design and Nefertiti hair styling for the bride, one of the few female monsters of the time, would become as iconic as Karloff's creature, a distinctly beautiful counterpart who, tellingly, is as horrified by the creature's appearance as everyone else. *Bride of Frankenstein*, camper and even more audacious, also imagined a new character, Doctor Septimus Pretorius (Ernest Thesiger), who helps Frankenstein birth the 'bride' in what has been read as a relatively open expression of the director's 'homosexual sensibility' (Benshoff 1997: 49–51).

Bride of Frankenstein also carried through the Gothic spaces of the first film, adding a creepy crypt to the franchise's list of dark architectural spots. These were deliberately expanded in *Son of Frankenstein*, a superproduction that starred both Karloff and Lugosi, had the longest run of any Universal horror film and, initially, was planned as a colour picture (Mallory 2009: 76). In an early scene that shows Baron Wolf von Frankenstein (Basil Rathbone) travelling with his family to their ancestor's home during a tempestuous night, a superstitious and 'strange looking country', Europe, is juxtaposed with modern America. The baron's innocent and fanciful wife (Josephine Hutchinson) hopes for 'a medieval castle' with a moat, a drawbridge and a 'great tall dark tower' with 'battlements'. Although this is not what she gets, the house operates as an architectonic substitute. The place, in which characters fear they might 'get lost', is dramatically lit from angles that cast long shadows onto walls and accentuate its unreality. Its Gothic potential is tapped when the baron, visiting the ruins of the laboratory and its sulphurous pit, is taken by body snatcher Ygor (Bela Lugosi) into the crypt where his father's sarcophagus is currently stored. The door leading to it channels the architectural improbabilities of German expressionism, and the pervading darkness, only punctuated by the light coming from the open door and a torch on the wall, aligns the space with the mummy's tombs and vampire lairs of previous Universal films. As Ygor succinctly puts it in a line that captures the spirit of the mise-en-scène, '[t]his is [the] place of the dead. We're all dead here'. At this point, the monster, sleeping, is introduced as immortal and Frankenstein as a copycat descendant intent on cleaning up his father's name. To emphasise this, the film even has the baron strike out the epithet written in what looks like chalk on the tomb, 'maker of monsters', and replace it with 'maker of men'.

Son of Frankenstein thus emphasises the Gothic aesthetics of the previous two Frankenstein films and revives the franchise's well-known scientist in the figure of his legacy-obsessed son. The parental connection is spelled out for the viewer when, early on, the baron is depicted staring at the portrait of his father in the living room and reading his notebook. Although this Frankenstein does not personally 'make' anyone, he simply awakens or re-energises the old creature, there are obvious correspondences between his work and black magic, a notion underscored by the hysterical reactions of the locals. The film attempts to further clarify what it was that brought the creature back to life – 'cosmic rays' harnessed through lightning with special properties. In so doing, Son of Frankenstein paved the way for the model of the indestructible monster that always returns. If lack of closure would be a more obvious feature of the postmodern Gothic film, Son of Frankenstein already displayed two of the key aspects of successful franchising: the further development of the history behind Gothic myths (more background story) and the endless revival of the, at one point, apparently finished creature.

The latent queerness of Bride of Frankenstein was also perceptible in the first of the Dracula sequels, Dracula's Daughter. Despite picking up where the first film ended, Dracula's Daughter dispensed with the count fairly speedily. He is shown only briefly inside his coffin (an unconvincing mannequin that stands in for Lugosi) as the police arrive.[12] Von Helsing, again played by Van Sloan, serves as a narrative bridge and, within the first seven minutes, the main events of the previous film are recapped. Safely stowed away in Whitby jail, the corpse of Dracula is, however, extracted by a mysterious caped woman who turns out to be his daughter. Burning the body in a purifying ritual intended to release her from the vampiric spell, Countess Marya Zaleska (Gloria

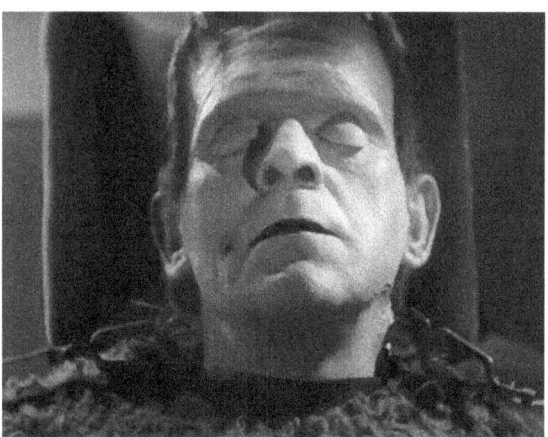

Figure 3.3 Boris Karloff reprised his iconic 'monster' role for the second and last time in Son of Frankenstein (1939), an example of Gothic franchising.

Holden) goes back to London. With Countess Zaleska, Universal introduced another of its few female monsters, an innovative move. Even more subversive was the tacit suggestion of the countess's apparent bisexual inclinations. It is not just that she appears to be happy to bite both men and women. In a revealing scene, she asks a woman brought home by servant Sandor (Irving Pichel) to remove her blouse because she is allegedly working on 'a study of a young girl's head and shoulders'. Her hungry and melancholic stare is naturally the result of her bloodlust, but it may also conceal a deep-rooted desire for the scantily clad model. The connections between vampirism and eroticism, incapable, given the Hays Code, of being anything more than a coded subtext, nevertheless point towards the gradually more explicit affairs of future queer texts, from Mrs Danvers' attraction to her mistress in *Rebecca* to the overtly lesbian scenarios of the continental 'Carmilla' adaptations of the 1960s and 1970s.[13] Given that psychoanalysis had recently theorised homosexuality as a psychosexual pathology, Dr. Garth's (Otto Kruger) psychiatric talk of how diseases of the mind may be cured via 'sympathetic treatment', the 'obsession' given 'mental release', is particularly poignant.

Dracula's Daughter is interesting for its humanisation of the vampire at a very early stage in its cinematic career. Countess Zaleska desperately needs to find a cure for what is clearly framed as an illness or addiction, a situation that positions her as more sympathetic than strictly evil. Even more significant is the confirmation in this film of a paradoxical aesthetic that would become one of Universal's trademarks: the mingling of a very modern present, generally connected to urban America, with a superstitious past that lives on in a fantasised peasant middle-Europe. Countess Zaleska lives in a shiny Chelsea studio and the heart of the film's action takes place in an England where Von Helsing struggles to convince rational policemen that his vampiric beliefs are not the delusions a madman. At the same time, the film also capitalises on all the Gothic trappings for which Universal was quickly becoming well-known. The narrative begins in Castle Dracula and includes a ceremony in some lugubrious moor near Whitby. It also eventually returns to the dark medieval Transylvania where it all started. This Gothicisation of certain spaces, predominantly, but not exclusively, European, naturally leads to the establishment of an atmospherics of fear. The settings for *The Mummy* and *The Wolf Man* were very different from those of *Dracula* and *Frankenstein* – contemporary Egypt and Wales, respectively. However, because lighting (the prevalence of shadows), sound (ominous, dramatic scores), the use of the pathetic fallacy (storms, thunder and lightning) and the treatment of any given space, regardless of its lingering, decaying connections to the past, can be rendered horrific, they are eminently comparable. As Stacey Abbott notes, it is also worth considering that Universal's representations of Transylvania and London are 'studiobound versions' of the original places, 'mythic' in essence (2007: 62). The dreadful eerie quality previously attributed to the Gothic building was transferred to virtually any other in future films, from open expanses of land (swamps, moors, the foggy streets of London) to confining basements (crypts, Egyptian tombs). In this respect, the types of affects connected to a grandiose, belittling style of architecture soon travelled outside of their 'original' context.

By the time Universal's distinct monsters began to cross paths in the early-to-mid-1940s, in *Frankenstein Meets the Wolf Man* (1943), *House of Frankenstein* (1944) and *House of Dracula* (1945), realism had given way to the performative pleasures of the horror formula. Timelines were collapsed and, in some cases, characters seemed to return from the dead for no apparent reason. Inconsistencies piled up. For example, the Frankenstein creature, blinded due to blood incompatibilities after having Ygor's brain transplanted, would unexplainably regain his sight, his capacity to speak coming and going depending on the film. The degree of indeterminacy inherent to the drive for new sequels also entailed the recycling of sets and settings, if not their misuse. In *House of Frankenstein*, characters return to a blasted Frankenstein castle that no longer looks like the one presented a few years earlier. Of course, to judge these films by their narrative accuracy is to somewhat miss the point. Curt Siodmack and Edward T. Lowe Jr., the scriptwriters, were less interested in expanding certain myths than in recuperating what had made each individual monster emblematic, much in the same way that current reboots and remakes reintroduce characters and formulas to new audiences. It is nevertheless crucial to note the effects this had on the establishment of a Gothic netherworld around the fictitious peasant towns of Frankenstein and Vasaria/Visaria (spelling varies) and which drew on the iconography developed throughout the series. The ruins of Castle Frankenstein and the coastal castle where Dr. Edelmann (Onslow Stevens) lives in *House of Dracula* are architectural pastiches of their predecessors embalmed in a Gothic timelessness that renders periodisation irrelevant. Regardless of the relatively contemporaneous settings, the Gothic is noticeable in their high-ceilinged, superannuated buildings full of secret passageways, hidden laboratories and dark shadows.

Gothic settings would not be as popular as contemporary and urban ones for horror films, as the latter allowed for the channelling of more immediate fears that could best resonate with viewers. Additionally, a lot of the horror films made by Universal and competing studios from 1931 to the 1950s, such as *Doctor X* (1932), *The Crime of Dr. Crespi* (1935), *Dr. Cyclops* (1940), *The Man Who Wouldn't Die* (1942), *The Corpse Vanishes* and *The Spider Woman Strikes Back* (1946), were of the mad scientist variety, which demanded modern technologies and surgical or scientific procedures increasingly out of place in the remote alchemical past. Other Universal monsters, such as the invisible man, the ape woman, the Creeper or the Gill-man would therefore manifest in contexts which, if given a horrific treatment, were patently not Gothic. Regardless, American studios did not altogether leave the Gothic behind. Universal's championing of horror had made ripples in the industry and even led to obvious copycats. The most significant of these was *Mark of the Vampire* (1935), which, despite it technically being a remake of *London After Midnight* (1927), imitated the sets and characters in *Dracula* to the point of including an opossum and casting Bela Lugosi in the role of Count Mora. A sequence where he and his daughter Luna (Carroll Borland), candle in hand, are shown walking through a heavily cobwebbed, dark crypt is evidently moulded after

Dracula's descent of the castle stairs in the 1931 film. Similarly, the credibility-busting Gothic castle in *The Most Dangerous Game* (1932), set off the west coast of South America, was visually influenced by the first act of *Dracula*.[14]

Films given thorough Gothic treatments would remain those based on ideas that had proven successful or whose storylines could be compatible with a certain medieval remoteness. There were adaptations of novels that are now widely studied as Gothic, such as *Jane Eyre* (1934), *The House of the Seven Gables* (1940) and *The Hunchback of Notre Dame* (1939), but the Gothic elements in the original texts were downplayed in favour of romance or melodrama. For instance, there are no horrific moments in *Jane Eyre*, beyond a couple of scares that include the 'madwoman', and Thornfield Hall is not rendered visually Gothic. Neither is the Pyncheon mansion in *The House of the Seven Gables*, whose plot is reworked to include a strong abolitionist message, particularly scary and the family curse plotline is not played sensationally. Conversely, *Tower of London*, a historical drama following the rise to power of Richard, Duke of Gloucester (Basil Rathbone), in 1483, appears to parade all the accoutrements of the Gothic, including an exterior castle set that would be reused in other Universal films. As in the other adaptations, the film avoids horror, despite having a relatively high body count. It indulges in only one torture sequence which takes place in a dark dungeon equipped with a rack, whips and branding hot irons, and is orchestrated by Boris Karloff in his role as executioner Mord. The spectacle is underplayed here, with the camera cutting away when John Wyatt (John Sutton) is about to scream.[15] *The Devil and Daniel Webster* (1942) was an adaptation of a 1937 story by Stephen Vincent Benét, itself inspired by the Washington Irving story 'The Devil and Tom Walker' (1824). The Faustian pact at the heart of the film connects it to the German legend but also to Charles Maturin's *Melmoth the Wanderer*, even though the setting is largely contemporary.

Much more straightforwardly Gothic was *The Black Room* (1935), in which Boris Karloff played twins Gregor and Anton de Berghman, the last descendants of a Tyrolean baronial family plagued by a dark prophecy that states that the older brother will be slain by the younger in the castle's black room. Beginning in 1790, when the space is sealed up by a 'masonic wall of bricks' so the horrid destiny may be prevented, the film fast-forwards to the early nineteenth century, when the boys have grown up and both parents have passed away. Anton, a kind man with a paralysed right arm, is summoned by his roguish older twin, who, it transpires, has gained access to the black room and plotted Anton's demise in fear of his own murder. In a turn of events that can only be blamed on fate, Gregor ends up dying by his brother's hand when he is pushed into the same pit where he formerly killed Anton and is impaled on a knife sticking out of the corpse. The film conjures up an ominous atmosphere that complements the many Gothic trappings of the old de Berghman's castle: the secret room, opened by a hidden latch, is fitted with reflective onyx walls and a trapdoor. *The Black Room* is not explicitly supernatural, but Anton's promise to come back 'even from the dead' to take revenge on his brother is as uncanny as Gregor's impersonation of his brother. An original written by Henry Myers and Arthur Strawn, the film outdid *Dracula* and *Frankenstein* in its theatricality, but was not a commercial success.

It would only be in the early 1950s, after RKO's hit with *The Body Snatcher* (1945), that Universal would go full-house Gothic again in the also Karloff-led features *The Strange Door* (1951) and *The Black Castle* (1952). *The Strange Door*, based on the Robert Louis Stevenson short story 'The Sire de Malétroit's Door' (1878), tells the macabre tale of an eighteenth-century envious sire, Alain de Malétroit (Charles Laughton), a man traumatised by the fact that his young beloved favours the affections of his brother (Paul Cavanagh). Imprisoning him for twenty years after the woman's death (who passes away while giving birth) and taking care of their daughter, Blanche (Sally Forrest), his ultimate quest for revenge includes forcing the girl to marry a scoundrel. However, the chosen man, one Denis (Richard Stapley), proves to be of noble spirit, so Alain is forced to imprison them both. Their frustrated escape via the chateau's burial ground is rendered horrific, as does a subterranean passage leading to an armour room where Denis nearly meets his end. The scene where Blanche and Denis are trapped in a cell with water-activated walls designed to crush them includes a haunting moment where Blanche's face and that of her mother are superimposed to hint at a form of transgenerational haunting. The entrance to the castle is the 'strange door' of the title, which locks behind anyone foolish enough to enter the premises. Although Boris Karloff was billed significantly in the marketing of the film, he only plays a small role as Alain's rebellious helper, Voltan.

Karloff played a similar character in *The Black Castle*, where, as Dr. Meissen, he aims to help a pair of ailing lovers in the clutches of Count Carl von Bruno (Stephen McNally). In this film, reminiscent of *The Most Dangerous Game*, Richard Beckett (Richard Greene) travels to von Bruno's castle near the Black Forest in order to investigate the disappearance of two of his friends. The tyrant, who appears to want to kill his second wife Elga (Rita Corday) as he did his first, is more than just another Bluebeard. He is also a professional hunter who keeps in his possession, among other creatures, a wild leopard and who owns an alligator pit barring the only way out of the building. The film takes a decidedly Gothic turn after Richard and Elga, persuaded by Dr. Meissen, decide that egress may only be achieved by imbibing a serum that renders them temporarily catatonic. After their ploy is exposed, in a scene that returns to the beginning of the film, they narrowly avoid live burial. Apart from its eighteenth-century, barbaric European setting, *The Black Castle*, like *The Strange Door* and *The Black Room*, emphasises the architectural Gothic of its titular castle: not only is the building imposing and full of deadly secrets, it is also rendered scarier thanks to stormy atmospherics.

Yet, for all their Gothic qualities, neither *The Strange Door* nor *The Black Castle* were as influential as the films made in the more contemporary horrific vein or the hybrids produced by the *Dracula*, *Frankenstein* and *Wolf Man* franchises. Only one thing points towards the establishment of a genre/mode more strongly than the monster rallies of the 1940s: the parodies of the late 1940s and the early-to-mid-1950s. Although horror comedies were hardly new by then, it is interesting that Universal decided to treat its own property in this way. In *Abbott and Costello Meet Frankenstein* (1948), comedians Bud Abbott and Lou Costello were pitted against the count, the creature and the wolf man all at once. This conflation did not as much ridicule the monsters as it made the most of their respective characteristics. Abbott and Costello, especially Costello as baggage clerk Wilbur, could act as the source of comic relief while, in his ineptitude, still fall prey to the horrors of a decrepit castle or of the McDougal's House of Horrors' wax museum. Particularly noteworthy is the way in which the monsters were played both for screams (those of Wilbur, who struggles to get his partner Chick to believe him) and for laughter (the various vignettes contribute to portray Wilbur as superstitious and irritating). These films signalled the stagnation of the monster formula once fright had been dulled by overfamiliarity.

Universal did not just create an industry around horror that would be continued by the so-called Poverty Row Studios (Monogram, PRC and Republic) in films such as *The Devil Bat* (1940), *King of the Zombies* (1941), *Strangler of the Swamp* (1946) and *The Catman of Paris* (1946) in the 1940s.[16] They were also responsible for patenting visual formulas and narrative patterns around continuation (and resuscitation) that would be picked up by countries like England (see Chapter 5) or Italy and Spain (see Chapter 6) even decades later. One of the key figures responsible for the return of monsters like the wolf man and the vampiric count, Jacinto Molina (better known as Paul Naschy), claimed in his memoirs that he was deeply affected by watching *Frankenstein Meets the Wolf Man* (1997: 37–38) as a boy, and many of his films clearly replay scenarios and motifs extracted from Universal's horrors. Mexico, a country whose horror films post-1935 already showed the influence of the mad science film as developed in *Frankenstein*, *Bride of Frankenstein* and *The Invisible Man* (Rhodes 2003: 98–103), would, in its Gothic cycle of the 1950s and 1960s, take inspiration from Universal, sometimes going as far as to cite specific films. For example, when a light beam crosses

Count Karol de Lavud's (Germán Robles) eyes in *El vampiro* (*The Vampire*, 1957), this is clearly an explicit reference to Lugosi's similarly starkly lit stare in *Dracula*. Although Lavud sports the first fangs since *Drakula İstanbul'da* (*Dracula in Istanbul*, 1953), his attire is also reminiscent of Lugosi's, and Marta's (Ariadne Welter) arrival in her hometown and derelict hacienda, an apparently inhabited ruin, echoes Renfield's first few moments in Castle Dracula.[17] Films such as *El monstruo resucitado* (*The Monstrous Doctor Crimen*, 1953), *La bruja* (*The Witch*, 1954), *El ataúd del vampiro* (*The Vampire's Coffin*, 1958), *Misterios de ultratumba* (*The Black Pit of Dr. M*, 1959), *El mundo de los vampiros* (*The World of the Vampires*, 1961), *El vampiro sangriento* (*The Bloody Vampire*, 1962), *El barón del terror* (*The Brainiac*, 1962) and *La invasión de los vampiros* (*The Invasion of the Vampires*, 1963) contain a panoply of borrowings, direct and indirect, from Universal's horror catalogue. Actor and director Abel Salazar even self-consciously modelled his production company ABSA, responsible for many of Mexico's Gothic horrors, after the American studio (Wilt 1998: 142). Naturally, these films were not simply derivative, but rather adapted their stories to a Mexican context. In some cases, as in *Ladrón de cadáveres* (*The Body Snatcher*, 1957) or *Santo vs. las mujeres vampiro* (*Santo Versus the Vampire Women*, 1962), the Gothic elements in the films were seamlessly combined with *lucha libre* wrestling. In others, as Andrew Syder and Dolores Tierney (2005: 39) note, the use of indigenous monsters like 'la llorona' (the crying woman) or the replacement of Egyptian mummies with Aztec ones that focus on the pre-Columbian past, problematise a reading of these films as mere copies. Universal helped turn a number of tropes, characters and settings into conventions that could be reshaped into different national and transnational forms of Gothic cinema.

If trick films and early adaptations began to visualise and imagine the Gothic, and if early European, especially German, films found cinematic ways of conveying their main effects, it was Universal that ignited the horror film industry. Although the nightmares it proposed originated in Gothic fantasies, safely contained in the past, horror films would increasingly locate events in the present, especially in the mad scientist subgenre and in 1950s atomic monster films. Still,

Universal horror played a crucial role in founding formulas that would shape the aesthetics of the Gothic. Indigenously, they would make horror films viable; internationally, they would become a cinematic blueprint to expand upon and emulate.

FILMOGRAPHY

Abbott and Costello Meet Frankenstein (Charles Barton, 1948, USA)
Bride of Frankenstein (James Whale, 1935, USA)
Bride of Frankenstein (James Whale, 1935, USA)
Doctor X (Michael Curtiz, 1932, USA)
Dr. Cyclops (Ernest B. Schoedsack, 1940, USA)
Dracula (Tod Browning, 1931, USA)
Dracula's Daughter (Lambert Hillyer, 1936, USA)
Drakula İstanbul'da (*Dracula in Istanbul*, Mehmet Muhtar, 1953, Turkey)
El barón del terror (*The Brainiac*, Chano Urueta, 1962, Mexico)
El monstruo resucitado (*The Monstrous Doctor Crimen*, Chano Urueta, 1953, Mexico)
El mundo de los vampiros (*The World of the Vampires*, Alfonso Corona Blake, 1961, Mexico)
El vampiro (*The Vampire*, Fernando Méndez, 1957, Mexico)
El vampiro sangriento (*The Bloody Vampire*, Miguel Morayta, 1962, Mexico)
Frankenstein (James Whale, 1931, USA)
Frankenstein Meets the Wolf Man (Roy William Neill, 1943, USA)
House of Dracula (Erle C. Kenton, 1945, USA)
House of Frankenstein (Erle C. Kenton, 1944, USA)
Jane Eyre (Christy Cabanne, 1934, USA)
Gothic (Ken Russell, 1986, UK)
King of the Zombies (Jean Yarbrough, 1941, USA)
La bruja (*The Witch*, Chano Urueta, 1954, Mexico)
La invasión de los vampiros (*The Invasion of the Vampires*, Miguel Morayta, 1963, Mexico)
La voluntad del muerto (*The Will of the Dead Man*, George Melford and Enrique Tovar Ávalos, 1930, Mexico)

Ladrón de cadáveres (*The Body Snatcher*, Fernando Méndez, 1957, Mexico)
London After Midnight (Tod Browning, 1927, USA)
Man-Made Monster (George Waggner, 1941, USA)
Mark of the Vampire (Tod Browning, 1935, USA)
Metropolis (Fritz Lang, 1927, USA)
Misterios de ultratumba (*The Black Pit of Dr. M*, Fernando Méndez, 1959, Mexico)
Murders in the Rue Morgue (Robert Florey, 1932, USA)
Nosferatu, eine Symphonie des Grauens (*Nosferatu*, F. W. Murnau, 1922, Germany)
Rebecca (Alfred Hitchcock, 1940, USA)
Santo vs. las mujeres vampiro (*Santo Versus the Vampire Women*, Alfonso Corona Blake, 1962, Mexico)
Show Boat (James Whale, 1936, USA)
Son of Frankenstein (Rowland V. Lee, 1939, USA)
Strangler of the Swamp (Frank Wisbar, 1946, USA)
Svengali (Archie Mayo, 1931, USA)
The Black Castle (Nathan Juran, 1952, USA)
The Black Cat (Edgar G. Ulmer, 1934, USA)
The Black Room (Roy William Neill, 1935, USA)
The Body Snatcher (Robert Wise, 1945, USA)
The Cat and the Canary (Paul Leni, 1927, USA)
The Cat Creeps (Rupert Julian, 1930, USA)
The Catman of Paris (Lesley Selander, 1946, USA)
The Corpse Vanishes (Wallace Fox, 1942, USA)
The Crime of Dr. Crespi (John H. Auer, 1935, USA)
The Devil and Daniel Webster (William Dieterle, 1942, USA)
The Devil Bat (Jean Yarborough, 1940, USA)
The House of Fear (Joe May, 1939, USA)
The House of the Seven Gables (Joe May, 1940, USA)
The Hunchback of Notre Dame (Wallace Worsley, 1923, USA)
The Hunchback of Notre Dame (William Dieterle, 1939, USA)
The Invisible Man (James Whale, 1933, USA)
The Invisible Man Returns (Joe May, 1940, USA)
The Invisible Ray (Lambert Hillyer, 1936, USA)
The Jazz Singer (Alan Crosland, 1927, USA)

The Last Warning (Paul Leni, 1929, USA)

The Man Who Laughs (Paul Leni, 1928, USA)

The Man Who Wouldn't Die (Herbert I. Leeds, 1942, USA)

The Most Dangerous Game (Irving Pichel and Ernest B. Schoedsack, 1932, USA)

The Mummy (Karl Freund, 1932, USA)

The Phantom of the Opera (Rupert Julian, Lon Chaney, Ernst Laemmle and Edward Sedgwick, 1925, USA)

The Raven (Lew Landers, 1935, USA)

The Spider Woman Strikes Back (Arthur Lubin, 1946, USA)

The Strange Door (Joseph Pevney, 1951, USA)

The Wolf Man (George Waggner, 1941, USA)

Tower of London (Rowland V. Lee, 1939, USA)

Werewolf of London (Stuart Walker, 1935, USA)

NOTES

1 There was also an adaptation of *Les Misérables* (1862) which I am not including because it is not Gothic. The fact that the uniting factor here is Victor Hugo and not the Gothic reinforces the point that neither *The Hunchback of Notre Dame* nor *The Man Who Laughs* were conceived as horror films.

2 I consulted a copy of the original 1923 pressbook available at the Margaret Herrick Library. It is unpaginated, has no discernible author (other than the studio itself) and contains no publication details.

3 See, for example, Anon. (1927). The article does concede that the film was first envisaged as 'a monster production to be made in France' (808).

4 See Williams (1984).

5 Contemporary articles in *Universal Weekly* commented on the amount of preparation behind, and resources allocated to, *The Phantom of the Opera*, calling it 'the biggest production of 1925' (Anon. 1925a: 12), and speculated that the phantom's 'chamber of mystery' was 'the most unusual set ever built' (Anon. 1925b: 17).

6 The sensationalism and perceived gruesomeness of Stoker's novel and stage adaptation, upon first in-house assessment in 1927, met with

resistance from the studio's readers. It was only after Carl Laemmle Jr., who became chief executive in 1929, decided to make the film on a grand scale that his father greenlit the project (Riley and Turner 1990: 30, 35).

7 Dracula's black cape was introduced in the 1924 British stage adaptation.
8 For the legal battle between Lugosi's descendants and Universal regarding the commercial use of the actor's image, see Skal (2004: 251–254).
9 The exterior of the castle was literally assembled from pieces of medieval sets used in previous silent pictures (Riley 1990: 61).
10 As Martin Myrone notes, the set for *Frankenstein* echoes Piranesi's *Carceri d'invenzione* (*Imaginary Prisons*) print series, first published in 1750 and reworked in 1761 (2013: 79).
11 As Kyle Edwards argues, the success of *Frankenstein* is what strengthened Universal's production model and, if it was somewhat stalled by the arrival of Charles Rogers as head of production, was quickly resurrected because its characters were 'valuable assets' and 'presold properties' (2014: 25).
12 As Mallory (2009: 54) explains, this decision was prompted by a rejection of the initial R. C. Sherriff script, based, although only nominally, on the Bram Stoker short story 'Dracula's Guest' (1914) and deemed too horrific and sexual. Problems with the production led to the paying off of Bela Lugosi and to the removal of a Middle Ages storyline that chronicled the count's abduction and adoption of the woman who would become his daughter.
13 The Hays Code was an American set of production directives in operation between the 1930s and 1960s that restricted the representation in cinema of various subjects and topics, including homosexuality.
14 The Russian owner and his castle were already there in the original 1924 story by Richard Connell, but their cinematic depiction recalls *Dracula*.
15 There is a scene where a dead man falls out of an iron maiden, which is quite effective but incidental.
16 For more on the Poverty Row Studios, see Turner and Price (1979) and Weaver (1993).
17 I am referring to what we now understand as vampire fangs. Of course, films like *Nosferatu* and *London After Midnight* had already featured vampires, real or fake, with rat-like incisors or razor-sharp teeth.

BIBLIOGRAPHY

Abbott, S. (2007) *Celluloid Vampires: Life after Death in the Modern World*, Austin: University of Texas Press.

Anonymous (1925a) 'Statistics on Making of "Phantom of the Opera" Indicate It Will Be Biggest of 1925 Productions', *Universal Weekly*, 10 January, 12, 29.

Anonymous (1925b) '"Chamber of Mystery" in "Phantom of Opera" Said to Be Most Unusual Set Ever Built', *Universal Weekly*, 31 January, 17.

Anonymous (1927) 'Carl Laemmle's Twenty-First Year: Universal World-Wide in Its Activities', *Moving Picture World*, 2 May, 806–810.

Benshoff, H. M. (1997) *Monsters in the Closet: Homosexuality and the Horror Film*, Manchester: Manchester University Press.

Blake, M. F. (1993) *Lon Chaney: The Man behind the Thousand Faces*, New York: Vestal Press.

Edwards, K. (2014) '"House of Horrors": Corporate Strategy at Universal Pictures in 1930s', in Richard Nowell (ed.) *Merchants of Menace: The Business of Horror Cinema*, London and New York: Bloomsbury.

Hogle, J. E. (2002) *The Undergrounds of The Phantom of the Opera: Sublimation and the Gothic in Leroux's Novel and Its Progeny*, Basingstoke: Palgrave.

Hutchings, P. (2004) *The Horror Film*, Longman: Pearson.

Jackson, K. (2013) *Nosferatu: Eine Symphonie des Grauens*, Basingstoke: Palgrave Macmillan.

Landry, R. (aka Land.) (1928) 'The Man Who Laughs Review', *Variety*, 2 May, 14.

Mallory, M. (2009) *Universal Studios Monsters: A Legacy of Horror*, New York: Universe Publishing.

Myrone, M. (2013) 'Gothic Art's Cinematic Legacies', in J. Bell (ed.) *Gothic: The Dark Heart of Film*, London: BFI.

Naschy, P. (1997) *Memorias de un hombre lobo*, Madrid: Alberto Santos Editor.

Peirse, A. (2013) *After Dracula: The 1930s Horror Film*, London and New York: I.B. Tauris.

Rhodes, G. (2003) 'Fantasmas del cine Mexicano: The 1930s Horror Film Cycle of Mexico', in S. J. Schneider (ed.) *Fear without Frontiers: Horror Cinema across the Globe*, Godalming: FAB Press.

Riley, P. J. and G. Turner (1990) 'Production Background', in P. J. Riley (ed.) *Dracula: The Original 1931 Shooting Script*, Absecon, NJ: MagicImage Filmbooks.

Skal, D. (2004) *Hollywood Gothic: The Tangled Web of Dracula from Novel to Stage to Screen*, rev. edn, London: Faber & Faber.

Smith, A. (2012) *Hideous Progeny: Disability, Eugenics, and Classic Horror Cinema*, New York: Columbia University Press.

Spadoni, R. (2007) *Uncanny Bodies: The Coming of Sound and the Origins of the Horror Genre*, London and Berkeley, LA: University of California Press.

Syder, A. and D. Tierney (eds) (2005) 'Importation/Mexploitation, or, How a Crime-Fighting, Vampire-Slaying Mexican Wrestler Almost Found Himself in an Italian Sword-and-Sandals Epic', in S. J. Schneider (ed.) *Horror International*, Detroit, MI: Wayne State University Press.

Turner, G. E. (1982) 'The Phantom Set', *The American Cinematographer*, 63.7: 673–677, 733–740.

Turner, G. E. and M. H. Price (1979) *Forgotten Horrors: Early Talkie Chillers from Poverty Row*, London: Thomas Yoseloff; South Brunswick and New York: A. S. Barnes and Co.

Weaver, T. (1993) *Poverty Row Horrors: Monogram, PRC and Republic Horror Films of the Forties*, Jefferson, NC: McFarland.

Williams, L. (1984) 'When the Woman Looks', in M. A. Doane, P. Mellencamp and L. Williams (eds) *Re-Vision: Essays in Feminist Film Criticism*, Frederick, MD: University Publications of America.

Wilt, D. (1998) 'Masked Men and Monsters', in P. Tombs (ed.) *Mondo Macabro: Weird and Wonderful Cinema around the World*, New York: St. Martin's Griffin.

4

THE EXPLAINED SUPERNATURAL

It was not just the horror films of Universal which contributed to the shift in temporality that allowed Gothic cinema to escape its medieval trappings. By the 1910s and 1920s, the Gothic had already travelled to the domestic space via the old dark house mysteries and it would see a steady development in the Female Gothic films of the 1940s. Turning to these bodies of films, whose generic hybridity is evident from the various labels employed to define them ('thrillers', 'mysteries', 'melodramas' and 'women films'), is important to a general understanding of Gothic cinema for two reasons. Firstly, their foregrounding of suspense and rational explanations over supernatural happenings mounts a challenge to the truism that the Gothic is inherently anti-realist. The old dark house mysteries owed much to the detective novels and plays of the early twentieth century, but may be productively recuperated as organic updates of the 'realist' school of Gothic writing championed by Ann Radcliffe.[1] Secondly, the films *The Bat*, *The Cat and the Canary* and *Rebecca* reveal that new suspense-driven films were instrumental in the migration of Gothic aesthetics from archaic times and their visual correlates (Gothic churches, decaying aristocratic castles) to the spatial confines of Victorian mansions and Edwardian manor houses in texts set in contemporary times. These buildings inherited the machinery and theatrics of fear that once characterised spaces such as Otranto and Udolpho. Taken together, the old dark house mystery and the Female Gothic film constitute a much-ignored missing link between the monster films of the 1930s and 1940s and the return to period Gothics catapulted by Hammer Film Productions in the UK and Roger Corman in the United States. They are also an important reminder that the Gothic, as an aesthetic marker, can manifest alongside comedy and romance and that its claustrophobic associations can be socially committed.[2]

There is a tendency to think about the Gothic tradition as a literature and cinema of 'fear' and thus to distinguish it from crime fiction and thrillers, considered a literature and cinema of 'suspense'. This dyadic model, although quite a contemporary one, stretches back to early nineteenth-century critical attempts at defining the various emotional reactions generated by different objects of terror. To Ann Radcliffe's famous separation between horror's annihilating powers and terror's inclination towards the sublime covered in the introduction, one could add Nathan Drake's suggestion that terror based on material sources cannot 'induce that thrilling sensation of astonishment, apprehension and delight' caused by 'mysterious incidents which indicate the ministration of beings mightier far than we' (1798: 245–246). Naturally, these theorisations of Gothic effects have little to do with the moment when a character first encounters the object of terror and more with their ultimate reveal as either really fantastic, as in Matthew Lewis's *The Monk* and Charles Maturin's *Melmoth the Wanderer*, or as only apparently so, as in Radcliffe's *The Mysteries of Udolpho*. The school of the 'explained supernatural', where the perceived threat turns out to be either a hoax (a character pretending to be a ghost) or the result of sensorial confusion (the heroine mistaking a wax figure for a real corpse) would be tremendously popular in Europe, even in countries like Spain, where the Gothic's concessions to the fantastic and morbid struggled to get approval from censorious religious bodies preoccupied with the mode's potential reification of superstition. The explained supernatural had the benefit of allowing the characters and readers to indulge in the spectacle of the uncanny and the numinous while didactically returning them to the rational world in their empirical resolutions. Radcliffe's fictions introduced readers to this narrative device (Clery 1995: 106–107) and, importantly, inaugurated the mystery genre.[3] As Catherine Spooner notes, the resolved 'mysteries' at the heart of Udolpho 'are a kind of precursor of the *denouement* of the detective plot' and Radcliffe's heroines 'proto-detective[s]' (2010: 248). More generally, a sizable proportion of Gothic writings followed the realist strand.

The old dark house mystery play that became popular in Broadway in the early twentieth century and which would lead to a number of successful film adaptations and to its own intrinsic cinematic subgenre developed from the explained supernatural and borrowed a number of the Gothic's tropes and settings. The roster of characters would usually include a young woman and an apparently supernatural creature (a ghost or monster) who would, in reality, be a murderer, escaped lunatic or crook in disguise. The scary encounters would typically take place in an old (Victorian) family mansion full of trapdoors, sliding panels, hidden passages and chambers. This setting would be lighted following the chiaroscuro techniques popularised by early German cinema and its spaces exploited for their affective possibilities. The action would normally circle around a voice from the past or a resurfacing family secret. The narrative would manipulate events to generate suspense, tension and fear, although direct violence would ultimately be eschewed, with any murders taking place off-camera and hair-raising face-offs counterpointed by moments of comic relief. Most importantly, all supernatural events would be ultimately explained away as elaborate ploys to steal valuables or cheat people out of their inheritances. The old dark house mystery's hotchpotch of horror, comedy, melodrama and thrills sometimes made for odd results, but its resistance to easy generic demarcation was part of its appeal and popularity. Since the most consequential examples were adapted from already successful plays, directors could also rely on a ready-made market and on cheap production costs. In the case of a classic like *The Cat and the Canary*, Paul Leni's achievement was largely visual and dynamic, and overcame the limitations of the stage. The film's brilliance resides in the director's capacity to use camera movement, depth and lighting to enhance events in a way unique to cinema that would simultaneously further entrench Gothic aesthetics into otherwise realist settings.

The first of the old house mysteries to make it to the big screen was *The Ghost Breaker*, based upon the 1909 melodramatic farce of the same title by Charles W. Goddard and Paul Dickey. Warren Jarvis (H. B. Warner) escapes from the police with his trusted servant Rusty (John Burton) after taking revenge on the man who killed his father. In the fourth act, he ends in an imposing Spanish castle belonging to the princess of Aragon (Rita Stanwood), where he, as a modern American man, stands for reason and the Spanish princess for Old World superstitious beliefs. Some of the comic-horrific moments that ensue stem from Warren's attempt to disprove that the castle is jinxed, and include a fight with a 'living' suit of armour. Contemporary reviews made much of *The Ghost Breaker*'s attempts to mingle comic episodes with frightening ones, especially during the final part of the film. *Motion Picture News* wrote that the scenes where the characters 'explore the treacherous rooms of the haunted castle, while mainly humorous, are both exciting and fearful' (Milne 1914: 62), and *Variety* opined that '[i]t is this air of gentle joshing that saves the story from ridicule' (Anon. 1914: 28). The trade journal *The Moving Picture World* perhaps best captured the film's composite formula when describing it as '[h]umor, pathos, thrills, genuine melodrama, novelty' (Bush 1914: 1692). Not a direct trendsetter, *The Ghost Breaker*'s experiment in the comedy-thriller set in an old dark castle was nevertheless followed by other films exploiting similar atmospherics and scenarios in domestic settings: the eccentric owners of an imposing house leave their estates to successors who prove their worth by living there for a period of time in *The House of a Thousand Candles* (1915), its remake *Haunting Shadows* (1919) and *The House of the Tolling Bell* (1920); either robbers or men left-for-dead (often husbands) are discovered to be responsible for apparent hauntings in *Das unheimliche Haus* (*The Eerie House*, 1916), *The Ghost House* (1917), *The Haunted Bedroom* (1919), *At the Villa Rose* (1920), *Love Without Question* (1920), *The House of Whispers* (1920), *A Midnight Bell* (1921) and *Terror Mountain* (1928); séances become a tantalising means of unmasking murderers in *The Thirteenth Chair* (1919), adapted from the 1916 play, *The Barton Mystery* (1920), *Luring Shadows* (1920) and *The Terror* (1928), adapted from the Edgar Wallace play of 1927.[4] Only a minority of films, such as the remake of *The Ghost Breaker* in 1922, *The Magician* (1926), *Tin Hats* (1926) and *London After Midnight*, would feature medieval castles and towers until the success of Universal's *Dracula* and *Frankenstein* made them fashionable again.

None of these films had the audience and critical success or influence of *The Bat* and John Willard's *The Cat and the Canary*, adapted from plays by Mary Roberts Rinehart and Avery Hopwood, and John Willard, respectively. The Broadway run for *The Bat* lasted two years and the play was performed a staggering 867 times. In fact, pioneer silent era director D. W. Griffith was so taken with it that, when he was refused the rights, he wrote his only 'horrific' film, *One Exciting Night* (1922), which crystallised the storm as crucial piece of Gothic atmospherics. *The Cat and the Canary* was performed 349 times and both it and *The Bat* would be staged in London, where they were also met with critical and popular enthusiasm (Lachman 2014: 130–131). Their film adaptations were equal box office successes and, for the most part, praised by critics. These were both key aspects in ensuring that a number of other successful Broadway plays were adapted in the 1920s: *The Monster* (1925), after the 1922 Wilbur Crane play; *The Gorilla* (1927), after the 1925 Ralph Spence play; and *The Last Warning*, after the 1922 Thomas F. Fallon play. The industry peaked in the 1930s and 1940s, during which period both *The Bat* and *The Cat and the Canary* saw more than one talkie remake. The former would be revisited by West in *The Bat Whispers* (1930) and the latter would be made into *The Cat Creeps* in 1930, along with its Spanish-language version *La voluntad del muerto*. It would be remade again in 1939. However, if the fact that *The Bat* and *The Cat and the Canary* were profitable and critically acclaimed is significant and explains the influx of similar titles in the years to follow, it is their iconoclastic cinematography, atmospherics and further entrenchment of the explained supernatural that makes them fascinating. As silent films adapting verbose plays, *The Bat* and *The Cat and the Canary* also took on the serious task of transporting their habitual repertoire of spooks to the screen without sound.

The play *The Bat* was itself based on Roberts Rinehart's 1908 novel *The Circular Staircase*, already made into a different film in 1915. Chief among the alterations the source material underwent was the introduction of a criminal who dresses up in a bat-shaped costume and refers to himself by the name of the animal. The film boasted a new prologue set in a bank in which viewers were shown the Bat's peculiar silhouette, marked by two big ears and what appears to be a snout. Narratively, the scene makes little sense, as the events have no connection to those that come immediately after, but it serves to establish a specific mood. The contrasting use of stark shadows with shafts of light and the building's imposing size and superhuman windows offer a taster of the type of architectonic dread elicited by the 'lonely mansion' which constitutes the Bat's next target. Famous production designer William Cameron Menzies created the set for the house with the intention that its scope and vastness would exceed those of the stage (Curtis 2015: 62): the floor space is immense and the tall ceilings and gigantic staircases dwarf the characters. In fact, the Fleming mansion, first portrayed in an imposing establishing shot, resembles a turreted castle rather than a peaceful country house. The maid (Louise Fazenda) is quick to define the place as the 'happy home of the Heebee-Jeebees', where '[d]oors slam – loose feet roam around – lights go out'. She is right on at least one account: lights do go out eventually and the corresponding effect, whereby characters move in pools of light, contributes to the spooky atmosphere. *The Bat* cleverly plays with lighting and composition to place the characters in vulnerable situations and thus enhance the dark aesthetics of a mansion that, functionally, becomes a domestic version of the Gothic castle.

As interesting as *The Bat*'s aesthetics was the language used in its publicity campaign. Referred to as a 'mystery melodrama' and as a 'comedy-mystery-drama' in contemporary adverts and theatre lobby cards, it is striking that the emphasis often fell upon the film's capacity to generate fear and not humour.[5] For example, a 1926 ad entitled '*The Bat* Thrilled Even the Critics on Broadway', which pulled together soundbites from newspapers such as *Daily News* or *The Times*, deliberately selected the parts of the reviews that foregrounded the chilling aspects. *The Evening Journal* wrote: '[f]or gorgeous entertainment that keeps you in suspense and thrills see *The Bat*. Lights flare and darken, shadows on the wall. Secret Passages. Suspects. Clews. And the audience is taken in'.[6] Similarly, *The Evening World* declared *The Bat* '[a] thrilling picture. Shivers up your spine', and *The Telegram* rather histrionically suggested that the film was so 'electric' the critic's 'teeth rattled like a skeleton on the roof with a cold in its head'.[7] In an echo of the hot and cold showers typical of the French Grand Guignol plays, reviewers such as George T. Pardy, writing for *Motion Picture News*, commented on how

> [t]here probably isn't a human creature, young or old, hard-boiled enough to sit through a session of *The Bat* without having spinal chills develop as a result of its eerie, creepy, blood-curdling atmosphere, or experiencing a sense of welcome relief when a thrust of slapstick comedy momentarily changes horror to hilarity. (1926: 1418)

The Bat's attempt to harness horrific suspense through its use of setting, lighting and action was celebrated as its greatest accomplishment; it even overshadowed the performances of the brilliant cast and made up for the convoluted plot. Utilising and shooting the Bat as a de facto monster, especially in the scene where he approaches Dale (Jewel Carmen) and the camera switches to a medium close-up of his grotesque mask, The Bat brought the formula of the explained supernatural into the era of mystery films. A particularly noteworthy scene in this respect features the silhouette of a bat overflying the mansion, an echo of previous ones in which it is fleetingly hinted at that the Bat may actually be able to metamorphose into the animal.[8] This moment is suggestively appropriate of the old dark mystery's tension between its conscious exploitation of the titillations of the supernatural and its moral obligation to offer a rational explanation.[9]

The Cat and the Canary would tread similar ground but, thanks in large part to Paul Leni's deft camerawork and innovative visual ideas, such as a hand wiping off a cobwebbed surface to clear the film title during the credits scene, it would shine in its own right. Once more, the most noticeable aspect about this film is not its thin, convoluted plot, but the gloomy spaces and its many mood-enhancing vignettes. The Cat and the Canary would set the scene for the Universal horrors I covered in the previous chapter – quite literally so, as set designer Charles D. Hall would go on to work in Dracula, Frankenstein and Bride of Frankenstein.

Figure 4.1 In The Bat (1926), the trappings of the Gothic castle travelled virtually unchanged into the structures of the mysterious old dark house.

The Gothic look of the West mansion, where the descendants of the dying owner gather in the hope of inheriting his fortune, was even more remarkable than the house in *The Bat*. Paul Gulick, in a contemporary article for *Amateur Movie Makers*, commented on how the 'Gothic design' of the film's architecture and furniture complemented the shadow play, 'lend[ing] a strange sinister atmosphere to the backgrounds' and, when coupled with the pantomimic acting, became 'intensely expressive of mystery' (1927: 11). The effect was such that, for modern horror and science fiction film critic Carlos Clarens, with *The Cat and the Canary* Leni had effectively 'updated *The Castle of Otranto*' (1997: 56). It would be more correct, given the thematic concerns of the film, to say that *The Cat and the Canary* had revamped Radcliffe's fictions: its heroine, beautiful and young heiress Annabelle West (Laura La Plante), may be read as a modern take on the wealthy inheritors of the Gothic romance, the maniac killer as an update of the tyrannical male figure prepared to kill or torture the heroine. The film includes apparently supernatural happenings, most of which are shown to be part of an elaborate plot to drive Annabelle insane; the revolving walls, secret chambers and various other trappings of Udolpho are recreated in the West mansion's fireplace buttons and removable panels.

The last point is particularly important because *The Cat and the Canary* is, like *The Bat*, at pains to portray its house as an old Gothic castle. The various shots of its façade actually display a medieval-looking building made up of a series of towers ending in spires that feel out of place in the context of the 'lonely, pine-clad hill overlooking the Hudson' where the mansion sits.[10] Additionally, its doors have large brass doorknobs ridden with cobwebs and the floors hide a crypt. The opening sequence also strives to introduce the West residence as haunted. After a title card explains there are rumours that 'the tormented ghost of Cyrus West wander[s] nightly through the deserted corridors', the camera seemingly embodies the spirit's point of view, tracking a shadowy, empty corridor with billowing curtains for no other apparent reason than to create a sinister ambiance. Many other effective tricks are used: underlighting underscores Mammy Pleasant's (Martha Mattox) ominous expression when she justifies her years of solitude as not needing the company of 'the living ones'; orbs of light dance in the darkness when characters start searching the place with torchlights; shadows heighten suspense when cast against starkly lit walls (there is even an echo of *Nosferatu* in the bedroom scene when the villain's hand hovers over Annabelle's chest); an elongating lens distorts the face of Aunt Susan (Flora Finch); the letters in the title cards sometimes shake, as if shivering with fear; the painting of Cyrus is depicted from a low angle and with a point of light falling on a malignant eye; irises and doors frame and encage the heroine and help connote her vulnerability; the corpse of the lawyer (Tully Marshall) falls towards the camera when a wall is accidentally lifted; the thief wears hairy claw gloves, tusks and a glass eye and, in the scene where he attacks Annabelle, his grotesque face is shot in an extreme and dramatically lit close-up. In short, *The Cat and the Canary* channelled the haunted castle's long literary tradition and the Gothic's set-based machinery, expertly adapting its chills to the screen in decidedly cinematic ways. Similar props would appear in a host of mystery films throughout the 1930s and 1940s and would be parodied in countries like Mexico, Britain and Spain.[11]

The Gothic in the old dark house mystery film primarily manifested on a surface level, yet operated on an affective one too. Setting could not be easily extricated from plot. More than a simple backdrop to the action, characters would interact with the mansion's secretive and surprising spaces – with what its clockwork props would work to conceal and reveal. To simply position the Gothic in these films as decorative or operational would be to do it a disservice. Much like the castle has been construed as a symbol of female oppression, of an extension and metaphorical engagement with 'the home as place of danger and imprisonment' (Ferguson Ellis 1989: x), the archaic sphere of the old dark house, often a token of patriarchy and male power, is susceptible of a more subversive reading. In *The Cat and the Canary*, Annabelle triumphs by virtue of her capacity to keep a straight mind when faced with the machinations of the villain and, if ultimately saved by her future fiancé, she also inherits the family fortune. Cyrus West, portrayed as an unsympathetic and scheming man whose fallen portrait is never replaced, does not return: his haunting presence has either been exorcised or forgotten. At the time of the film's release, and throughout the 1930s, when the old dark house mystery would thrive on screen, the representation of women in cinema was hardly progressive. In fact, as Veronica Pravadelli argues, 'outside of the screwball comedy, female independence [was] typically frustrated' and 'strong women' were deliberately 'depicted as bad, so they could be rightfully punished' (2017: 368). In films like *The Bat* and *The Cat and the Canary*, and in later ones like *Bachelor Brides* (1926), *Easy Pickings* (1927), *Something Always Happens* (1928), *The Haunted House* (1928), *The House of Horror* (1929), *The Old Dark House* (1932), *The Monster Walks* (1932), *Geheimnis des blauen Zimmers* (*Secret of the Blue Room*, 1932), *One Frightening Night* (1935), *The Ghost Breakers* (1940), *The Night Monster* (1942) and *One Body Too Many* (1944), women (albeit, admittedly, primarily those of an upper-middle class upbringing) would be granted a modicum of independence and mobility, a modern cinematic equivalent of Radcliffe's heroines.[12] Only in a minority of examples, such as in *Murder by the Clock* (1931), *Double Door* (1934) and *Sh! The Octopus* (1937), would the culprits turn out to be devious or mad women.

Like the Gothic novels from which they partly drew inspiration, films such as *The Bat* and *The Cat and the Canary* were also distinctive for their heavy reliance on comedy and romance. These elements served to counterbalance and somewhat diffuse tense and unpleasant atmospheres that may have otherwise been frowned upon. It is important to remember that violence in film was a contentious issue at the time, both for the regional censors and the subsequent industry regulatory bodies after 1930 (Prince 2003: 23–29), and that the experience of aesthetic horror in film did not yet exist. As the publicity materials for *The Bat* demonstrate, the inclusion of humour and of rational explanations for the spooks made raising objections to these films harder, since superstitious beliefs would be ineluctably dispensed with and their entertainment value reified. While humour would continue to mingle with the ghost story in subsequent 'haunted' house comedies such as *You'll Find Out* (1940) and *Spooks Run Wild* (1941), and even evolve into the parodic spoof, romance and its disillusionments became an appreciable part of the Female Gothic films that appeared in the 1940s.[13] The term 'Female Gothic' deliberately pulls together a number of films which would not have been marketed or received as such – some were referred to in the press as '(gaslight) melodramas', 'murder thrillers', 'suspenseful dramas', 'cinematic psycho-thrillers' and even 'horror' (Barefoot 2001: 1–5; Hanson 2007: 40; Jancovich 2013: 28–32).[14] However, films such as *Rebecca*, *The Spiral Staircase* (1946), *The Woman in White* (1948) and *Dragonwyck* (1946) may be productively read as engaging with the legacy of the Female Gothic and the old dark house mystery regardless of their precise generic ascription.[15] In fact, a number of the films covered below are hybrids of sorts, drawing thematically and aesthetically from cinematic traditions as varied as the melodrama (especially the period drama), film noir, romance and horror. Crucially, the Female Gothics may be understood as a valid cinematic category because they share contextual coordinates: they blossomed during a period that saw a redefinition of social roles and cinema audiences following two world wars.

The path-opener was Alfred Hitchcock's *Rebecca*, which was immensely profitable despite cost overruns (Adair 2002: 70) and garnered critical acclaim, eventually winning an Academy Award for Best Picture. Sumptuously filmed and intended as a quality production, *Rebecca* was adapted from the novel of the same title by Daphne du Maurier. Much like the 1940s Female Gothics have only recently been recuperated by Gothic Studies, du Maurier was not necessarily received as a Gothic novelist during her time despite the fact that many of her works, such as the novels *Jamaica Inn* (1936), *My Cousin Rachel* (1951) and *The Scapegoat* (1957), as well as some of the short stories in *The Apple Tree* (1952, later *The Birds and Other Stories*) and *Not After Midnight* (1971, later *Don't Look Now and Other Stories*), engaged directly with its literary tradition.[16] *Rebecca* itself is a rewriting of Charlotte Brontë's *Jane Eyre*, with its titular character susceptible of being read as a ghostly descendant of Bertha, the madwoman in the attic secreted by Mr Rochester. Arguably, both texts also belong to a wider literary tradition of abusive, older husbands and investigative (sometimes captive) wives that may be traced back to, at least, the Bluebeard fairy tale. In these fictions, especially in their revival in the Female Gothic film cycle of the 1940s, the husband tends to either harbour a dark past he wishes to conceal or else has been psychologically damaged by an unresolved traumatic experience. His new wife, upon finding herself an outcast in his ancestral mansion, must uncover the truth or suffer the same misfortune as the other women who came before her. *Rebecca* certainly follows this narrative blueprint. The positioning of the heroine (Joan Fontaine) as a possession is evident: as in the novel, she is never named, remaining the second Mrs de Winter throughout. Not only does this signal subservience, that she can never aspire to be anything more than her husband's partner, but also that she cannot escape the memory of his previous wife. Enshrined in the minds of those who occupy the de Winter household as well as in the furnishings (the monogrammed pillow and the gigantic painting are two good examples), Rebecca commands ownership from beyond the grave. *Rebecca* thus effectively married the Bluebeard formula with the ghost story; its narrative constantly calling to mind a haunting without ever summoning an actual apparition.

Rebecca's evocation of the Gothic takes place on various levels, all of which would be imitated or taken up by the Female Gothics that followed. On the one hand, the mode continues to manifest architectonically, much like it did in the old dark house mystery. Manderley, the estate belonging to the de Winter family, has so much personality that it is possible to interpret it as a character in its own right. After all, its imposing and vast façade is the first thing the film shows. After a series of suggestive stills of foggy fields (presumably the gardens), the moon glimmers on a dark and cloudy sky. The voice-over, relating the narrator's recurring dream of Manderley, accompanies a very interesting use of a disembodied camera, which travels spirit-like through a dark iron gate and up the meandering and misty drive to a 'secretive and silent' mansion covered in shadows. Lights appear to shine in the windows of the magnificent building, but this impression is soon corrected by the narrator, who explains this is only an illusion as the camera moves rightwards to reveal 'a desolate shell' of a house 'with no whisper of the past about its walls'. The film's mantra, '[w]e can never go back to Manderley again', is then intoned. The scene is full of symbolism, but its meaning is hard to discern this early on. Only after *Rebecca*'s last suggestive image, the pillow with Rebecca's initial engulfed in flames, does the true import of the statement gain significance: it is impossible to return to Manderley because it no longer exists. The ruins of the opening scene are real and the estate is no more, having burnt to the ground after a crazed Mrs Danvers (Judith Anderson), the housekeeper, set fire to it.

Yet this scene may be read in more complex ways. Firstly, like the grandiose stately past it appears to symbolise, Manderley stands for the passing of time, its carcass an architectonic *memento mori*. As we age, we are left with memories of the past, which are fallible and unreliable. In this respect, Manderley resonates with its first mistress, Rebecca, whose story may only be pieced together from the accounts of those who knew her personally. Through her character, it becomes obvious that the past is not just what has happened but how we choose to remember and honour it. Finally, Manderley, especially its Victorian architecture, is also a Gothic embodiment of the patriarchal, old-fashioned codes according to which the house is still run. As the new Mrs de Winter gains confidence, especially after the turning point represented by an exchange with Mrs Danvers that nearly ends in suicide, she begins to confront the legacy of silence around her. Eventually dragging a confession out of her husband, who admits he hated Rebecca for her licentious behaviour and may have had a hand in her death, the woman's memory, and the story of repression it spells out, can be put to rest.[17] The new relationship that ensues, the film implies, will be much more equal and companionate. One can never go back to Manderley again because Mrs de Winter has come of age, overcome her trials and fought a system that refused to grant her any agency. In this reading, Manderley embodies the asphyxiating gender roles that must be left behind if women are to find self-fulfilment and freedom.

The figure of the heroine is important here, especially because *Rebecca*'s engagement with the Gothic canon cannot be reduced to a question of symbolic architecture. The film takes great pains to chronicle Mrs de Winter's journey from gullible young girl to understanding grown woman at peace with herself. Her tribulations and disappointments, especially the feelings of inadequacy brought on by class guilt and ignorance of the etiquette of polite society, are dramatised throughout, but they find their most open Gothic externalisation in Mrs Danvers, a gatekeeper of custom and propriety and main preserver of Rebecca's memory. Her confrontation with Mrs de Winter, especially the balcony scene where she beckons the latter to jump to her death because she has nothing to live for, symbolises Mrs de Winter's battle with her own demons. She will never be able to fill Rebecca's shoes and the process of trying to live up to the expectations set by her predecessor can only lead to tragedy. It is the realisation that she must stop pretending to live someone else's life that gives her the strength to confront her husband and make him confess to the secret behind Rebecca's death. This process involves the development of investigative competence, moral rectitude and determination, skills once learnt by first wave Gothic heroines. Thematically, the Female Gothics of the 1940s draw from the Bluebeard Gothic, yet add the trappings of film noir, horror and melodrama to the mix, especially following the success of the adaptation of Patrick Hamilton's play *Gaslight* (1938) into two successful films in 1940 and 1944.

In these, as in the source text, the husband, Paul/Gregory (Anton Walbrook/Charles Boyer), is a completely irredeemable and predatorial character prepared to psychologically torture his wife for financial gain. Minor plot deviations aside, the core of the narrative treads familiar ground – abuses of male power that result in a terrible situation for female partners – but introduces the notion of madness as another key element. As Bella/Paula (Diana Wynyard/Ingrid

Bergman) notices strange happenings in their new Victorian house, such as weird noises and the dimming of the gaslight, she begins to suspect she may be losing her mind. As it turns out, these phenomena have a natural cause: the husband's search for another woman's jewels in the attic and his deliberate attempt to drive Paula insane. Madness, an illness which has long been constructed by male social and psychiatric discourses as a 'female malady' (Showalter 1987: 19), is here connected to the male space of the mansion. Much like Manderley becomes a species of prison for the new Mrs de Winter, the house in the *Gaslight* films brings together notions of physical and mental entrapment. The films also resort to the narrative machinery of the explained supernatural. The disavowal of the apparently fantastic is perhaps what differentiates the more Gothic titles from similar thrillers that explore female captivity at home and, by extrapolation, marriage, such as *Caught* (1949). However, the *Gaslight* films, like Gainsborough Pictures' *The Man in Grey* (1943), rely on a neo-Victorian mise-en-scène that points to the Female Gothic and connects domesticity with imprisonment. This overlap between architecture and the position of women very specifically engages with the 'madwoman in the attic' tradition.[18] Unsurprisingly, *Jane Eyre* was itself adapted in 1943.

In the new Female Gothic narratives, the heroine is an investigator, even a prototype for the 'final girl' of the later 'slasher' film, as her survival often depends upon her capacity to expose and outsmart her potential male murderers.[19] This happens in *The Spiral Staircase*, where mute Helen (Dorothy McGuire) must escape a killer obsessed with disabled young women. Appropriately, the husbands are revealed as the potential killers in *Suspicion* (1941), *Sleep, My Love* (1948) and *Sorry, Wrong Number* (1948).[20] Although a number of the women in them do not survive or must be rescued by a male character, their capacity to at least fight back and thus take an active role in their own salvation is very important in terms of the evolution of the capable, independent heroine who will eventually save herself from danger. Other heroines follow the path of the new Mrs de Winter and Jane Eyre and seek to cure their partners, embodying the more traditional female stereotype of the nurturing mother. These are, however, the least satisfying examples of the Female Gothic, at least at the narrative level. For example, in *Secret Beyond the Door*, where Celia (Joan Bennett) decides to help her husband back into a happy marriage upon discovering that he strangled his previous wife, the resolution feels strained. The reason for this is that, unlike Anthony (Gregory Peck) in *Spellbound*, whose psychoanalytic treatment ultimately proves his innocence, Celia's husband did indeed kill his previous wife. Even these less progressive narratives show women's capacity to forgive and forget, to move on and overcome problems.

Key to the development of the resourceful and self-reliant heroine in the Female Gothic films of the 1940s is her awareness of the past, as well as her ability to learn from it to change the course of present events. The return of the repressed often manifests through pictorial remnants of the heroine's predecessors, usually a deceased wife about whom little is mentioned. Secrecy kick-starts the desire to know more, especially given that the introduction of a portrait normally coincides with the heroine's realisation that their husband hides a secret or else entertains murderous intentions. In *Dragonwyck* and *The Two Mrs. Carrolls* (1947) portraits arouse suspicion about the tragic fate of the women depicted in them and thus operate as warnings. Clear bonds are established between the heroines and other women in a process of transhistorical doubling. This form of feminine lineage, if correctly interpreted, offers a way out from, and stands in stark contradistinction to, the patriarchal system embodied by the tyrannical husband and their house, the Gothic space. Sometimes, the identification may be literalised, as in *Rebecca*, where the new Mrs de Winter puts on a costume previously worn by Rebecca (itself a reference to an ancestor) and thus momentarily becomes three women. This staging signifies more than 'a struggle to differentiate herself from the woman in the past' (Hanson 2007: 96). The fear of repetition in the Female Gothic literalises the relationship between the heroines and the generations that came before them, between new and old notions of gender roles. It is not a coincidence that the Female Gothics are often set in the nineteenth century (*The Man in Grey, Dragonwyck*, 1944's *Bluebeard* and *Experiment Perilous*), in Victorian houses (*Rebecca, Jane Eyre,* 1944's *Gaslight*), American backwaters and plantations (1943's *I Walked with a Zombie*, 1944's *Dark Waters*) or in claustrophobic spaces stuck in time (the farm and mansion in 1946's *Undercurrent*). In fighting a villainous husband, the Gothic heroine goes against the social structures that have traditionally enabled male control and contributed to female oppression. Portraits, often the only female concession in otherwise archaic and male-dominated environments, become turning points.

Critics have responded with reflective readings to the blossoming of these new cinematic heroines and their male counterparts at this point in the history of American and British cinema. The 1940s was a decade marked by the changing roles of women brought about by the war years. For Molly Haskell, 'the influx of women into the job market (and their obvious success) … contributed to that sense of instability,

Figure 4.2 Portraits establish female lineages and act as forewarnings in Female Gothics like *Gaslight* (1944).

of disease and even impotence that lurked beneath the surface of male characters' (1974: 194). For Marjorie Rosen, the rise of the femme fatale occurred simultaneously with the rise of the female as victim, an indication that 'women were finally a threat to the status quo' (1975: 224). Her outlook on these films is not a positive one, as she reads the helplessness of most of their heroines as a reification of 'female weakness, mental and physical' (224). In this view, women do not always follow their initial intuitions, are incapable of thinking for themselves and maintain idealistic dreams about marriage even when faced with incontrovertible evidence that their partners are monsters. Haskell's position is not sustained by a close analysis of the films, however, as even in the few cases where women do not uncover the murderers themselves, the films rarely fail to typify the husband as villainous. It is, in fact, possible to argue that these Gothic heroines, and the Female Gothic more generally, are representationally more important and subversive than has been granted. As Andrea S. Walsh brilliantly argues, the power of these narratives lies in their portrayal of a 'powerful cultural current of feminine suspicion and distrust' (1984: 184), where husbands are doubted – either by heroines or the film – and where, predominantly, wives are proven right. On the one hand, these films may be reflecting context-specific concerns about rushed wartime marriages or the changes suffered by men returning from war (Walsh 1978: 6), but the critique can be extended to the macrosystem of female repression. Beyond the previously mentioned equations between home and prison, male power and patriarchy, fragility and (female) madness, the Female Gothic renders patriarchy a barbaric throwback, a Gothic intrusion which manifests architectonically and behaviourally.

The realist aesthetics of the explained supernatural, as well as the focus on strong women characters, can be located in terms of an industry response to market changes that were by no means confined to Britain and America. The melodrama *Malombra* (1942), based on Antonio Fogazzaro's novel of 1881 about the apparent possession of Marina by a dead woman once oppressed by a male ancestor, is a great example of an Italian Female Gothic of the time. The gloomy mansion in Lake Como where Marina (Isa Miranda) is caused to stay until her marriage of convenience is finalised operates as a modern version of the Radcliffean castle, and her perception that she is a reincarnated Cecilia is clearly in dialogue with Mrs de Winter's momentary impersonation of Rebecca. The disavowal of the apparent supernatural happenings as madness brought on by the limitations put on Marina's freedom by her unmovable and dominating uncle are clearly connected to the position of women in a phallocentric society where their future is determined by men. In the French *La Fiancée des ténèbres* (*Bride of Darkness*, 1945) a similar imposition is made on Sylvie (Jany Holt) by her adoptive guardian (Édouard Delmont), a man obsessed with the Cathars who eventually persuades Sylvie to renounce the world in favour of the secrets lying in a secluded underground Albigensian sanctuary. Gothic trappings also appear in de Poligny's mystery melodrama *Le Baron fantôme* (*The Phantom Baron*, 1943) and in Jean Cocteau's spellbinding and lusciously shot *La Belle et la Bête*, a retelling of Gabrielle-Suzanne Barbot's fairy tale. In the UK, the adaptation *Uncle Silas* (1947) pitted a young teenage heiress against her scheming uncle and his partners in crime. Even Spain, reluctant to embrace the Gothic due to censorship, would produce realist Gothic melodramas with strong female characters like *El clavo* (*The Nail*, 1944), a nineteenth-century murder mystery about a woman with a double identity, and the adaptation of the Enrique Jardiel Poncela play *Eloísa está debajo de un almendro* (*Eloísa Is Under an Almond Tree*, 1943), where the Ojeda castle hides a number of secrets connected to a traumatic family past. These films, imbued with a strong sense of atmosphere and sentimentalism, evince more than the global impact of Hitchcock's *Rebecca*.[21] They demonstrate the pervasiveness and transnational appeal of Gothic realism, as it manifested in the old dark house first and in the Female Gothics later, and how the strong ties between the mode and new forms of gender identity spoke to changes in social attitudes and audience demographics.

Naturally, it is important to resist a reductive revision of female viewers in the 1940s as automatically ideologically progressive. As Walsh (1984: 38) herself shows in her analysis of contemporary sources (journalistic pieces, testimonials and surveys), it is quite simply not the case that female cinemagoers were overly feminist or even overwhelmingly less traditionalist. Having said this, the period was indeed 'transitional' (Waldman 1984: 30) and marked by the realisation that there might be a space for women outside the house, in the public sphere. The changing make-up of audiences and their gender shaped the types of films that were made, and access to the job market, as well as a growing awareness of birth control and knowledge about sex, had a profound impact on how women perceived themselves. The Female Gothic film updated Radcliffean heroinism by planting the seeds of discord into a previously sacrosanct institution, marriage. Men and their violent and abusive behaviours began to be doubted and women given the narrative, and thus imaginative, space to dispute them. Their victories and the fact that the heroines tended to prosper or else cure their husbands point to more than a simple case of crowd-pleasing entertainment. Cinema had to evolve to suit changing attitudes towards women, propriety, accountability within marriage and sisterhood. If the domestic space became the new Gothic castle – and the dark cinematography, carried over from the old dark house film and influenced by film noir, certainly suggests this – then Gothic artifice moved from the buildings' trappings to the machinations of patriarchal figures who treated their wives as a means to wealth.

Films like *Rebecca* did more than intimate that gender dynamics had not materially evolved since the eighteenth and nineteenth centuries, especially in terms of the prevailing political and economic straightjackets curtailing the freedoms of women. The Gothic horror of Universal's monster films had created a temporal ambiguity that collapsed centuries together and forced the Gothic to migrate to anachronistic settings. The Female Gothic, and the old dark house mystery as its cinematic predecessor, continued to firmly position the Gothic within the contemporary because its ideological nightmares could conceivably manifest in the context of the 1940s. On a practical level, the Gothic did not have to limit its fantasies to times gone by; now it could rear up its atavistic head whenever and wherever. By the 1960s, when *The Innocents* and *The Haunting* returned to the trappings of the Female Gothic, supernatural elements already had a stronger hold on the popular imagination, but its female characters were still to move past the social constraints of the family home.

FILMOGRAPHY

A Midnight Bell (Charles Ray, 1921, USA)
Ask a Policeman (Marcel Varnel, 1939, UK)
Au secours! (*The Haunted House*, Abel Gance, 1924, France)
Bluebeard (Edgar G. Ulmer, 1944, USA)
Bride of Frankenstein (James Whale, 1935, USA)
Cada loco con su tema (*Every Madman to His Specialty*, 1939, Mexico)
Caught (Max Ophüls, 1949, USA)
Dark Waters (Andre DeToth, 1944, USA)
Das unheimliche Haus (*The Eerie House*, Richard Oswald, 1916, Germany)
Double Door (Charles Vidor, 1934, USA)
Dracula (Tod Browning, 1931, USA)
Dragonwyck (Joseph L. Mankiewicz, 1946, USA)
Easy Pickings (George Archainbaud, 1927, USA)
El clavo (*The Nail*, Rafael Gil, 1944, Spain)
Eloísa está debajo de un almendro (*Eloísa Is Under an Almond Tree*, Rafael Gil, 1943, Spain)
Experiment Perilous (Jacques Tourneur, 1944, USA)
Frankenstein (James Whale, 1931, USA)
Gaslight (Thorold Dickinson, 1940, UK)
Gaslight (George Cukor, 1944, USA)
Geheimnis des blauen Zimmers (*Secret of the Blue Room*, Erich Engels, 1932, Germany)
Haunting Shadows (Henry King, 1919, USA)
Immediate Possession (Arthur Varney, 1931, UK)

I Walked with a Zombie (Jacques Tourneur, 1943, USA)
Jane Eyre (Robert Stevenson, 1943, USA)
La Belle et la Bête (*Beauty and the Beast*, Jean Cocteau, 1946, France)
La Fiancée des ténèbres (*Bride of Darkness*, Serge de Poligny, 1945, France)
La voluntad del muerto (*The Will of the Dead Man*, George Melford and Enrique Tovar Ávalos, 1930, USA)
Le Baron fantôme (*The Phantom Baron*, de Poligny, Serge de Poligny, 1943, France)
Le Déménagement (*Spooks Do the Moving*, Segundo de Chomón, 1908, France)
London After Midnight (Tod Browning, 1927, USA)
Love Without Question (B. A. Rolfe, 1920, USA)
Luring Shadows (Joseph Levering, 1920, USA)
Mahal (*The Mansion*, Kamal Amrohi, 1949, India)
Malombra (Mario Soldati, 1942, Italy)
Murder by the Clock (Edward Sloman, 1931, USA)
One Body Too Many (Frank McDonald, 1944, USA)
One Exciting Night (D. W. Griffith, 1922, USA)
One Frightening Night (Christy Cabanne, 1935, USA)
Rebecca (Alfred Hitchcock, 1940, USA)
Secret Beyond the Door (Fritz Lang, 1947, USA)
Sh! The Octopus (William C. McGann, 1937, USA)
Sleep, My Love (Douglas Sirk, 1948, USA)
Something Always Happens (Frank Tuttle, 1928, USA)
Sorry, Wrong Number (Anatole Litvak, 1948, USA)
Spellbound (Alfred Hitchcock, 1945, USA)
Spooks Run Wild (Phil Rosen, 1941, USA)
Suspicion (Alfred Hitchcock, 1941, USA)
Thark (Tom Walls, 1932, UK)
Terror Mountain (Louis King, 1928, USA)
The Barton Mystery (Harry T. Roberts, 1920, UK)
The Bat (Roland West, 1926, USA)
The Bat Whispers (Roland West, 1930, USA)
The Beechwood Ghost (Powers Picture Plays (producer), 1910, USA)
The Cat and the Canary (Paul Leni, 1927, USA)
The Cat Creeps (Rupert Julian, 1930, USA)

The Club Pest (Biograph (producer), 1915, USA)
The Ghost (James Kirkwood, 1913, USA)
The Ghost Breaker (Cecil B. DeMille and Oscar C. Apfel, 1914, USA)
The Ghost Breaker (Alfred E. Green, 1922, USA)
The Ghost Breakers (George Marshall, 1940, USA)
The Ghost House (William C. deMille, 1917, USA)
The Gorilla (Alfred Santell, 1927, USA)
The Haunted Bedroom (Fred Niblo, 1919, USA)
The Haunted House (William F. Haddock, 1911, USA)
The Haunted House (Benjamin Christensen, 1928, USA)
The Haunting (Robert Wise, 1963, UK)
The House of a Thousand Candles (Arthur Lubin, 1915, USA)
The House of Horror (Benjamin Christensen, 1929, USA)
The House of the Tolling Bell (J. Stuart Blackton, 1920, USA)
The House of Whispers (Ernest C. Warde, 1920, USA)
The Innocents (Jack Clayton, 1961, UK)
The Last Warning (Paul Leni, 1929, USA)
The Magician (Rex Ingram, 1926, USA)
The Man in Grey (Leslie Arliss, 1943, UK)
The Monster (Roland West, 1925, USA)
The Monster Walks (Frank R. Strayer, 1932, USA)
The Night Monster (Ford Beebe, 1942, USA)
The Old Dark House (James Whale, 1932, USA)
The Spiral Staircase (Robert Siodmak, 1946, USA)
The Terror (Roy Del Ruth, 1928, USA)
The Thirteenth Chair (Léonce Perret, 1919, USA)
The Two Mrs. Carrolls (Peter Godfrey, 1947, USA)
The Uninvited (Lewis Allen, 1944, USA)
The Woman in White (Peter Godfrey, 1948, USA)
Tin Hats (Edward Sedgwick, 1926, USA)
Una mujer en peligro (*A Woman in Danger*, José Santugini, 1936, Spain)
Uncle Silas (Charles Frank, 1947, UK)
Undercurrent (Vincente Minnelli, 1946, USA)
You'll Find Out (David Butler, 1940, USA)

NOTES

1 I am not suggesting that the Gothic did not also manifest in supernatural films, like *The Uninvited* (1944), only that the realist tradition deserves more critical attention.

2 As Tania Modleski (1982: 59–65) notes, Gothic and Harlequin romances show some similarities. However, the treatment of their characters and formulae is different.

3 Radcliffe did write one novel with a real ghost in it, her posthumously published *Gaston de Blondeville* (1826), but the novels that made her famous developed the explained supernatural.

4 These films were also influenced by early ghost-debunking comedies such as *Le Déménagement* (*Spooks Do the Moving*, 1908), *The Beechwood Ghost* (1910), *The Haunted House* (1911) and *The Ghost* (1913). The subgenre would continue in films like *The Club Pest* (1915) and *Au secours!* (*The Haunted House*, 1924).

5 I am referring to the materials made available in the Exhibitors Campaign Book published by United Artists Corporation (available on microfiche at the Margaret Herrick Library). The book is not paginated and does not include any publication details.

6 These reviews are taken from the advert as run in *Moving Picture World* on 8 May 1926, 158.

7 These reviews are taken from the source detailed in the previous entry.

8 Some of them show the crook's face framed by bat wings and another shows a bat with a man's head mid-flight.

9 A similar case in point is the hypnotist (Lon Chaney) in *London After Midnight*, who looks and dresses like a vampire.

10 The quotation comes from a film's intertitle in the standard version of the film.

11 See *Immediate Possession* (1931), *Thark* (1932), *Una mujer en peligro* (*A Woman in Danger*, 1936), *Cada loco con su tema* (*Every Madman to His Specialty*, 1939) and *Ask a Policeman* (1939).

12 Ellen Moers referred to this imaginary freedom as 'Gothic heroinism' or 'traveling heroinism' and proposed that Radcliffe's novels 'became a

female substitute for the picaresque, where heroines could experience all the adventures and alarms that masculine heroes had long experienced, far from home, in fiction' (1978: 1926).

13 For an overview of some of the key comedy horrors of these two decades, see Hallenbeck (2009: 15–53).

14 As Jancovich notes, horror in the 1940s was not as clearly demarcated a genre as it is today. It overlapped significantly with the 'mystery' (2008: 28) or what we now refer to as the 'thriller'.

15 See Doane (1987: 123–124). In fact, one could go as far as to suggest that the texts of the explained supernatural could equally be understood as 'melodramas', 'murder thrillers', 'suspenseful dramas' and 'psycho-thrillers'.

16 The same applies to du Maurier's critical reception. Avril Horner and Sue Zlosnik, in their brilliant study of du Maurier as Gothic writer, complained that, by the late 1990s, '[c]ritical work on [her] skill as Gothic novelist and writer of short stories ha[d] hardly begun' (21).

17 I realise that this reading ultimately depends on the viewer accepting that Rebecca was an unhappy wife who used the only weapon at her disposal, her sexuality, to challenge the stifling circumstances of her marriage. Given the Bluebeard connection, and since the film creates visual associations (pictorial and otherwise) between the two Mrs de Winters, there are enough arguments to suggest the film favours a sympathetic portrayal of Rebecca – especially after it is revealed she was dying of cancer.

18 See Gilbert and Gubar (1979).

19 The slasher horror subgenre, which developed in the 1970s and peaked in popularity in the 1980s, involves the stalking and murder of a group of characters by a, sometimes supernatural, psychopath.

20 In the ending of *Suspicion*, the husband is exonerated, a change encouraged by the studio. I would, however, like to acknowledge the original intended ending, where Lina (Joan Fontaine) is legitimised in her misgivings about her husband's behaviour (Hitchcock, quoted in Truffaut and Scott 1985: 142).

21 It is tempting to trace the *Rebecca* effect as far as India, where *Mahal* (*The Mansion*, 1949), a tale of ghostly reincarnation, was responsible for introducing the Gothic romance and Gothic aesthetics to Bollywood cinema.

BIBLIOGRAPHY

Adair, G. (2002) *Alfred Hitchcock: Filming Our Fears*, Oxford: Oxford University Press.

Anonymous (1914) 'The Ghost Breaker', *Variety*, 12 December, 28.

Barefoot, G. (2001) *Gaslight Melodrama: From Victorian London to 1940s Hollywood*, London and New York: Bloomsbury.

Bush, S. (1914) 'The Ghost Breaker: A Multiple Reel Lasky Production of Unusual Merit – Has Many Thrills and Much Humor', *The Moving Picture World*, 19 December, 1692.

Clarens, C. (1997) *An Illustrated History of Horror and Science Fiction Films*, Cambridge, MA: Da Capo Press.

Clery, E. J. (1995) *The Rise of Supernatural Fiction, 1762–1800*, Cambridge: Cambridge University Press.

Curtis, J. (2015) *William Cameron Menzies: The Shape of Films to Come*, New York: Pantheon.

Doane, M. A. (1987) *The Desire to Desire: The Woman's Film of the 1940s*, London: Macmillan Press.

Drake, N. (1798) *Literary Hours, or Sketches Critical and Narrative*, London: Printed by J. Burkitt and sold by T. Cadell, Junior and W. Davies.

Ferguson Ellis, K. (1989) *The Contested Castle: Gothic Novels and the Subversion of Domestic Ideology*, Urbana and Chicago, IL: University of Illinois Press.

Gilbert, S. M. and S. Gubar (1979) *The Madwoman in the Attic: The Woman Writer and the Nineteenth-Century Literary Imagination*, New Haven, CT: Yale University Press.

Gulick, P. (1927) 'Shadows as a Movie Motif', *Amateur Movie Makers*, 24 March, 10–11.

Hallenbeck, B. G. (2009) *Comedy-Horror Films: A Chronological History, 1914–2008*, Jefferson, NC: McFarland.

Hanson, H. (2007) *Hollywood Heroines: Women in Film Noir and the Female Gothic Film*, London: I.B. Tauris.

Haskell, M. (1974) *From Reverence to Rape: The Treatment of Women in the Movies*, New York: Holt, Rinehart and Winston.

Horner, A. and S. Zlosnik (1998) *Daphne du Maurier: Writing, Identity and the Gothic Imagination*, Basingstoke: Macmillan; New York: St. Martin's Press.

Jancovich, M. (2008) 'Pale Shadows: Narrative Hierarchies in the Historiography of 1940s Horror', in L. Geraghty and M. Jancovich (eds) *The Shifting Definitions of Genre: Essays on Labeling Film, Television Shows and Media*, Jefferson, NC: McFarland.

Jancovich, M. (2013) 'Bluebeard's Wives: Horror, Quality and the Gothic (or Paranoid) Woman's Film in the 1940s', *The Irish Journal of Gothic and Horror Studies*, 12: 20–43.

Lachman, M. (2014) *The Villainous Stage: Crime Plays on Broadway and in the West End*, Jefferson, NC: McFarland.

Milne, P. (1914) 'The Ghost Breaker', *Motion Picture News*, 19 December, 62.

Modleski, T. (1982) *Loving with a Vengeance: Mass-Produced Fantasies for Women*, London and New York: Routledge.

Moers, E. (1978) *Literary Women*, London: The Women's Press.

Pardy, G. T. (1926) 'Pre-release Reviews of Features: The Bat', *Motion Picture News*, 27 March, 1418.

Pravadelli, V. (2017) 'Classical Hollywood and Modernity: Gender, Style, Aesthetics', in K. L. Hole, D. Jelača, E. A. Kaplan and P. Petro (eds) *The Routledge Companion to Cinema and Gender*, London and New York: Routledge.

Prince, S. (2003) *Classical Film Violence: Designing and Regulating Brutality in Hollywood Cinema, 1930–1968*, New Brunswick, NJ, and London: Rutgers University Press.

Rosen, M. (1975) *Popcorn Venus: Women Movies and the American Dream*, London: Peter Owen.

Showalter, E. (1987) *The Female Malady: Women, Madness and English Culture, 1830–1980*, London: Virago.

Spooner, C. (2010) 'Crime and the Gothic', in C. J. Rzepka and L. Horsley (eds) *A Companion to Crime Fiction*, Oxford and Malden, MA: Wiley-Blackwell.

Truffaut, F. and H. G. Scott (1985) *Hitchcock*, rev. edn, London and New York: Simon & Schuster.

Waldman, D. (1984) '"At Last I Can Tell It to Someone!": Feminine Point of View and Subjectivity in the Gothic Romance Film of the 1940s', *Cinema Journal*, 23.2: 29–40.

Walsh, A. S. (1978) 'Films of Suspicion and Distrust: Undercurrents of Female Consciousness in the 1940s', *Film and History*, 8.1: 1–8, 15.

Walsh, A. S. (1984) *Women's Film and Female Experience, 1940–1950*, London and New York: Praeger.

5

GOTHIC IN TECHNICOLOUR

The opening credits for Hammer's Dracula are a true statement of aims. A still image of a large stone eagle, silhouetted against a blue sky, dominates the centre of the first shot as the words 'a Hammer Film Production' and then the name of the lead actor, Peter Cushing, appear in bright red. This is followed by the film's title, Dracula, presented in an ornate Gothic font, the 'D' encased within an imitation seal (or perhaps a family shield) decorated with etchings of dragons and other winged beasts.[1] As the rest of the credits fade in and out, a rightwards pan and simultaneous sideways tilt circle around the regal statue to reveal an imposing castle gate in the background. The journey continues towards a crypt franked by a small, prison-like iron door. A dissolve then takes the viewer into a dark underground space boasting an ominous coffin with the name 'Dracula' engraved on its surface. As the scene settles on a close-up, the letters are suddenly spattered with red paint, in imitation of blood, seemingly dripping from an unknown source located above the camera.

This sensational opening, a spectacular mood piece with no direct narrative connection to the rest of the film, is enhanced by the loud orchestral score composed by James Bernard, organised around a memorable 'repeated, three–note brass and percussion motif (one sustained note followed by two repeated notes an octave lower)' (Larson 1996: 22) which takes its rhythm and pattern from the syllables that form the count's family name. The piece is intense and atmospheric, and it is clearly intended to add to the scene's other aristocratic signifiers by emphasising ideas of predatorial power and faded grandeur. Overall, the sequence does more than simply advertise its monster via architectural metaphor; it also expertly summarises the film's ethos. *Dracula* is a fast, short affair that goes for the jugular, and is distinguishable from previous adaptations of Stoker's novel by its spectacle and bloody treatment of the myth. Importantly, its type of Gothic horror is one bathed in highly saturated colour. Only one other film, also produced by Hammer the previous year, could lay claim to this modern formula.

The Curse of Frankenstein opened with a similarly strident credits sequence. A lugubrious drum roll and a slow burning string accompaniment plays in the background as a series of intertitles situate the events of the film '[m]ore than a hundred years' in the past (thus the early nineteenth century) 'in a mountain village in Switzerland'. The legend of Frankenstein, viewers also learn, is 'still told with horror the world over'. Both the retrojected remoteness, spatial and temporal, and the shocking

Figure 5.1 The colourful and sensational opening credits for *Dracula* (1958) were a veritable statement of aims for Hammer's brand of Gothic cinema.

aspects of the narrative are emphasised aesthetically by a white Gothic typeface shot against a vivid crimson screen as well as by a musical climax punctuated by cymbals. The background is noticeably smoky, perhaps an echo of the 'strange experiments' of the mad scientist clearly foregrounded in the colourful laboratory scenes. This is important, since one of the film's many strokes of genius, albeit one motivated, at least in part, by Universal's aggressive protection of their own *Frankenstein* franchise, would be to make the doctor the central villain. A selfish aristocrat, not unlike Dracula, Baron Frankenstein (Cushing) is a man who, despite initially appearing to be interested in science for the good of humankind, reveals himself to be emotionally aloof, delusional and driven by obsession, typical characteristics of the mad scientist in horror films (Skal 1998: 18; Frayling 2005: 115–116). The monster (Christopher Lee) is an abject creature who, despite remaining in the periphery of the action, is central to two of *The Curse of Frankenstein*'s most well-known scenes. In one of them, the reveal sequence, Fisher indulges in a fast and jittery track shot towards the wrapped-up monster that stands out as a striking diversion from the film's otherwise 'sober and restrained' camerawork (Hutchings 2001: 85). In the other, the scene in the woods, the monster is shot in the right eye at close range. Although tame by today's standards – all that is shown is the monster holding his eye with a hand and gore pooling around it – this moment is one of Gothic cinema's most important, signalling the possibility of bloodier approaches to the source material. Colour photography, accentuated by the striking look of blood, was a calling card that set Hammer's period films apart from the Gainsborough historical black-and-white melodramas and Female Gothics and signalled that Gothic cinema was ready to leave behind restraint in lieu of profitable risqué ventures.[2]

Strictly speaking, nothing about *The Curse of Frankenstein* and *Dracula* was really that inventive. Although problems with overzealous censors meant that a horror industry did not develop in the UK in the 1930s and 1940s, British cinema had nevertheless managed to produce atmospheric Gothic period films adapted from literary sources, such as *Sweeney Todd: The Demon Barber of Fleet Street* and *The Queen of Spades* (1949), as well as films that made use of the architectural Gothic of the old Victorian estate – in *Crimes at the Dark House* – or comparable modern spaces – in *The Dark Eyes of London* (1939). The supernatural had been mined extensively in Europe and America, as the previous chapters in this book demonstrate, and even in Britain ghostly affairs had been the subject of horror in Ealing's portmanteau film *Dead of Night*. The explicit nature of *The Curse of Frankenstein*'s 'sadistic' antics had clear predecessors in visceral and violent American horror films such as *Doctor X* and *Murders in the Zoo* (1933) and Universal's Poe adaptations *The Murders in the Rue Morgue*, *The Black Cat* and *The Raven*.[3] Although enthusiastic critics sometimes bill *The Curse of Frankenstein* as the first colour horror film, *The Phantom of the Opera* (1925), *The Great Gabbo* (1929) and *The Picture of Dorian Gray* (1945) had already included colour inserts, and at least *Dr. Jekyll and Mr. Hyde* (1913), *Doctor X*, *Mystery of the Wax Museum* (1933), *Scared to Death* (1947) and *House of Wax* (1953) had been shot using either Kinemacolor, two-strip Technicolor, Cinecolor or Warnercolor. *House of Wax* had also been shot in 3D, a costly process that aimed to bring the visual experience of horror closer to the viewer. *The Curse of Frankenstein* and *Dracula* did not constitute a radical break for horror so much as the refinement and entrenchment of certain cinematic techniques. The films' originality, and that of Hammer's subsequent output, lay in their capacity to amalgamate and streamline, to diversify by reframing familiar stories and a genre that was by then recognisable. This point is key, so it needs some elaboration.

Both *The Curse of Frankenstein* and *Dracula* returned to the Gothic myths already exploited by Universal, a transnational connection that would be cemented for good after a copyright agreement allowing Hammer to legally remake Universal's horror classics was struck in 1958 (Kinsey 2005: 86). And yet, well-known monsters such as Frankenstein's creature, Count Dracula or those that would come to join them – the mummy, the wolf man and Jekyll/Hyde, among others – would be given an intrinsically different treatment that was initially unique to Hammer. This involved shooting well-known narratives in colour-saturated stock – especially the beautiful *The Mummy* (1959) – penning often dynamic scripts and relying on increasing levels of violence and eroticism.[4] While horror, Universal's or otherwise, had occasionally delved in the gruesome, this had often manifested in either mad science flicks or in films where the action was relatively modern or even contemporary. The hybrid concept of Victorian and Edwardian Gothic period melodramas, supernatural creatures and sensational set pieces was ripe for expansion. Iconography via casting decisions was important too, a lesson learnt from Karloff's defining performance as the monster in Whale's *Frankenstein*. Terence Fisher's directorial involvement in a total of sixteen of Hammer's horrors between 1957 and 1974, of which at least thirteen could be considered Gothic, alongside the recurring participation of British actors Peter Cushing and Christopher Lee, helped solidify a distinctive aesthetic and modus operandi for the studio. As a matter of fact, Hammer's many successes and low-budgeted, independent approach laid the ground for a form of Gothic filmmaking which would remain popular and influential throughout the rest of the 1950s and most of the 1960s.

Drawing on Universal's development of monster franchising, Hammer followed up their breakthrough films with sequels. *The Revenge of Frankenstein*, apparently influenced by the brain transplant shenanigans of *The Ghost of Frankenstein* (1942), came out in 1958 and *The Brides of Dracula*, this time without Christopher Lee, two years later. Neither constituted a wild departure, but their enthusiastic reception and, in the case of *The Brides of Dracula*, good worldwide box office takings galvanised Hammer's approach to the Gothic: period settings and British casts, Manichean fights between good and evil and, above all, alluring colour. The impact of these films in the global perception of the horror genre was truly transformational. As early as 1958, journalist Richard Gertner, writing for the American magazine *Motion Picture Daily*, noted that

> [t]he most notable contribution the Hammers have made to the genre [of the horror picture] is the stunning use of color for

frightening effects. Blood dripping from a dismembered arm looks 13 times as gory in Technicolor, and there is nothing so chilling as the sight of a green light thrown over a corpse. The Hammers have demolished once and for all the theory that horror films should always be in black and white. (1958: 5)

In the British context, bar some accomplished black-and-white Gothics like *Night of the Demon* (1957), *The Innocents*, *Night of the Eagle* (1962) and *The Haunting*, the chromatic approach would prevail. This is in no small part due to the fact that Hammer's unrelenting production schedule led to many more colour iterations of the Frankenstein and Dracula myths during the 1960s. Vampiric interest was kept alive by *Dracula: Prince of Darkness* (1966), *Dracula Has Risen from the Grave* (1968), *Taste the Blood of Dracula* (1970), a particularly interesting entry in terms of its striking deployment of red, and *Scars of Dracula* (1970), as well as the independent *The Kiss of the Vampire* (1963). Frankenstein returned four more times during this period, in *The Evil of Frankenstein* (1964), *Frankenstein Created Woman* (1967), which flirted with the rape-revenge formula popular in the 1970s, *Frankenstein Must Be Destroyed* (1969) and *The Horror of Frankenstein* (1970). These franchise entries were complemented by individual films, some – *The Mummy*, *The Hound of the Baskervilles* (1959), *The Two Faces of Dr. Jekyll* (1960), *The Curse of the Werewolf* (1961) and *The Phantom of the Opera* (1962) – were adaptations of long-established Gothic myths (in the case of *The Mummy*, a Universal remake), others – *The Man Who Could Cheat Death* (1959), *The Gorgon* (1964) and *The Plague of the Zombies* (1966) – looked to different sources for inspiration.[5] With a few exceptions, namely *The Witches* (1966) and the Dennis Wheatley adaptation *The Devil Rides Out* (1968), both of which take place in the twentieth century, Hammer would set its Gothic plots in a fantastic version of the Victorian past. Remoteness manifested primarily at the architectonic level, in settings that inherited a lot visually from the old dark house mysteries and the Female Gothics.

Before exploring Hammer's impact, it is important to acknowledge that it is possible to support the case that the studio's idiosyncrasies were as much the result of a series of smart decisions on the part of their producers and directors as they were the sign of a rapidly changing cinema industry. For example, in 1950, Eastmancolor introduced a new colour negative process which did much to democratise and commercialise the use of colour on film. Although Technicolor's quality control could not be replicated on their stock, their innovative single-strip process allowed for in-house lab treatment and was more cost-efficient for distributors (Haines 1993: 54). Also that year, a consent decree forced Technicolor to license patents and offer technical information on their systems, thus effectively putting an end to the company's monopoly over colour cinematography (Balio 1985: 426).[6] Over the next decade, colour would become more widespread, with Hollywood already shooting 50% of its films in colour by 1955 (Lev 2003: 108). An ever-increasing number of Gothic films would welcome its exciting potential. The late 1940s and early 1950s also saw the beginnings of full-scale commercial television broadcasting, so colour, wider screens, cinematic gimmicks like those of William Castle and the focus on more titillating spectacles need to be understood, to some degree, as cinema's way of adapting to the pressures exerted by what quickly became its main competing medium.[7] Colour, like larger aspect ratios, became less the province of carefully orchestrated in-studio cinematography and much more an inherent part of filmmaking. Excess, violent and erotic, would be exploited by gore cinema – cemented in 1962 by Herschell Gordon Lewis's *Blood Feast* – and sexploitation flicks, especially from the late 1960s onwards. In a sense, Hammer's Gothic productions were a few years ahead of their time. When some of their techniques were adopted by other studios and directors, their formula inevitably became diluted.

Hammer's development of a period Gothic gave them an initial unique selling point, but it would also prove a difficult one to shake off, especially when the success of horror films set in modern times started to indicate a potential shift in public taste. Attempts to emulate profitable modern Gothics like *Count Yorga, Vampire* (1970) in *Dracula A.D. 1972* (1972) and *The Satanic Rites of Dracula* (1973) were not widespread successes. A trilogy of films from the early 1970s, the Karnstein trilogy loosely based on Sheridan Le Fanu's novella 'Carmilla', was Hammer's last attempt at renovating their sexy Gothic brand via the adaptation of yet another well-known literary myth, one that did not deviate substantially from that of their tried-and-tested previous efforts and offered room for more licentious shenanigans like full-frontal nudity (notably that of Ingrid Pitt in 1970's *The Vampire Lovers*). Although *The Vampire Lovers* did well, Hammer's Gothic brand of horror would soon come to a natural standstill. The first Hammer horrors were so controversial for their 'sensationalist' and 'exploitative' nature that the BFPA (British Film Producers Association) at one point requested that the BBFC (British Board of Film Classification) consider reinstating the 'H for Horrific' certificate which had been phased out in 1951.[8] By the early 1970s, the relaxation of censorship laws around the portrayal of violent and sexual material on film had brought about dramatic changes. As Sue Harper has noted (2012: 28), the liberal treatment of *Frightmare* (1974), which deals with cannibalism and mutilation but received an 'X' certificate and only a few cuts, indicates how rapidly and fundamentally the boundaries of the permissible were moving. Dramatic décolletages, colourful gore or licentious villains were no longer as shocking as they once had been.

Hammer also suffered from genre saturation. By the mid-to-late 1960s, it was no longer the only British studio producing colour horrors. Anglo-Amalgamated had caused an uproar with three visceral films whose contemporary, crueller spectacles distinguished them from Hammer's Gothics. *Horrors of the Black Museum* (1959), replete with gratuitous torture scenes, had come first. It had been shot in colour and using CinemaScope widescreen technology. In its American release, it had also included 'Hypnovista', a suggestively hypnotic introduction given by a psychologist that prepared audiences for the spectacle to come. This was an echo of the many promotional gimmicks developed by William Castle in the States in films such as

Macabre (1958), The Tingler (1959) and House on Haunted Hill and which would include anything from insurance policies protecting members of the audience against death by fright during screenings to electrified buzzers in theatre seats.[9] Horrors of the Black Museum proved popular, so Circus of Horrors (1960), shot in Specta-Color, and Peeping Tom, with its immersive first-person point-of-view shots, followed suit. The latter, whose main premise involves the actions of a voyeuristic serial killer obsessed with capturing the moment of death in the face of his female victims, was so vehemently criticised for its violence that it effectively ended director Michael Powell's career in Britain.[10] These films would not be Hammer's sole competitor.

In 1961, Americans Milton Subotsky and Max Rosenberg, who had initially tried to sell their Frankenstein script to Hammer, founded rival company Amicus Productions in Britain in order to take advantage of the tax benefits provided by the Eady Levy, a 'fund ... intended to aid in the production of British commercial films for the domestic and international market' (Heffernan 2004: 46). After an initial atmospheric black-and-white horror film about witchcraft, The City of the Dead (1960), was released by their one-off company Vulcan, Amicus began to copy Hammer's style, going as far to hire some of their actors – Cushing, Lee and Pitt – directors and crew. However, they had to differentiate their output if they were to stand out in a crowded market, especially because Hammer were firmly established as the main British studio. They made a small number of standalone Gothic films, such as the atmospheric The Skull (1965), based on the Robert Bloch story 'The Skull of the Marquis de Sade' (1945); I, Monster (1971), a faithful adaptation of Strange Case of Dr Jekyll and Mr Hyde; and And Now the Screaming Starts! (1973), a Radcliffean tale based on the contemporary David Case novella Fengriffen (1971). What ended up characterising Amicus, however, would be their honing of portmanteau horror. By 1965 the anthology film had a long and critically lauded history (Hallenbeck 2014: 11–38) and at least three other horror anthologies had been shot in colour in the early 1960s: the American Tales of Terror (1962) and Twice Told Tales (1963), based on the works of Edgar Allan Poe and Nathaniel Hawthorne, and the Japanese *Kaidan*, adapted from Lafcadio Hearn's short stories. Amicus managed to give the format a personal touch by incorporating black humour and favouring light-hearted scares. Over the course of nine years, the studio released seven portmanteau horror films, all of them shot in colour, with four to five stories each tied together by a framing narrative. These were *Dr. Terror's House of Horrors* (1965), *Torture Garden* (1967), *The House That Dripped Blood* (1971), *Tales from the Crypt* (1972), *Asylum* (1972), *Vault of Horror* (1973) and *From Beyond the Grave* (1974). Intermittently successful and adapting, during their 1970s phase, the equally episodic 1950s EC comics, they only occasionally resorted to the Gothic.

Of their pioneering *Dr. Terror's House of Horrors* only two stories exhibit a Gothic aesthetic, 'Werewolf' and 'Vampire', and of these only the former attempts to evoke architectonic remoteness through a Hebridean seventeenth-century ancestral home. Even these, like the stories in Amicus's other portmanteau films, can only partially be understood as Gothic, insofar as *Dr. Terror's* contemporary settings forestall a true retrojection to the Victorian past. The characters resolutely inhabit the present, so their segments are bound up with the temporal accoutrements of the twentieth century. The same applies to the 'The Man Who Collected Poe' segment in *Torture Garden*, adapted from the 1951 Robert Bloch story, or 'The Cloak' segment in *The House That Dripped Blood*, adapted from another Bloch story from 1939. These are important because they demonstrate that, by the 1960s, Gothic monsters were inhabiting the contemporary world with ease. They also show that, when Amicus attempted to do Gothic, it still relied on Hammer's formula (archetypal monsters, Victorian settings, vivid red blood) even when the source material was eminently American (Hutchings 2002: 132). Their most aesthetically distinct Gothic piece was, in fact, the aforementioned *And Now the Screaming Starts!*, which, despite receiving some enthusiastic reviews and managing respectable first week box office returns, did not come remotely close to the earnings of *Scream and Scream Again* (1970), *Tales from the Crypt* and *Asylum*, all set in modern times. The film's lukewarm performance is perhaps an indication that, as Allan Bryce notes, in the early 1970s 'Gothic horror simply wasn't guaranteed box office any longer' (2016: 116). Given that *The Exorcist* was the success horror film of that same year and that others with modern themes, such as *Jaws* (1975) and *The Omen* (1976), would follow shortly, it is hard not to concede that colour Gothic horror eventually lost its novelty value.

Another company making British colour horrors during the late 1960s and early 1970s was Tigon British Film Productions, initially a grindhouse and film distributor whose founder, Tony Tenser, had previously produced a Hammer-esque Gothic, *The Black Torment* (1964), through the short-lived company Compton Films. Although, like Amicus, the studio only very occasionally worked on Gothic films, these are the best remembered of their cinematic catalogue. *Curse of the Crimson Altar* (1968), which starred Boris Karloff, Christopher Lee and Barbara Steele, takes place in the present, but the haunting of ancestral family home Craxted Lodge involves colourful hallucinogenic scenes set in a strangely medieval, Satanic neverwhere. The shocking events in *Witchfinder General* (1968) and *Blood on Satan's Claw* (1971) occur in seventeenth- and eighteenth-century England, but the films are more obviously interested in the superstitious fear generated by paganism, Satanism and witchcraft than in the architectural and narrative trappings of the Gothic. This is one of the reasons they have been studied as examples of 'folk horror' and their exploits, certainly those of *Witchfinder General*, seem to engage more actively with the 'revenger motifs' of the Western (Forshaw 2013: 111). More straightforwardly Gothic are *The Blood Beast Terror* (1968), an atmospheric Victorian period featuring a 'were-moth', and *The Creeping Flesh* (1973), Tigon's last film as a production company. The latter's aesthetic invokes Hammer's and the film even concludes with a finale that returns to the possibility of madness hinted at in the conclusion of *The Curse of Frankenstein*. Tigon's more openly exploitative style – Andy Boot goes as far as to call exploitation 'Tigon's *raison d'être*' (1996: 174) – saw their films receive numerous cuts, and would find immediate British continuity in the films of Pete Walker, with their explicit combination of horror and erotic titillation. *House of Whipcord* (1974), *Frightmare* and *House of Mortal Sin* (1975), in particular, have been read by Steve Chibnall as updates of the Gothic literary tradition, relying as they do on tropes like the 'persecuted woman', oppressive and repressed 'privileged men' and the sinister house, a reconfiguration of the Gothic castle (2002: 168–169).

The development of a colour form of the Gothic was not limited to Britain, although attempts elsewhere would be a lot more atomised and experimental. Roger Vadim's exquisite adaptation of 'Carmilla' … *Et mourir de plaisir* (*Blood and Roses*, 1960) was shot in Technicolor, but in two instances it lapses into black and white. The first of these is the opening credits, where pictures of Carmilla (Annette Stroyberg, as Anette Vadim) provide the background to the names of the cast and crew. The switch to a very vivid colour photography in the plane and arrival scenes that follow has a contrastive function: its lushness connotes the film's reigning atmosphere of barely concealed eroticism. Although unknown to the viewer at this point, the potential vampire (it is never revealed whether Carmilla is actually possessed by her vampiric ancestor, Millarca) is also subtly introduced as a relic of the past and as dangerously latent as the munitions left over from World War II that eventually destroy a parcel of the estate.[11] The second instance is located towards the end of the film and revolves around Georgia's (Elsa Martinelli's) dream. As we enter her subconscious, the colour fades to grey. Yet not all colour disappears: blood, rendered in a very bright red, drips from Carmilla's neck; Georgia observes from the other side of a black-and-white wall a small door of colour encasing a horse rider (perhaps her fiancé) and, finally, surgical gloves on the hands of nurses are singled out (also in red) in an operation scene where Carmilla, explaining she is really Millarca, lifts the breathing mask of the patient (Carmilla). The nightmare sequence ends with Georgia and Carmilla/Millarca in a gyrating embrace and apparent vampiric kiss that exudes pent-up desire. Colour tricks enhance the unearthly nature of the events and the film's tentative and allegorical approach to the story. Similar hallucinogenic, sometimes psychedelic, colour scenes would be inserted in later Gothic-flavoured horror films of the period, most notably in the Coffin Joe (Zé do Caixão) vehicles *Esta noite encarnarei no teu cadáver* (*This Night I Will Possess Your Corpse*, 1967) and *O ritual dos sádicos* (*Awakening of the Beast*, 1970).

1960 was also the year of the release of another film that experimented with colour and optical technologies. William Castle's 13 *Ghosts* tells the story of a haunted house whose spectres are only visible through a set of special goggles left behind by the previous owner. The film is largely in black and white, but its main gimmick, 'Illusion-O', involved providing audiences with their own version of the goggles, needed in order to 'see' the supernatural events in the film. Unlike 3D glasses, the 'ghost viewer' had blue and red cellophane strips and required people to look through a single colour at a time. Since the ghostly elements were shot in red with a blue background, the blue filter would remove them, while the red would make them visible (Law 2000: 82). The gimmick aligned camera, character and audience, thus shortening the distance between the three. As is clear from Castle's own opening sequence, where he addresses viewers directly, 13 *Ghosts* wanted to make people believe in ghosts while also giving the sceptical the illusion of agency.[12] Some of the promotional materials also referred to the film's 'ectoplasmatic color', playfully evoking a long history of mediumship and alleged evidence of spiritual contact.[13] As Murray Leeder has noted, what is striking is not the fact that the supernatural was coloured but rather that it became '*colour itself*' and thus a reflection on 'cinematic colour's own suppressed ineffability, intangibility and uncontainability (through projective dimensionality)' (2018: 194, italics in original). 13 *Ghosts* is a modern horror film, rather than a Gothic one, yet its visual tricks signal a sea change in the perception of the value and potential of colour as a catalyst of the repressed and invisible. Only two months later, *House of Usher* would premiere in the States and literalise these concerns for Gothic cinema.

The gravitas and often poetic nature of the films of Roger Corman, the quintessential independent American filmmaker, made them Hammer's real Gothic rival in the early 1960s. For *Sunday Times* reviewer Dylis Powell, for example, Hammer's Gothics were funny, '[b]ut a guffaw isn't enough; if I am to have horror in Technicolor I want the kind of Gothic dream-horror which Roger Corman can do, eg. *The Fall of the House of Usher*' (quoted in Huxley 2012: 52). In the 1950s Corman had produced a number of black-and-white horror films for AIP (American International Pictures).[14] *It Conquered the World* (1956) or *Attack of the Crab Monsters* (1957) had, like Hammer, capitalised on the 1950s market for science fiction and appealed to the younger audiences for whom films like *I Was a Teenage Werewolf* (1957), *I Was a Teenage Frankenstein* (1957) and *Blood of Dracula* (1957) had been made. The comedy horrors *A Bucket of Blood* (1959) and *The Little Shop of Horrors* (1960) are also indicative of Corman's capacity to reinvent the genre and push it forward. However, only one film, the medieval witchcraft melodrama via psychic regression to a past life *The Undead* (1957), pointed towards the thematic leap the director would take with his Poe films. Corman has claimed that it was only after he had made *House of Usher* that he saw Mario Bava's *Black Sunday* (1960) and Hammer's early efforts and that his drive to shoot the film was both a long-held passion for the American author and the desire to direct a more ambitious and competitive project (Corman, quoted in Silver and Ursini 2006: 128).[15] Like Stoker and Shelley's work, Poe's well-known horror stories had been adapted a number of times for the big screen before 1960, but no one had previously attempted to do so in colour. Corman, in collaboration with scriptwriter Richard Matheson, would attempt to translate over Poe's discombobulated psychologies, unreliable narrators and recurrent hallucinations and dreams.[16]

House of Usher, sometimes given the full title of the story it adapts, 'The Fall of the House of Usher', opens with an experimental credits sequence that belies the excitement and possibilities of colour cinematography. Plumes of purple, green, red and blue smoke take turns travelling across the screen over a pitch-black background. The images are so fluid that the small clouds look almost liquid, like splashes of paint spreading over a canvas, a visual metaphor fleshed out in the opening credits for *The Pit and the Pendulum* (1961), where actual rivulets of paint are used. These suggestive will-o'-the-wisps are expressionistic and evoke the excesses of feeling suffered by the film's characters. They also echo the ground fog engulfing the arid and desolate land which Philip (Mark Damon) slowly rides across on his approach to the Usher mansion.[17] Interestingly, the lush Les Baxter score accompanying the titles, somewhat romantic and invigorating, is at odds with the horror genre. Perhaps this inviting gesture nods to the romantic elements of the film, but it is also possible that it is meant to contrast with the more dramatic music that follows once the story discloses Roderick Usher's (Vincent Price) hypochondriac disposition and incipient insanity (van Elferen 2012: 52). This short and simple sequence, distinctively atmospheric, creates a strong sense of identity for *House of Usher* and for the Poe films. Shot in CinemaScope and in colour, cinematography and mise-en-scène would become equally salient traits. If the trailer's suggestion that the 'house is the monster' may have been a tongue-in-cheek trick to get AIP to invest in an otherwise monsterless horror film, the Usher mansion really does become the protagonist. On a narrative level, its ornate opulence, the claustrophobic arrangement of the props and its airless, cobwebbed family crypt all reflect the Ushers' mental descent into madness and the terminal state of the family line. On a surface level, it connects architecture, aesthetics and story. Cinematographer Floyd Crosby and art designer Daniel Haller's return to future Poes and the recomposition of the set's flats from film to film turned these particularities into trademarks for Corman's Gothic brand.

Colour expresses many things in *House of Usher*, and it is as important a series of signifiers as the crack running through the house. As Joaquín Vallet and Teresa Llácer propose, the use of primary colours is significant and striking, and may be an attempt to engage with the 'primitive side of the human condition' (2016: 120, my translation). Philip is dressed in stark blue, a symbol of his purity, while Roderick appears first in a vivid red, a symbol of passion, and then in a funereal black and a dark grey. Red, in fact, pervades the set and accessories, from the many candles to the curtains, the glasses, the chairs' backrests and the sofa. This is no coincidence, for red is also the colour of blood, a major motif. Death awaits the Ushers: the 'morbid acuteness of the senses', as Roderick puts it, ailing them is hereditary, their lineage tainted with the 'plague of evil'. This invisible inevitability, their destruction, is triggered by Philip's attempt to lay claim to Madeline's heart (Myrna Fahey) and manifests as a haunting.[18] Through a conversation with Roderick, we learn of the Gothic curse, of the Biblical visitation of the 'sins of the fathers' 'on their children to the third and fourth generation' that had already dominated Walpole's *The Castle of Otranto*. The history of the family's 'savage degradations' is retold while Roderick introduces Philip to his ancestors. The litany of their 'foul deeds' – the Ushers have been 'merchant[s] of flesh', thieves, professional assassins, blackmailers, slave-traders, usurers, harlots, swindlers, forgers and drug addicts – is punctuated by middle and close shots of their portraits. These are eminently impressionistic, distorted Burt Shonberg paintings which use predominantly red, black, grey and blue, and render their models evil caricatures of themselves. These figures return in Philip's dream sequence, where they are portrayed in a similarly grotesque manner. This fantasy scene is formally interesting, for it makes use of double printing (giving the illusion of triple vision), is tinted in an uncanny blue (and, at other points, purple and pink) and had its audio layered on in postproduction.[19] An exercise in cinematic technique, its whimsy would become one of the signatures of Corman's Poe films. The storm which marks the final bout of action is also accentuated by lightning, portrayed here in flashes of electric blue light that emphasise the colour scheme adhered to elsewhere in *House of Usher*.

Lighting, set design and even clothes are strongly determined by the overall intention to parade the lunacy of the last two members of the Usher family. In this sense, *House of Usher* plays as a story of the unconscious, reflecting the unreliability of a tormented mind (Roderick's) suffering from a nervous disease. The corruption of his lineage speaks to the Gothic's obsession with aristocratic decadence – also apparent in Hammer's profusion of barons and counts – a point emphasised by Roderick when he explains that the stately Usher home is a 'centuries old house, brought [t]here from England. And with it every evil rooted in its stones'. This evil is not just a word, however, but 'a reality'. The film's heavily staged, studio-bound feel contributes to the uncanniness elicited by the colour scheme and cloying settings; it mirrors the psychological entrapment of the main character. It highlights the fact that *House of Usher*, like many of the other Poe films, can be construed as a series of personal distortions or sick visions. Aside from the recurring fantasy sequences, Corman would centre on monomaniacs haunted by the past (who sometimes even become possessed by it) with only a thin grasp on reality: both Nicholas (Vincent Price) in *The Pit and the Pendulum* and Guy (Ray Milland) in *The Premature Burial* (1962) are driven to insanity by morbid thoughts of premature interment; both Mr. Locke (Price) in the 'Morella' segment of *Tales of Terror* and Verden (Price) in *Tomb of Ligeia* (1964) are unable to overcome their respective wives' deaths. Poe's intrinsic first-person narrative voices and subjective dreamscapes had found their perfect cinematic counterparts.

This new approach to Gothic cinema, which brought narrative intent, setting and cinematography together and exploited the opportunities offered by colour photography, proved very popular with both critics and the public. It would be finessed over seven more films and two aesthetically similar ones, the remake of *Tower of London* (1962) and *The Terror* (1963).[20] Corman would soon add more innovations to the reprised fantasy sequences in *The Pit and the Pendulum* and *The Premature Burial*, with in some instances heavier use of lens distortion and overlaying. In the 'The Facts of the Case of M. Valdemar' segment in *Tales of Terror*, a revolving lantern with multi-coloured glass panels, some of them primary, is used to mesmerise Valdemar (Price) at the point of death. The defamiliarising effect created by the alternating blue, red, yellow and green filters cast over the actor's face is both entrancing and unsettling, gently hinting at the supernatural turn events take after

Figure 5.2 The tortuous mindscapes of Poe's characters found cinematic equivalents in the set design and vivid colours of *House of Usher* (1960).

Valdemar's soul is deprived of corporeal release. The brief scenes that precede the different stories in this film also exploit the stark contrast of red on black: a disembodied heart beats in a void, apparently suspended in space, and a cat's bloody paw prints manifest on a dark floor. In its opening credits, *The Raven* (1963) inserts a totally gratuitous still of a coffin that has been filtered through a rainbow lens, and the film includes extreme close-ups of stone gargoyles bathed in eerie shades of green and pink. Red asphodels (the flowers of death) are one of the motifs in *Tomb of Ligeia*, showcased in a daydream sequence where Rowena (Elizabeth Sheperd) awakes surrounded by them. Finally, *The Masque of the Red Death* (1964), the apogee of Corman's colour experiments, is a real mosaic and feast for the eyes. Monochromatic rooms resonate with the various coloured deaths (white, yellow, golden, blue, violet, black and red), represented by men in dyed monastic cloaks. Red in this film signifies blood (and thus, the feudal lord's cruelty) and even moral corruption (soullessness) by dint of temptation. In fact, the red death is at first mistaken for the devil by Prospero (Price), who time and again pronounces the death of God. In all of Corman's Gothics, colour is closely connected to the psychological worlds of the films' characters; it externalises inner turmoil and desire.

On the one hand, Corman's experimental pushing of colour was markedly different from that of Hammer, Amicus or Tigon. In his amalgamation and distillation of Poe's themes and metaphysical preoccupations, he was interested in setting up cinematic tapestries that would compositionally explore and connote the warped recesses of the human mind, especially the diseased one.[21] The British studios were keener to exploit the affective capacity of colour, its potential to shock and disgust, and thus to inject life into the stultified black and white period Gothic. In this respect, Corman's colour Gothic may be said to be more auteuristic, Hammer, Amicus and Tigon's more functional. On the other hand, the films produced by all these different studios can be productively read as a cinematic corpus that reflects the opportunities opened up by a turn to colour photography during a period when Gothic cinema reinvented itself once again. The widespread idea that Gothic horror had to be shot in black and white, a perceived atmospheric requirement influenced by the chiaroscuro leanings of early German cinema, Universal horrors and old dark house mysteries, could no longer be plausibly maintained. Colour Gothic made money, it was enterprising and it could also offer new and artistic avenues for directors like Corman. The late 1950s and early 1960s, as well the 1970s, saw a flurry of Gothic activity that cannot be separated from the rise of colour photography and the entrenchment of horror cinema (and its Gothic subgenre) as profitable. In a natural cycle, innovation led to success, and success led to the production of more films like those that had proved most commercial. A connected development was the reach of this tried-and-tested type of cinema, that is, the subsequent growth of an inter- and transnational Gothic horror industry, especially across Europe. This topic, of enormous significance to the evolution of Gothic cinema, is inseparable from the British and American companies whose practices and films have been covered in this chapter. Yet the multifarious and context-specific qualities of the Gothic films that followed grant them separate attention.

FILMOGRAPHY

13 Ghosts (William Castle, 1960, USA)
A Bucket of Blood (Roger Corman, 1959, USA)
And Now the Screaming Starts! (Roy Ward Baker, 1973, UK)
Asylum (Roy Ward Baker, 1972, UK)
Attack of the Crab Monsters (Roger Corman, 1957, USA)
Black Sunday (Mario Bava, 1960, Italy)
Blood Feast (Herschell Gordon Lewis, 1962, USA)
Blood from the Mummy's Tomb (Seth Holt and Michael Carreras, 1971, UK)
Blood of Dracula (Herbert L. Strock, 1957, USA)
Blood on Satan's Claw (Piers Haggard, 1971, UK)
Circus of Horrors (Sidney Hayers, 1960, UK)
Count Yorga, Vampire (Bob Kelljan, 1970, USA)
Crimes at the Dark House (George King, 1940, UK)
Curse of the Crimson Altar (Vernon Sewell, 1968, UK)
Curse of the Mummy's Tomb (Michael Carreras, 1964, UK)
Dead of Night (Alberto Cavalcanti, Charles Crichton, Robert Hamer and Basil Dearden, 1945, UK)
Doctor X (Michael Curtiz, 1932, USA)
Dr. Jekyll and Mr. Hyde (Charles Urban (producer), 1913, UK)
Dr. Terror's House of Horrors (Freddie Francis, 1965, UK)
Dracula (Terence Fisher, 1958, UK)
Dracula A.D. 1972 (Alan Gibson, 1972, UK)
Dracula: Prince of Darkness (Terence Fisher, 1966, UK)
Dracula Has Risen from the Grave (Freddie Francis, 1968, UK)
Esta noite encarnarei no teu cadáver (*This Night I Will Possess Your Corpse*, José Mojica Marins, 1967, Brazil)
…Et mourir de plaisir (*Blood and Roses*, Roger Vadim, 1960, France/Italy)
Frankenstein and the Monster from Hell (Terence Fisher, 1974, UK)
Frankenstein Created Woman (Terence Fisher, 1967, UK)
Frankenstein Must Be Destroyed (Terence Fisher, 1969, UK)
From Beyond the Grave (Kevin Connor, 1974, UK)

Frightmare (Pete Walker, 1974, UK)
Horrors of the Black Museum (Arthur Crabtree, 1959, UK)
House of Mortal Sin (Pete Walker, 1975, UK)
House of Usher (Roger Corman, 1960, USA)
House of Wax (Andre DeToth, 1953, USA)
House of Whipcord (Pete Walker, 1974, UK)
House on Haunted Hill (William Castle, 1959, USA)
I, Monster (Stephen Weeks, 1971, UK)
I Was a Teenage Frankenstein (Herbert L. Strock, 1957, USA)
I Was a Teenage Werewolf (Gene Fowler Jr., 1957, USA)
It Conquered the World (Roger Corman, 1956, USA)
Jaws (Steven Spielberg, 1975, USA)
Kaidan (Kwaidan, Masaki Kobayashi, 1964, Japan)
Macabre (William Castle, 1958, USA)
Murders in the Zoo (A. Edward Sutherland, 1933, USA)
Mystery of the Wax Museum (Michael Curtiz, 1933, USA)
Night of the Demon (Jacques Tourneur, 1957, UK)
Night of the Eagle (Sidney Hayers, 1962, UK)
O ritual dos sádicos (*Awakening of the Beast*, José Mojica Marins, 1970, Brazil)
Peeping Tom (Michael Powell, 1960, UK)
Scared to Death (Christy Cabanne, 1947, USA)
Scars of Dracula (Roy Ward Baker, 1970, UK)
Scream and Scream Again (Gordon Hessler, 1970, UK)
Sweeney Todd: The Demon Barber of Fleet Street (George King, 1936, UK)
Tales from the Crypt (Freddie Francis, 1972, UK)
Tales of Terror (Roger Corman, 1962, USA)
Taste the Blood of Dracula (Peter Sasdy, 1970, UK)
The Black Cat (Edgar G. Ulmer, 1934, USA)
The Black Torment (Robert Hartford-Davis, 1964, UK)
The Blood Beast Terror (Vernon Sewell, 1968, UK)
The Brides of Dracula (Terence Fisher, 1960, UK)
The City of the Dead (John Llewellyn Moxey, 1960, UK)
The Creeping Flesh (Freddie Francis, 1973, UK)
The Curse of Frankenstein (Terence Fisher, 1957, UK)

The Curse of the Werewolf (Terence Fisher, 1961, UK)
The Dark Eyes of London (Walter Summers, 1939, UK)
The Devil Rides Out (Terence Fisher, 1968, UK)
The Evil of Frankenstein (Freddie Francis, 1964, UK)
The Ghost of Frankenstein (Erle C. Kenton, 1942, USA)
The Gorgon (Terence Fisher, 1964, UK)
The Great Gabbo (James Cruze and Erich von Stroheim, 1929, USA)
The Haunted Palace (Roger Corman, 1963, USA)
The Haunting (Robert Wise, 1963, UK)
The Horror of Frankenstein (Jimmy Sangster, 1970, UK)
The Hound of the Baskervilles (Terence Fisher, 1959, UK)
The House That Dripped Blood (Peter Duffell, 1971, UK)
The Innocents (Jack Clayton, 1961, UK)
The Kiss of the Vampire (Don Sharp, 1963, UK)
The Little Shop of Horrors (Roger Corman, 1960, USA)
The Man Who Could Cheat Death (Terence Fisher, 1959, UK)
The Masque of the Red Death (Roger Corman, 1964, USA)
The Mummy (Terence Fisher, 1959, UK)
The Mummy's Shroud (John Gilling, 1967, UK)
The Murders in the Rue Morgue (Robert Florey, 1932, USA)
The Omen (Richard Donner, 1976, UK and USA)
The Phantom of the Opera (Rupert Julian, 1925, USA)
The Phantom of the Opera (Terence Fisher, 1962, UK)
The Plague of the Zombies (John Gilling, 1966, UK)
The Premature Burial (Roger Corman, 1962, USA)
The Picture of Dorian Gray (Albert Lewin, 1945, USA)
The Pit and the Pendulum (Roger Corman, 1961, USA)
The Quatermass Xperiment (Val Guest, 1955, UK)
The Queen of Spades (Thorold Dickinson, 1949, UK)
The Raven (Lew Landers, 1935, USA)
The Raven (Roger Corman, 1963, USA)
The Revenge of Frankenstein (Terence Fisher, 1958, UK)
The Satanic Rites of Dracula (Alan Gibson, 1973, UK)
The Skull (Freddie Francis, 1965, UK)

The Terror (Roger Corman, 1963, USA)
The Tingler (William Castle, 1959, USA)
The Two Faces of Dr. Jekyll (Terence Fisher, 1960, UK)
The Undead (Roger Corman, 1957, USA)
The Vampire Lovers (Roy Ward Baker, 1970, UK)
The Witches (Cyril Frankel, 1966, UK)
Tomb of Ligeia (Roger Corman, 1964, USA)
Torture Garden (Freddie Francis, 1967, UK)
Tower of London (Roger Corman, 1962, USA)
Twice Told Tales (Sidney Salkow, 1963, USA)
Vault of Horror (Roy Ward Baker, 1973, UK)
Witchfinder General (Michael Reeves, 1968, UK)
X the Unknown (Leslie Norman and Joseph Losey, 1956, UK)

NOTES

1 The American version of the film does not use this more ornate font for its title, *Horror of Dracula*. Instead, it presents the title in the same style as the rest of the credits.
2 Both *The Curse of Frankenstein* and *Dracula* were shot using Eastmancolor.
3 A lot has been written about the censors' impact on the stalled development of early British Gothic cinema. See Boot (1996: 9–17), Conrich (2002) and Forshaw (2013: 22–32).
4 Higher levels of more intense violence are particularly evident in later films made by Hammer, especially in *Scars of Dracula* (1970), which includes a completely gratuitous dismemberment scene, and *Frankenstein and the Monster from Hell* (1974).
5 There were three other mummy films – *Curse of the Mummy's Tomb* (1964), *The Mummy's Shroud* (1967) and *Blood from the Mummy's Tomb* – but, although they were aesthetically linked, none of them was related to the 1959 film.
6 An antitrust suit against Technicolor and their suppliers, Eastman Kodak, had been filed by the Department of Justice following complaints from the

industry that the companies were restraining trade and preventing other studios from developing their own colour photography processes.

7 In fact, television, which was in black and white at the time and would not adopt colour until the mid-1960s, is responsible for a slump in colour cinema production in the late 1950s (Neale 1985: 143).

8 The BFPA felt that Hammer's marketisation of the once-feared 'X' certificate, eminently so in the cases of the science fiction horrors *The Quatermass Xperiment* (1955) and *X the Unknown* (1956), was bringing into disrepute the quality adult films intended to be covered by it (Aldgate 1995: 51–52).

9 For more on Castle's gimmicks, see Leeder (2011).

10 Powell was, at one point, even compared to the Marquis de Sade (Hamilton 2013: 83).

11 The explosion is responsible for exposing the family's ancestral tomb. The film thus suggests repression inevitably leads to cathartic release.

12 This premise is contradictory and contrived, as the existence of ghosts is proven at the diegetic level (the ghosts do exist in the film). As Leeder notes, this opening sequence is best understood as a dare to the viewer (2018: 191).

13 Ectoplasm is a supernatural, viscous substance that putatively dribbles out of the medium's body during trance and forms the manifestation of spirits.

14 Corman had already worked in an impressive array of genres by the 1960s, including Westerns and adventure films, and his subsequent career would be just as eclectic. I recuperate him here in his capacity as Gothic horror director only.

15 See, for example, his commentary on the 2013 Arrow Blu-ray release of *House of Usher*.

16 For a detailed exploration of these key elements of Poe's fiction, see Fisher (2002: 78–91).

17 This scene was not shot in a set. It made the most of a real forest fire that had broken out in the Hollywood hills.

18 After Madeline's sudden death, Usher intones 'one candle left to burn now', further associating these objects, and their redness, with the inexorable passing of time and the demise of the Usher family.

19 When writing about *House of Usher*, Corman claimed he used 'either gel over the lights or a colored filter over the lens' (1990: 79) to achieve the eerie blue and red look of the dream sequence, but he has since also mentioned postproduction methods like colour desaturation.
20 As is well known, *The Haunted Palace* (1963) is only nominally a Poe adaptation, having been deliberately (and disingenuously) marketed as such by AIP to capitalise on the success of Corman's previous Poe ventures (McGee 1988: 51). The film largely adapts H. P. Lovecraft's short novel *The Case of Charles Dexter Ward* (1943). It is also important to note that *Tower of London* was, unlike the other films, shot in black and white.
21 Corman has often spoken of how the Poe films were influenced by his reading of Freud at the time. See Corman and Jerome (1990: 77, 80).

BIBLIOGRAPHY

Aldgate, A. (1995) *Censorship and the Permissive Society: British Cinema and Theatre, 1955–65*, Oxford and New York: Oxford University Press.

Balio, T. (1985) *The American Film Industry*, rev. edn, Madison, WI: University of Wisconsin Press.

Boot, A. (1996) *Fragments of Fear: An Illustrated History of British Horror Films*, London: Creation Books.

Bryce, A. (2016) *Amicus: The Friendly Face of Fear*, South Cheam: Ghoulish Publishing.

Chibnall, S. (2002) 'A Heritage of Evil: Pete Walker and the Politics of Gothic Revisionism', in S. Chibnall and J. Petley (eds) *British Horror Cinema*, London and New York: Routledge.

Conrich, I. (2002) 'Horrific Films and 1930s British Cinema', in S. Chibnall and J. Petley (eds) *British Horror Cinema*, London and New York: Routledge.

Corman, R. and J. Jerome (1990) *How I Made a Hundred Movies in Hollywood and Never Lost a Dime*, New York: Random House.

Fisher, B. F. (2002) 'Poe and the Gothic Tradition', in K. J. Hayes (ed.) *The Cambridge Companion to Edgar Allan Poe*, Cambridge: Cambridge University Press.

Forshaw, B. (2013) *British Gothic Cinema*, Basingstoke: Palgrave Macmillan.

Frayling, C. (2005) *Mad, Bad and Dangerous? The Scientist and the Cinema*, London: Reaktion Books.

Gertner, R. (1958) 'Review: *The Revenge of Frankenstein*', *Motion Picture Daily*, 18 June, 5.

Haines, R. W. (1993) *Technicolor Movies: The History of Dye Transfer Printing*, London and Jefferson, NC: McFarland.

Hallenbeck, B. C. (2014) *The Amicus Anthology*, Baltimore, MD: Midnight Marquee Press.

Hamilton, J. (2013) *X-Cert: The British Independent Horror Film 1951–1970*, Baltimore, MD: Midnight Marquee Press.

Harper, S. (2012) *British Film Culture in the 1970s: The Boundaries of Pleasure*, Edinburgh: Edinburgh University Press.

Heffernan, K. (2004) *Ghouls, Gimmicks and Gold: Horror Films and the American Movie Business, 1953–1968*, London and Durham, NC: Durham University Press.

Hutchings, P. (2001) *Terence Fisher*, Manchester and New York: Manchester University Press.

Hutchings, P. (2002) 'The Amicus House of Horrors', in S. Chibnall and J. Petley (eds) *British Horror Cinema*, London and New York: Routledge.

Huxley, D. (2012) 'Depressing, Degrading! The Reception of the European Horror Film in Britain 1957–1968', in P. Allmer, E. Brick and D. Huxley (eds) *European Nightmares: Horror Cinema in Europe since 1945*, London and New York: Wallflower Press.

Kinsey, W. (2005) *Hammer Films: The Bray Studios Years*, Richmond: Reynolds and Hearn.

Larson, R. D. (1996) *Music from the House of Hammer: Music in the Hammer Horror Films, 1950–1980*, London and Lanham, MD: Scarecrow Press.

Law, J. (2000) *Scare Tactic: The Life and Films of William Castle*, Lincoln, NE: Writers Club Press.

Leeder, M. (2011) 'Collective Screams: William Castle and the Gimmick Film', *The Journal of Popular Culture*, 44.4: 773–795.

Leeder, M. (2018) *Horror Film: A Critical Introduction*, London andNew York: Bloomsbury.

Lev, P. (2003) *The Fifties: Transforming the Screen, 1950–1959*, London and Berkeley, CA: University of California Press.

McGee, M. T. (1988) *Roger Corman: The Best of the Cheap Acts*, London and Jefferson, NC: McFarland.

Neale, S. (1985) *Cinema and Technology: Image, Sound, Colour*, London and Basingstoke: Macmillan Education.

Silver, A. and J. Ursini (2006) *Roger Corman: Metaphysics on a Shoestring*, Beverly Hills, CA: Silman-James Press.

Skal, D. J. (1998) *Screams of Reason: Mad Science and Modern Culture*, London and New York: W. W. Norton.

Vallet, J. and T. Llácer (2016) *Roger Corman: Poe, monstruos y extraterrestres*, Madrid: T&B Editores.

van Elferen, I. (2012) *Gothic Music: The Sounds of the Uncanny*, Cardiff: University of Wales Press.

6

EXPLOITATION GOTHIC

From the early 1960s to the end of the 1970s some countries in continental Europe produced a multitude of Gothic films in an attempt to capitalise on the success of Hammer's period Gothics and Corman's Poe cycle. The two key players, Italy and Spain, had dabbled in Gothic cinema before the 1960s. Italy actually beat Hammer with the release of Riccardo Freda's *I vampiri*, the screenplay and original story for which were Italian, and Spain's own *La torre de los siete jorobados* (*The Tower of the Seven Hunchbacks*, 1944), based on the 1920 novel by Spanish writer Emilio Carrère, appeared during the early years of Francisco Franco's military dictatorship.[1] Neither led to a noteworthy revival of the Gothic in their respective countries, where they were received with lukewarm interest and modest revenues (Di Chiara 2016: 31). *I vampiri* actually raised eyebrows at home, where audiences did not associate Italian filmmaking with an ostensibly foreign cinematic tradition, especially after Universal's horrors started playing there in the early 1950s. The colour Gothics of England and America changed the game. Horror's popularity and easily recouped investments made it a relatively safe and appealing genre, especially to independent filmmakers and producers. As a notable case in point,

Spanish director Jesús (Jess) Franco allegedly managed to convince his producers to back his Gritos en la noche (The Awful Dr. Orlof, 1962), a breakthrough in Spanish cinema, after taking them to a screening of Terence Fisher's sequel to Dracula, 1960's The Brides of Dracula (Lázaro-Reboll 2012: 56). This new era would lead to record highs for national horror filmmaking that are impressive even by today's standards.[2] While Hammer and Corman's interventions did not constitute strict points of origin, they did mark a new utilitarian beginning premised on the economic principles of supply and demand. Horror became plentiful and polymorphic, manifesting in the most gruesome examples of the nascent *giallo* genre and in the modern occult trends of the 1970s. The Gothic remained, at least initially, a key horrific strand because those making genre films sought to replicate familiar formulas that had proved profitable and would appeal to North American and European markets and tastes.

Italy was the first, and perhaps most significant, example of a country to rapidly develop a Gothic horror industry.[3] The release of 1958's *Dracula* had caused a real furore that translated into an almost immediate and truly transformative commercial response.[4] Only a year later, the horror comedy *Tempi duri per i vampiri* (*Uncle Was a Vampire*, 1959) parodied many of the elements in Fisher's film from a contemporary perspective (1950s Italy) and even included the presence of Christopher Lee, who virtually reprised his Count Dracula role. A middling colour farce following the adventures of Baron Osvaldo (Renato Rascel), driven in his time of need to turn his ancestral home into a hotel, the film is less interesting for its re-treading of well-known vampiric lore (the protections offered by garlic, crosses and daylight) than for its humour, largely derived from the explicit sensualisation of vampirirism. After the baron is 'turned' by his uncle (Lee), he becomes a sensation among the holidaying crowd. Bikini-clad women snub their husbands and extol his virtues: 'he is wonderful ... He really makes other men ridiculous', they exclaim as they hypnotically stroke their necks and hope for another 'bite'.[5] In a telling scene, the vampire's hunger is crudely compared to his sexual prowess when the dial of a clock is substituted, on an hourly basis, with images of his nocturnal visits to female victims.

The increasingly explicit rendering of the Gothic's erotic undercurrents, this time without the tongue-in-cheek irreverence of *Tempi duri per i vampiri*, would become one of the key trademarks of continental cinema throughout the 1960s and 1970s.[6] As early as 1960, *L'ultima preda del vampiro* (*The Playgirls and the Vampire*) and *L'amante del vampiro* (*The Vampire and the Ballerina*) paired their respective aristocratic monsters with beautiful young women happy to parade their curvaceous bodies in musical numbers that, in *L'ultima preda del vampiro*, even sees one of the playgirls stripping down to her underwear. In the same film, a vampirised Katia (Maria Giovannini) walks naked at one point, her nipples visible in the lower frame, and this after her legs – the 'best … in Europe', according to one of the men – have already been amply exposed. Vampirism's once subtextual associations were foregrounded in the continental Gothic, all-too-often blurring the lines between fear, violence and sex. In *L'amante del vampiro*, after a man introduces the vampire to a captive female audience as a man who likes to possess his victims, a girl proposes that he sounds like a 'principe azzurro' (prince charming). Later, in a replay of *Dracula*'s bedroom scene, Luisa (Hélène Rémy) massages her neck and left breast in anticipation of the monster's attack. *L'amante del vampiro* sensationalised Hammer's Gothic films, keeping their core mechanics but upping the erotic ante.

The dozens of continental films that followed need to be understood as an industry-led reaction, with Gothic films made in continental Europe being shaped by time-specific modes of production that simultaneously allowed for a type of experimentation and exploration of the Gothic not previously conceivable or perceived as cost-effective. The 1960s and 1970s were defined by the rise of exploitation cinema, of 'cheap, sensational movies distributed to a sectionalised market' (Hunter 2009: 9) which normally privileged the key ingredients of violence and sex or else openly imitated other successful films (Hunter 2013: 32–33).[7] Connected to B-movies (cheaper, shorter films that would be paired up with 'A' pictures up until the 1950s) through their low budgets, less well-known actors, formulaic nature and fast-paced narratives, exploitation began to flourish in the 1950s thanks to changes in exhibition patterns (the increase in the number of drive-in theatres in the 1950s and the emergence of grindhouse cinemas and midnight movies in the late 1960s and early 1970s) and the explicit targeting of a younger demographic. Many of the films that would be played at such venues were made in Europe, with horror eventually leading as 'the most prevalent exploitation genre' (Mathijs and Sexton 2011: 150). Co-productions, a growing trend after the first bi-lateral agreement between continental countries was struck in 1949 (Di Chiara 2016: 34), made films safer and easier to finance, and distribution and co-production deals between America and Europe that could guarantee increased international sales of theatrical receipts had become de rigueur by 1960 (Heffernan 2004: 136). For American film studios like AIP, who imported Mario Bava's La maschera del demonio (1960) in a new cut as Black Sunday, the success of their international endeavours, as well as their outright purchases of completed films and co-production ventures, was crucial in terms of increasing the amount and quality of annual releases (Heffernan 2004: 135). This market logic also encouraged the employment of mixed casts, a demand for a small number of recognisable Gothic stars like Lee and Peter Cushing, who played in films such as the Spanish-British Pánico en el Transiberiano (Horror Express, 1974), and of cross-country screenwriting teams.[8] The horror industry was booming and it had become more trans- and international than ever.

All these contextual developments led to a surge of interest in films that would recycle recognisable Gothic myths and motifs easily marketable to the substantial audiences that had flocked to watch Hammer and Corman's films. Canonical characters like Dracula or Frankenstein and his/her creature appeared in continuations and reimaginings such as Lady Frankenstein (1971), El gran amor del conde Drácula (Count Dracula's Great Love, 1973) and La saga de los Drácula (The Dracula Saga, 1973), monster mashes like Drácula contra Frankenstein (Dracula, Prisoner of Frankenstein, 1972) and Los monstruos del terror (Assignment Terror, 1970) – albeit under different names to avoid copyright infringement in the latter – and in adaptations like *El conde Drácula* (*Count Dracula*, 1970), which featured Lee. Sheridan Le Fanu's novella 'Carmilla' was reinvented multiple times, most memorably in ...*Et mourir de plaisir*, covered in the previous chapter; in *La cripta e l'incubo* (*Terror in the Crypt*, 1964), which projects the characteristics particular to Carmilla onto Laura (Adriana Ambresi) in order to obfuscate the former's relationship to a long-dead vampire; in Harry Kümel's surprise success *Les Lèvres rouges* (*Daughters of Darkness*, 1971); and in the oft-surreal *La novia ensangrentada* (*The Blood Spattered Bride*, 1972). Films like *La marca del hombre lobo* (*Frankenstein's Bloody Terror*, 1968) and *La noche de Walpurgis* (*The Werewolf Versus the Vampire Woman*, 1971), two of Spain's most successful Gothic horrors, attempted something halfway between the borrowing and the expansion. Their main monsters, the tragic hero Count Waldemar Daninsky (Paul Naschy), Dr. Janos (Julián Ugarte) and Countess Wandessa (or Wandesa, depending on the film) Dárvula de Nadasdy (Patty Shepard) all had clear predecessors in Larry Talbot's wolf man and Fisher's Dracula, but were given different identities and histories. In the case of Countess Wandes(s)a, based on the real and allegedly murderous countess Elizabeth Báthory, the character even predated Hammer's *Countess Dracula* (1970).[9] Importantly, films would artistically cross-pollinate. For example, Georges Franju's *Les Yeux sans visage* (*Eyes Without a Face*, 1960) led to further face-grafting horrors in Spain and Italy.[10] A smaller number of the Gothic films of this period, like *Il mio amico Jekyll* (*My Friend, Dr. Jekyll*, 1960) and *Un vampiro para dos* (*A Vampire for Two*, 1965), are also sexy parodies, something which suggests the cultural currency of their respective Gothic myths. The hybridisation of Gothic motifs and situations resulted in patchwork pieces brimming with torture dungeons, bloodsuckers, disfigured hulks and damsels in distress such as *La strage dei vampiri* (*Slaughter of the Vampires*, 1962), *Metempsyco* (*Tomb of Torture*, 1963), whose Italian poster poignantly asked punters 'sesso o terrore?' ('sex or horror'?), and *Horror* (*The Blancheville Monster*, 1963).

Some of these Gothics were 'firsts' of sorts. *I vampiri*, for example, was the first sound Italian horror film and the first to introduce the figure of the sensual and supernatural female villainess that would become one of the country's trademark characters during the early to-mid-1960s. Closer to the police procedural than to the monster film, *I vampiri* does not actually feature any vampires, but rather takes its name from the life-draining crimes committed by Gisele Du Grand (Gianna Maria Canale), an ageing lady of society who cannot accept that her good looks are fading. Gisele employs the services of Professor Julian (Antoine Balpêtré) to transfer the youth of kidnapped women to her, something he only manages to achieve temporarily. It soon becomes apparent that Gisele and her aunt Marguerite, presumed suffering from a 'terrible' and 'incurable' disease and retired from society in her old castle, are one and the same person. Combining the fluid-exchanging rejuvenation experiments of *The Corpse Vanishes* with the metamorphoses of *Dr. Jekyll and Mr. Hyde* (1931), *I vampiri* weaves together mystery, melodrama and horror into a new hybrid that feels both familiar and original, distinctive not for its conglomerate narrative or characters but its setting, which mixes the modern present of the urban centre with the decaying architecture of its grandiose fortress. Although apparently the result of budgetary constraints as much as a desire to make the film's nightmare feel modern (Curti 2015: 22), the castle becomes the predominant source of the Gothic aesthetic. Access to Julian's dark laboratory is via a secret trapdoor behind a tomb in the family chapel, decorated with skulls and bones and various candles, and the main living room includes windblown curtains in the style of *La Chute de la maison Usher*, massive ceilings and the centrepiece, a huge fireplace with a trapdoor so striking that it would make a return a few years later in *La maschera del demonio*. The scene where a recently rejuvenated Gisele saunters down an impressive, shadow-laden stairwell crowned with a grotesque, bare-breasted gryphon is a Gothic masterpiece of composition, lighting and acting that conjures up a strong sense of menace and anticipates the future aesthetic achievements of its cinematographer, Mario Bava.

After working on *I vampiri* and *Caltiki – Il mostro immortale* (*Caltiki – The Immortal Monster*, 1959), Bava would eventually get a chance to direct

Figure 6.1 The incipient eroticism characteristic of the continental Gothic is manifest in I vampiri (The Vampires, 1957), Italy's first sound horror film.

his first film, La maschera del demonio, a title which echoed the recent The Curse of Frankenstein, retitled in Italy as La maschera di Frankenstein ('the mask of Frankenstein'). If Bava's previous work with Freda had been impressive, it had not achieved international success. This would come with La maschera del demonio, a film loosely based on Nikolai Gogol's novella 'Viy' ('The Viy', 1835) and which would become known as Black Sunday in its edited American version. It would actually turn out to be one of the most influential continental Gothics ever made. Shot in black and white at Bava's request, the film begins in 1630 Moldavia, where the witch Asa Vajda (Barbara Steele) is condemned to a gruesome death by her persecutors. In its iconic opening scene, Asa curses his executor and descendants, threatening to use the powers of darkness to 'return throughout the night of time' just before the nail-studded mask of the Italian title is hammered into her face.[11] 200 years later, Asa's remains, protected by a huge cross, rest in the derelict, medieval-looking chapel of the current Vajda family. When awakened by the blood of a curious stranger, the witch revives her dead lover and attempts to kill her descendant, Katia, who is, uncannily, also played by Steele.

The list of Gothic motifs and tropes in La maschera del demonio, from family curses to secret passageways, bat-ridden crypts and a ruinous castle, is so extensive as to constitute a veritable compendium. These all add to the overall feeling of dread and apprehension, solidifying around aesthetic vignettes that showcase Bava's incredible eye for depth of space, use of shadows and experience with special effects. Especially significant is Dr. Kruvajan's (Andrea Checchi) lamp-lit descent into the bowels of the castle. Inside the crypt, Asa's tomb implodes, as if from pent-up tension, to reveal the heavy-breathing witch. Kruvajan is compelled to kiss her on the lips, a daring action that seals his fate. The scene is not just remarkable for its construction and execution but for its barely contained eroticism. Compelling and visibly aroused, the image of Asa as she awakes from her long slumber is both horrific and sensual. Witches and female reincarnations, often visually doubled through the casting of the same actress in two roles, would recur in other Gothic filoni such as I lunghi capelli della morte (The Long Hair of Death, 1964), Amanti d'oltretomba and Un angelo per satana (An Angel for Satan, 1966), and in the form of a full coven in the later Suspiria (1977).[12] These characters are often presented as temptresses bent on revenge, an archetype in dialogue with that of the innocent heroine in a diaphanous white gown sauntering through dark corridors and spiral stairs inherited from the Female Gothic tradition. They represent the dichotomous roles to which women were commonly relegated in continental Gothic cinema: endangered, childlike victims or dangerous sex fiends.

The continental Gothic's key addition to the formula was its amplification and exploitation of sensuality and violence. While these elements were not exclusive to the cinema of Italy and Spain, they were developed more steadily and resolutely by these countries in the 1960s and 1970s.[13] The gratuitous nipple and aestheticised dead female bodies in Il mulino delle donne di pietra (Mill of the Stone Women, 1960), the first Italian horror film shot in colour, would soon be joined by other more macabre and controversial scenarios. L'orribile segreto del Dr. Hichcock (The Horrible Dr. Hichcock, 1962), the first Italian horror film to receive the new VM18 rating ('vietato a i minori di diciotto anni', or 'no one under 18 allowed'), featured a surgeon who drugs his wife into a deathlike state with a special serum in order to fulfil his necrophiliac desires. Its provocative combination of sex and corpses would reappear in *La residencia* (*The House That Screamed*, 1969), the Italian-French co-production directed by Paul Morrissey *Flesh for Frankenstein* (1973) and in the modern-day splatter *Buio omega* (*Beyond the Darkness*, 1979). Sadism featured strongly in *La mano de un hombre muerto* (*The Sadistic Baron Von Klaus*, 1962) and Bava's *La frusta e il corpo* (*The Whip and the Body*, 1963). Lesbianism was implied, and in places acted out, in *Danza macabra* (*Castle of Blood*, 1964), *La cripta e l'incubo* and *Contronatura* (*The Unnaturals*, 1969). The titillating aspects of the Gothic had become central by the time French director Jean Rollin made his erotic-surreal films *Le Viol du vampire* (*The Rape of the Vampire*, 1968), *La Vampire nue* (*The Nude Vampire*, 1970), *Le Frisson des vampires* (*The Shiver of the Vampires*, 1971), *Requiem pour un vampire* (*Requiem for a Vampire*, 1971), *Lèvres de sang* (*Lips of Blood*, 1975) and *Fascination* (1979). The gratuitous nudity in Rollin, complete or partially veiled by paper-thin gowns, softcore sex scenes and flimsy lesbian affairs are symptomatic of a market logic dictated by the gradual relaxation of laws around onscreen sexuality and violence.[14] The mingling of brutal, sometimes sexualised, torture of women with the explicit objectification of their bodies in continental Gothics like *Hexen bis aufs Blut gequält* (*Mark of the Devil*, 1970) and *Inquisición* (*Inquisition*, 1976) remains problematic, the underlying misogyny at play hard to ignore.

Despite stemming from industrial booms that are easy to demarcate, the incredibly varied corpus of Gothic films that emerges from Europe in the 1960s and 1970s resists homogenisation, their boundaries more porous than it might at first appear (Hawkins 2000: 53–64). The overall output includes melodrama adaptations of Gothic books, such as *Rękopis znaleziony w Saragossie* (*The Saragossa Manuscript*, 1965) and *Le moine* (*The Monk*, 1972); artistic films like *Valerie a týden divů* (*Valerie and Her Week of Wonders*, 1970), *Malpertuis* (1971), *Morgiana* (1972) and Herzog's *Nosferatu: Phantom der Nacht* (*Nosferatu the Vampyre*, 1979); and the experimental avant-garde of *Vampir – Cuadecuc*. In fact, studies highlighting the peculiarities of key directors like Mario Bava, Jesús Franco, Paul Naschy or Jean Rollin, all of whom have been connected to exploitation cinema, make compelling cases for the positioning of their respective oeuvres as auteuristic.[15] The comparable social and historical cinematic contexts of Italy and Spain (and, to a lesser degree, France) did, on the whole, translate into a specific type of Gothic cinema defined by low budgets, a vibrant co-production system and a distinct transnational appeal and projection that turned graphic depictions of violence and eroticism into the main attraction. Indeed, the excesses of the continental Gothic are also what makes these texts transgressive in a way that recuperates the spirit of the Gothic literary tradition and its indulgence in libidinous passions. These films pushed the envelope time and again, both thematically (in their reliance on sexual and moral taboos) and visually (in their anti-realistic explorations of colour, movement and light, in their unleashing of aggressive violence and mad mindscapes). It is, in fact, possible to argue that the continental Gothic's moral excesses often mirrored bold aesthetic ones. For example, in *Lo spettro* (*The Ghost*, 1963), Margaret (Barbara Steele) has an affair with her husband's doctor (Peter Baldwin), but, unbeknownst to them both, the ailing cuckold is planning his revenge. The film's many morally reprehensible acts find cinematic echoes in the portrayal of murder, most notably when crazed Margaret slashes at her lover with a razor. The moment is portrayed through a short/reverse shot dynamic that aligns the viewer with the victim and is memorable for the blood that splashes, trickles down and eventually covers the camera lens. The scene plays like an explicit retake of the famous shower scene in Alfred Hitchcock's *Psycho* (1960) – it is even accompanied by a similarly strident score. The makers of *5 tombe per un medium* (*Terror-Creatures from the Grave*, 1965) went as far as to shoot two additional gore scenes – in one, a face is savaged by a horse kick; a man impales himself in the other – that were only included in the American version of the film.[16] It is important to note that the gruesomeness of the continental Gothic did not develop in a vacuum and that, if it necessarily influenced the rise of the horror genre and the nudie film, it was also, in turn, shaped by cinema's growing interest in the sexually and violently explicit. The varied works of Lucio Fulci, Dario Argento, León Klimovsky and Narciso

Ibáñez Serrador often straddled various types of horror, even other genres like the Western, the *giallo* and science fiction.

The continental Gothic borrowed many monsters from Anglo-American cinema and literature — vampires, mad scientists, werewolves, mummies and ghosts — because these were internationally recognisable, but filmmakers also sporadically developed more *sui generis* characters to suit the exploitative nature of the industry. The most Gothic of these is, without a doubt, the punisher, who, despite not manifesting cohesively or sequentially, reared his resuscitated head in a few films of the period. This monster is a male revenant, actual or apparent, descended from a barbaric past and who intends on visiting violence upon predecessors or reckless passersby. Tied up aesthetically and thematically to the setting, his horrors are perpetrated upon a suitably archaic stage, typically a torture dungeon. His first significant appearance was in *La vergine di Norimberga* (*The Virgin of Nuremberg*, 1963), based on a 1960 pulp novel by Frank Bogart (Maddalena Gui), as a mysterious presence who roams the dark passages of a German family castle. The ancestral 'il giustiziere', or executioner in Italian, played by Mirko Valentin, is said to have lived 300 years ago and gained notoriety for his punishment of disobedient women 'impenitent of their sins'.[17] As it turns out, the monster is actually an ex-SS officer general punished for plotting against Hitler by being turned into a 'living skull', that is, by having most of the flesh on his face surgically removed. This hardly matters, as he effectively plays the part of the punisher, going as far as to wear his signature red mantle and hood. In *Il boia scarlatto* (*Bloody Pit of Horror*, 1964), the merciless 'crimson executioner' is described by a voice-over as a man who 'dared to take into [his] own hands the laws of both God and men' and 'caused inhuman suffering not from any sense of justice but from hatred and self-gratification'.[18] Judged, sentenced to death and entombed by a tribunal in 1648, he swears he will return to be avenged and reign as 'the supreme law'. When a group of models and members of a pulp publishing house attempt a quick photoshoot in the castle where he died, the crimes resume. The ghost is ultimately proven to be human, nothing more than an assumed identity taken by a mentally unstable man with a strong (and rather convenient) resemblance to the executioner. The later *Gli orrori del castello di Norimberga* (*Baron Blood*, 1972) treads similar ground with its seventeenth-century baron, Otto von Kleist. Known for his passion for impaling his enemies, he is accidentally revived by a descendant and embarks on a mission to restore the 'devil's castle', as the locals call it, to its former greatness.[19]

In these three films, the punisher serves the clear narrative and dramatic purpose of dishing out visceral numbers. The opening scene of *La vergine di Norimberga*, which follows a gowned heroine's (Rossana Podestà) wandering from her bed to a display torture chamber upon being awakened by a scream, climaxes with her discovery of a corpse inside an iron maiden, the dead woman's eyes gouged out by metal spikes. In *Il boia scarlatto*, one of the instruments of torture is a rotating contraption with blades conspicuously placed to tear through the female victims' bras and breasts. The objectification of the scantily clad women in this film is not unique – the executioner is also shown oiling up his muscled body in some detail – but it powerfully resonates with earlier sequences where the same models pose suggestively for male photographers. Appropriately, and metafictionally, the shoot happens to be for the covers of a lurid erotic horror comic.[20] In *Baron Blood*, the inventive murder and chase sequences are not too different in pace and structure from those of the *gialli* Bava was directing at the time, notably *Reazione a catena* (*A Bay of Blood*, 1971). The supernatural element resonates with the gloomy Gothic mise-en-scène and enables an unexpected monstrous reveal at the end, but does not significantly alter the overall slasher dynamics. The Gothic in the punisher films opens the doors to visual and moral excesses that can be retrojected to the Middle Ages while catering to the libidinous, where not salacious, tendencies of exploitation cinema. In other words, the actions of the punisher are wrong and actively condemned, but they also hypocritically enable licentious spectacles. At the same time, the unforgiving moral codes expounded by the punishers, and mirrored by the austere and dilapidated look of their castles, can be read as a critique of the censorship that has routinely repressed Gothic titillation; they are grotesque reflections of religious views on indecency, especially the sins of the flesh.[21] The repressed past is here also a repressed present, with the gratuitous macabre acts of justice encouraging modern viewers to question their own reasons for watching.

The punisher figure also surfaced in Spain in a series of films starring horror legend Paul Naschy (Jacinto Molina). Carlos Aured's *El espanto surge de la tumba* (*Horror Rises from the Tomb*, 1973), filmed from a script by Naschy, introduced Alaric de Marnac, a medieval French warlock killed for evil crimes like drinking 'human blood, of both the living and the dead', cannibalism and the sacrifice of new-borns and young girls in black masses.[22] Sentenced to death by beheading, he vows to return to wreak his vengeance upon humanity and those who dared to stand against him and his mistress Mabille de Lancré (Helga Line). According to the rules of Gothic reanimation, Alaric is brought back from the dead after his head is dug out from a coffer in the grounds of a nearby monastery and reattached to the rest of his body. The character was inspired by the real Gilles de Rais, the fifteenth-century knight and alleged serial killer of children said to have inspired the Bluebeard fairy tale. Like its Italian counterparts, the film is notoriously violent and has even been called one of Spain's first splatters (Pulido 2015: 243). Some of its scenes, especially those where hearts are ripped out of chests with the help of a sickle, would only remain untouched in the international cut. The second film to explore this figure, albeit under the name of Gilles de Lancré, was *El mariscal del infierno* (*Devil's Possessed*, 1974). Although it was not directly linked to the 1972 film, set as it is entirely in the fifteenth century, it covered similar thematic ground. Gilles (Naschy) is a knight with ambitions to overthrow the king and who, taking heed from his mistress, resorts to the black arts in his search for power and immortality. The film is more historical in its approach and renders the despot a sad and tragic figure, driven to madness by the voices of those he has tortured and killed. Naschy would return to Alaric one last time in the sequel *Latidos de pánico* (*Panic Beats*, 1983), which he directed himself.

The apparently non-supernatural premise – a descendant of de Marnac, Paul (Naschy) successfully scares his frail wife to death by staging the return of his ancestor – is overturned when the knight actually comes back from the dead. *Latidos de pánico* lays bare its exploitational nature in the very opening scene, which tracks the persecution of a fully naked woman by an armoured Alaric, flail in hand.[23]

If the early-to-mid-1960s were the golden age of Italian horror films, Spain would not lag behind, quickly entering a feverish period of overproduction that would last until the mid-1970s.[24] Many of its films recycled classic monsters – the mummy, in *La venganza de la momia* (*The Mummy's Revenge*, 1975), or the werewolf, in the Waldemar Daninsky series, which saw Paul Naschy play the role of the tragic lycanthrope in at least eight films between 1968 and 1980.[25] Films like *El jorobado de la morgue* (*Hunchback of the Morgue*, 1972), which drew inspiration from the Frankenstein myth and from other filmic Quasimodos but also contained a Lovecraftian monster, continued to mash together characters and scenarios borrowed from the wider horror pool. As happened in Italy, this frenzy of activity also led to more original projects. For example, *La cruz del diablo* (*Cross of the Devil*, 1975), a Spanish film directed by the Brit John Gilling, adapted the much-neglected Gothic legends of Spanish Romantic writer Gustavo Adolfo Bécquer.

Some of the most distinctive Gothic characters of the period were the knights Templar in Amando de Ossorio's low-budget independent *La noche del terror ciego* (*Tombs of the Blind Dead*, 1972), a co-production with Portugal. Its resuscitated twelfth-century crusaders cannot see, their eyes having been pecked by crows after the king of Spain had the men hanged for sacrificing virgins. The legend, retold by the musty-looking Professor Canal (José Thelman), 'an authority on the Middle Ages', allows for the showdown between the superstitious past and the modern science-driven present that characterises the Gothic.[26] In a scene where the possible reason for Virginia's (María Elena Arpón) death is discussed openly, the coroner (Juan Cortés) proposes that she may have been 'the victim of a death ritual', an idea immediately refuted by Roger (César Burner) on the grounds that it is 'impossible' for black masses to still be taking place in the twentieth century.[27] The characters' clothes, modish and bright-coloured, and liberated attitudes towards sexuality stand in direct contrast to the murderous hordes of the Blind Dead. The latter first manifest in the ruins of an old church to a plucky young girl in a scene that clearly juxtaposes the new and modern with the obsolete and derelict. The Gothic here stages a generational conflict between old-fashioned and contemporary ideals regarding social behaviours and, especially, impropriety as perceived by the stalwarts of religion and patriarchy. The knights Templar would return in three sequels that rewrote and muddled their mythology, becoming imbricated with Lovecraft's fictional grimoire the Necromonicon in *La noche de las gaviotas* (*Night of the Seagulls*, 1975).

Despite their uniqueness and subsequent cult following, neither Alaric de Marnac nor the knights Templar were technically that new, deriving many of their characteristics from other Gothic monsters and formulae. Alaric looks and acts like a vampire for the last third of *El espanto surge de la tumba*, donning a long black cape, sucking the blood of

Figure 6.2 The knights Templar in *La noche del terror ciego* (*Tombs of the Blind Dead*, 1972) stage the Gothic confrontation between the liberal present and ossified moral attitudes.

his victims and recoiling in terror at the sight of an amulet in the shape of Thor's Hammer that, to all intents and purposes, operates as a crucifix. His revival is derived from folklore (the superstition that vampires may be destroyed by beheading) and from other vampire films like *Dracula Has Risen from the Grave* and *Taste the Blood of Dracula*, where the touch or imbibement of blood is enough to restore supernatural life to a corpse. As for the knights Templar, Ángel Gómez Rivero proposes that their look and costumes were inspired by Bécquer's legends 'El monte de las ánimas' ('The Forest of the Souls in Purgatory', 1861) and 'El miserere' ('The Miserere', 1862), writings de Ossorio admired (2009: 265–266). Yet the Blind Dead's connections to zombie films, especially to George A. Romero's *Night of the Living Dead* (1968), are apparent: they slowly lurch forward, are unable to speak, feed on their victims and their skeletons are reminiscent of the putrescent bodies of the living dead.[28] De Ossorio's brilliance was to create a new fictional monster that was inherently Catholic in its history and censorial leanings but whose qualities were intelligible to an international audience. The Gothic in *La noche del terror ciego* and *El espanto surge de la tumba* evokes a number of aesthetic and thematic connotations that both help sell the films and codify traditional tropes such as the evil return of the past or the tensions between superstition and science.

The late 1960s marked the beginning of what has come to be known as the 'New Hollywood', a renaissance period in American cinema epitomised by films like *Bonnie and Clyde* and *The Graduate* (1967) that caused controversy thanks to their daring themes and graphic depictions of violence (Krämer 2006: 1). The early 1970s also saw the release of auteuristic films like *The Devils*, *Straw Dogs* (1971), *A Clockwork Orange* (1971) and, a little later, *Salò o le 120 giornate di Sodoma* (*Salò, or the 120 Days of Sodom*, 1975), which pushed the envelope of what was permissible on screen. Their contentious topics and depictions of brutal acts and sexualised violence even led to bannings and withdrawals in some countries. It is therefore to be expected that, for all the continuity between exploitation Gothic in the 1960s and the 1970s, the films of the latter decade would accentuate explicitness and exhibit a few distinctive traits. One of these was that the setting began to be only intermittently retrojected and would more commonly become the present, with Gothic architecture (ostentatious old villas and castles) once again standing in for outdated belief systems, returning curses and repressed traumas. Another was that black-and-white filmmaking, with its emphasis on evocative chiaroscuro and shadow play, would be left behind in favour of bright and vivid colours. A third characteristic of this new exploitation Gothic was its dilution and hybridisation with other genres like the popular *giallo*, especially as practised by Argento. This meant that some Gothics suddenly gained black-gloved killers and a focus on suspense and gruesome set pieces. *Il rosso segno della follia* (*A Hatchet for the Honeymoon*, 1970), *La notte che Evelyn uscì dalla tomba* (*The Night Evelyn Came Out of the Grave*, 1971), *Un bianco vestito per Marialé* (*Spirits of Death*, 1972), *La dama rossa uccide sette volte* (*The Red Queen Kills Seven Times*, 1972), *Tutti i colori del buio* (*All the Colors of the Dark*, 1972), *La morte ha sorriso all'assassino* (*Death Smiles on a Murderer*, 1973) and *La morte negli occhi del gatto* (*Seven Deaths in the Cat's Eye*, 1973) all updated the Female Gothic tradition in narratives where the scares and uncanniness of previous horrors were replaced by sometimes heavily stylised murders that ultimately dispelled the supernatural in favour of surprise culprits.

The fourth of the changes the Gothic underwent in the early 1970s is perhaps the most noticeable: what had previously manifested as 'suggestive eroticism and mild nudity' (Curti 2017: 1) turned, after the relaxation of censorship in 1968, into the ubiquitous inclusion of (where possible, full frontal) nudity and softcore sex scenes. The Gothic in films such as *Las vampiras* (*Vampyros Lesbos*, 1971), *Byleth (Il demone dell'incesto)* (*Byleth – The Demon of Incest*, 1972), *Il plenilunio delle vergini* (*The Devil's Wedding Night*, 1973), *Riti, magie nere e segrete orge nel Trecento* (*The Reincarnation of Isabel*, 1973), *Nuda per Satana* (*Nude for Satan*, 1974), *Vampyres* (1974), *La Bête* (*The Beast*, 1975), *La pelle sotto gli artigli* (*The Skin Under the Claws*, 1975), *La sanguisuga conduce la danza* (*The Bloodsucker Leads the Dance*, 1975), *La Comtesse noire* (*Female Vampire*, 1975) and *L'osceno desiderio – Le pene nel ventre* (*Obscene Desire*, 1978) is not completely disconnected from horror, but is, above all, made to accommodate erotic and sexual elements that follow clearly exploitative parameters: a voyeuristic and fetishistic male gaze, lesbian sex scenes and sadistic tableaux where women are tied up and either killed or tortured.[29] The lines between erotic cinema and pornography became decidedly blurred in cases like that of *Malabimba* (*The Malicious Whore*, 1979), a sex-horror where the Gothic is really mere window-dressing for a series of interlinked explicit sex scenes.[30] These sex-horrors, or 'horrotica', would begin to decline after the arrival of actual hardcore films rendered the hybrid redundant (Tohill and Tombs 1995: 5). In Spain, the introduction of the 'S' certificate, which permitted the wide distribution of softcore pornography after democracy was restored, meant that the industry focused on sex-oriented films, encouraging one-time sleazy-horror directors to pursue more openly erotic ventures (Kowalski 2004).

Exploitation Gothic shows that, by the 1970s, Gothic cinema no longer belonged in the mainstream – it had moved away from big screens into smaller 'adults only' venues ('seconda' and 'terza' vision theatres). The same had happened in America, where drive-in and grindhouse cinemas had become the home of sexploitation, blaxploitation films – some of which, like the memorable *Blacula* (1972), *Blackenstein* (1973) and *Dr. Black, Mr. Hyde* (1976), reconceptualised classical Gothic characters for new audiences – and Euro horror.[31] In the 1970s, horror began a process of transformation, especially after the critical successes of *The Exorcist* and *Jaws*, both of which were nominated for the Academy Award for Best Picture. If the Gothic's trappings had once allowed for the exploration of repressed desires, the gradual liberation cinema had undergone since the 1960s would make its aesthetic trimmings unnecessary, even passé. What few exploitation Gothics surfaced in the early 1980s were either essentially nostalgic and did poorly, as in the Naschy-led *El retorno del hombre lobo* (*Night of the Werewolf*, 1980) and *El aullido del diablo* (*Howl of the Devil*, 1987), or else displayed the Gothic ornamentally and sparingly, as in Argento's *Inferno* (1980) and *Opera* (1987) or Lucio Fulci's *Paura nella città dei morti viventi* (*City of the Living Dead*, 1980) and

Quella villa accanto al cimitero (*The House by the Cemetery*, 1981). These films represent the last throes of a by-then redundant way of shooting horror and of a struggling independent industry that would flounder after the 'decreto Miró' (Miró decree), intended to promote 'quality' pictures, was enforced by the socialist government in Spain in 1982 and the Eady Levy was terminated in the UK in 1985. As the rise of the slasher and of body horrors in the 1980s indicate, markets were changing and the times demanded a certain degree of contemporaneity, something diametrically opposed to the Gothic's preference for vague and nebulous pasts. The Gothic horrors of the 1960s would give way to occult supernaturalism, zombie gore and animal terrors, but would not disappear completely.

FILMOGRAPHY

5 tombe per un medium (*Terror-Creatures from the Grave*, Massimo Pupillo, 1965, Italy/USA)
A Clockwork Orange (Stanley Kubrick, 1971, UK/USA)
Amanti d'oltretomba (*Nightmare Castle*, Mario Caiano, 1965, Italy)
Blackenstein (William A. Levey, 1973, USA)
Blacula (William Crain, 1972, USA)
Bonnie and Clyde (Arthur Penn, 1967, USA)
Buio omega (*Beyond the Darkness*, Joe D'Amato, 1979, Italy)
Byleth (Il demone dell'incesto) (*Byleth – The Demon of Incest*, Leopoldo Savona, 1972, Italy)
Caltiki – Il mostro immortale (*Caltiki – The Immortal Monster*, Riccardo Freda, 1959, Italy/France)
Contronatura (*The Unnaturals*, Antonio Margheriti, 1969, Italy/West Germany)
Danza macabra (*Castle of Blood*, Antonio Margheriti and Sergio Corbucci, 1964, Italy/France)
Die Nackte und der Satan (*The Head*, Victor Trivas, 1959, Germany)
Dr. Black, Mr. Hyde (William Crain, 1976, USA)
Dr. Jekyll and Mr. Hyde (Rouben Mamoulian, 1931, USA)
Dracula (Terence Fisher, 1958, UK)

Drácula contra Frankenstein (Dracula, Prisoner of Frankenstein, Jesús Franco, 1972, Spain/France/Liechtenstein)
Dracula Has Risen from the Grave (Freddie Francis, 1968, UK)
Fascination (Jean Rollin, 1979, France)
Flesh for Frankenstein (Paul Morrissey, 1973, Italy/France)
Gli orrori del castello di Norimberga (Baron Blood, Mario Bava, 1972, Italy/West Germany)
Gritos en la noche (The Awful Dr. Orlof, Jesús Franco, 1962, Spain/France)
Ein Toter hing im Netz (Horrors of Spider Island, Fritz Böttger, 1960, Germany)
El aullido del diablo (Howl of the Devil, Paul Naschy, 1987, Spain)
El conde Drácula (Count Dracula, Jesús Franco, 1970, Spain/Italy/West Germany/Liechtenstein/UK)
El espanto surge de la tumba (Horror Rises from the Tomb, Carlos Aured, 1973, Spain)
El gran amor del conde Drácula (Count Dracula's Great Love, Javier Aguirre, 1973, Spain)
El jorobado de la morgue (Hunchback of the Morgue, Javier Aguirre, 1972, Spain)
El mariscal del infierno (Devil's Possessed, León Klimovsky, 1974, Spain/Argentina)
El retorno del hombre lobo (Night of the Werewolf, Jacinto Molina, 1980, Spain)
...Et mourir de plaisir (Blood and Roses, Roger Vadim, 1960, France/Italy)
Hexen bis aufs Blut gequält (Mark of the Devil, Michael Armstrong, 1970, West Germany)
Horror (The Blancheville Monster, Alberto de Martino, 1963, Italy/Spain)
House on Bare Mountain (Lee Frost, 1962, USA)
I lunghi capelli della morte (The Long Hair of Death, Antonio Margheriti, 1964, Italy)
I vampiri (The Vampires, Riccardo Freda, 1957, Italy)
Il boia scarlatto (Bloody Pit of Horror, Massimo Pupillo, 1964, Italy/USA)
Il mio amico Jekyll (My Friend, Dr. Jekyll, Marino Girolami, 1960, Italy)
Il mulino delle donne di pietra (Mill of the Stone Women, Giorgio Ferroni, 1960, Italy/France)
Il plenilunio delle vergini (The Devil's Wedding Night, Luigi Batzella and Joe D'Amato, 1973, Italy)
Il rosso segno della follia (A Hatchet for the Honeymoon, Mario Bava, 1970, Italy/Spain)
Inferno (Dario Argento, 1980, Italy)

Inquisición (Inquisition, Paul Naschy, 1976, Spain)
Jaws (Steven Spielberg, 1975, USA)
L'amante del vampiro (The Vampire and the Ballerina, Renato Polselli, 1960, Italy)
L'orribile segreto del Dr. Hichcock (The Horrible Dr. Hichcock, Riccardo Freda, 1962, Italy)
L'osceno desiderio – Le pene nel ventre (Obscene Desire, Giulio Petroni, 1978, Italy/Spain)
L'ultima preda del vampiro (The Playgirls and the Vampire, Piero Regnoli, 1960, Italy)
La Bête (The Beast, Walerian Borowczyk, 1975, France)
La cara del terror (Face of Terror, Isidoro M. Ferry, 1962, Spain)
La Chute de la maison Usher (The Fall of the House of Usher, Jean Epstein, 1928, France)
La Comtesse noire (Female Vampire, Jesús Franco, 1975, Belgium/France)
La cripta e l'incubo (Terror in the Crypt, Camillo Mastrocinque, 1964, Italy/Spain)
La cruz del diablo (Cross of the Devil, John Gilling, 1975, Spain)
La dama rossa uccide sette volte (The Red Queen Kills Seven Times, Emilio Miraglia, 1972, Italy/West Germany)
La frusta e il corpo (The Whip and the Body, Mario Bava, 1963, Italy/France)
La mano de un hombre muerto (The Sadistic Baron Von Klaus, Jesús Franco, 1962, Spain)
La marca del hombre lobo (Frankenstein's Bloody Terror, Enrique López Eguiluz, 1968, Spain)
La maschera del demonio (Black Sunday, Mario Bava, 1960, Italy)
La morte ha sorriso all'assassino (Death Smiles on a Murderer, Joe D'Amato, 1973, Italy)
La morte negli occhi del gatto (Seven Deaths in the Cat's Eye, 1973, Antonio Margheriti, Italy/West Germany/France)
La noche de las gaviotas (Night of the Seagulls, Amando de Ossorio, 1975, Spain)
La noche de Walpurgis (The Werewolf Versus the Vampire Woman, León Klimovsky, 1971, Spain/West Germany)
La noche del terror ciego (Tombs of the Blind Dead, Amando de Ossorio, 1972, Spain/Portugal)
La notte che Evelyn uscì dalla tomba (The Night Evelyn Came Out of the Grave, Emilio Miraglia, 1971, Italy)

La novia ensangrentada (The Blood Spattered Bride, Vicente Aranda, 1972, Spain)
La pelle sotto gli artigli (The Skin Under the Claws, Alessandro Santini, 1975, Italy)
La residencia (The House That Screamed, Narciso Ibáñez Serrador, 1969, Spain)
La saga de los Drácula (The Dracula Saga, León Klimovsky, 1973, Spain)
La sanguisuga conduce la danza (The Bloodsucker Leads the Dance, Alfredo Rizzo, 1975, Italy)
La strage dei vampiri (Slaughter of the Vampires, Roberto Mauri, 1962, Italy)
La torre de los siete jorobados (The Tower of the Seven Hunchbacks, Edgar Neville, 1944, Spain)
La Vampire nue (The Nude Vampire, Jean Rollin, 1970, France)
La venganza de la momia (The Mummy's Revenge, Carlos Aured, 1975, Spain)
La vergine di Norimberga (The Virgin of Nuremberg, Antonio Margheriti, 1963, Italy)
Lady Frankenstein (Mel Welles, 1971, Italy)
Las vampiras (Vampyros Lesbos, Jesús Franco, 1971, West Germany/Spain)
Latidos de pánico (Panic Beats, Jacinto Molina, 1983, Spain)
Le Frisson des vampires (The Shiver of the Vampires, Jean Rollin, 1971, France)
Le Moine (The Monk, Adonis Kyrou, 1972, France/Italy/West Germany)
Le Viol du vampire (The Rape of the Vampire, Jean Rollin, 1968, France)
Les Lèvres rouges (Daughters of Darkness, Harry Kümel, 1971, Belgium/France/West Germany)
Les Yeux sans visage (Eyes Without a Face, Georges Franju, 1960, France/Italy)
Lèvres de sang (Lips of Blood, Jean Rollin, 1975, France)
Los monstruos del terror (Assignment Terror, Hugo Fregonese and Tulio Demicheli, 1970, Spain/West Germany/Italy)
Malabimba (The Malicious Whore, Andrea Bianchi, 1979, Italy)
Malombra (Carmine Gallone, 1917, Italy)
Malombra (Mario Soldati, 1942, Italy)
Malpertuis (Harry Kümel, 1971, Belgium)
Metempsyco (Tomb of Torture, Antonio Boccacci, 1963, Italy)
Morgiana (Juraj Herz, 1972, Czechoslovakia)
Night of the Living Dead (George A. Romero, 1968, USA)
Nosferatu: Phantom der Nacht (Nosferatu the Vampyre, Werner Herzog, 1979, West Germany)
Nuda per Satana (Nude for Satan, Luigi Batzella, 1974, Italy)

Opera (Dario Argento, 1987, Italy)
Orgy of the Dead (Stephen C. Apostolof, 1965, USA)
Pánico en el Transiberiano (*Horror Express*, Eugenio Martín, 1974, UK/Spain)
Paura nella città dei morti viventi (*City of the Living Dead*, Lucio Fulci, 1980, Italy)
Psycho (Alfred Hitchcock, 1960, USA)
Quella villa accanto al cimitero (*The House by the Cemetery*, Lucio Fulci, 1981, Italy)
Reazione a catena (*A Bay of Blood*, Mario Bava, 1971, Italy)
Rękopis znaleziony w Saragossie (*The Saragossa Manuscript*, Wojciech Jerzy Has, 1965, Poland)
Requiem pour un vampire (*Requiem for a Vampire*, Jean Rollin, 1971, France)
Riti, magie nere e segrete orge nel Trecento (*The Reincarnation of Isabel*, Renato Polselli, 1973, Italy)
Salò o le 120 giornate di Sodoma (*Salò, or the 120 Days of Sodom*, Pier Paolo Pasolini, 1975, Italy/France)
Seddok, l'erede di Satan (*Atom Age Vampire*, Anton Giulio Majano, 1960, Italy)
Straw Dogs (Sam Peckinpah, 1971, UK/USA)
Suspiria (Dario Argento, 1977, Italy)
Taste the Blood of Dracula (Peter Sasdy, 1970, UK)
Tempi duri per i vampiri (*Uncle Was a Vampire*, Stefano Vanzina [Steno], 1959, Italy/France)
The Brides of Dracula (Terence Fisher, 1960, UK)
The Corpse Vanishes (Wallace Fox, 1942, USA)
The Devils (Ken Russell, 1971, UK)
The Exorcist (William Friedkin, 1973, USA)
The Graduate (Mike Nichols, 1967, USA)
Tutti i colori del buio (*All the Colors of the Dark*, Sergio Martino, 1972, Italy/Spain)
Un angelo per satana (*An Angel for Satan*, Camillo Mastrocinque, 1966, Italy)
Un bianco vestito per Marialé (*Spirits of Death*, Romano Scavoli, 1972, Italy)
Un vampiro para dos (*A Vampire for Two*, Pedro Lazaga, 1965, Spain)
Valerie a týden divů (*Valerie and Her Week of Wonders*, Jaromil Jireš, 1970, Czechoslovakia)
Vampir – Cuadecuc (*Vampire – Cuadecuc*, Pere Portabella, 1971, Spain)
Vampyres (José Ramón Larraz, 1974, UK)

NOTES

1 The Spanish film famously courted controversy for its fantastic scenario, which it was forced to dispel as a dream after encountering objections from the board of censors.

2 In Italy, thirty horror films were made between 1960 and 1966 alone (Hunter 2016: 35). In Spain, 1972 stands as the zenith of horror filmmaking, with nearly 25% of all Spanish films made that year – a whopping 25 out of 104 – belonging to the horror genre (Matellano 2009: 22).

3 To the two adaptations of *Malombra* in 1917 and in 1942, one must add a string of Poe adaptations in the 1910s by Arturo Ambrosio. For details, see Rigby (2016: 54–57).

4 This excitement travelled outside the filmic world too. Hammer's *Dracula* led to a veritable 'horror craze' (Curti 2015: 16) in the publishing world that included the release of vampire novels, photo novels and comic books.

5 Quotations are taken from the American releases of the films. Where these do not exist, the words are my own translation.

6 Eroticism in continental horror could be said to start with the German films *Die Nackte und der Satan* (*The Head*, 1959) and *Ein Toter hing im Netz* (*Horrors of Spider Island*, 1960), both of which feature underdressed women. I do not include them in this discussion because, despite being mad scientist films, they make few aesthetic concessions to the Gothic.

7 It is, of course, possible to trace the roots of exploitation cinema back to the early twentieth century and especially the 1950s, when teenage exploitation films dominated the market (Shaefer 1999).

8 Sometimes the names of scriptwriters from one of the co-producing countries would be included purely for the sake of obtaining subventions.

9 Naschy claimed in his memoirs that, although the character was fleshed out in *La noche de Walpurgis*, he already had Báthory in mind when he created Countess Wandesa in *La marca del hombre lobo* (Naschy 1997: 215).

10 In order of release, these post-Franju films are *Seddok, l'erede di Satan* (*Atom Age Vampire*, 1960), *Gritos en la noche* and *La cara del terror* (*Face of Terror*, 1962).
11 I am quoting the English subtitles in the Italian version of the film distributed by Arrow Video in 2013.
12 The Italian term *filone* (*filoni* in the plural) usually designates a type of popular cinema less concerned with stable notions of genre and more with speedy profiteering from trends.
13 The 'nudie cutie', where nudity was partially justified by an often very loose narrative, is considered to have begun in America in 1959. Very few of the nudie cuties were Gothic, although *House on Bare Mountain* (1962) and *Orgy of the Dead* (1965) are noteworthy exceptions.
14 The fact that Rollin directed actress Brigitte Lahaie both in a pornographic film and in two of his horrors literalises the generic blurring of sex and fear in his work.
15 For Bava, see Lucas (2007), Luigi (2011), Pezzotta (2013), Abad (2014) and Howarth (2014). For Franco, see Mesnildot (2004), Aguilar (2011), Serrano Cueto (2011) and Thrower and Grainger (2015). For Naschy, see Agudo (2009). For Rollin, see Odell and Le Blanc (2004), Marinone (2015) and Hinds (2016).
16 The second scene is technically a substitution. In the Italian version, Stinel (Ennio Balbo) more tactfully hangs himself.
17 I am quoting the American English-dubbed version of the film distributed by Shriek Show in 2004.
18 I am quoting the American English-dubbed version of the film distributed by Image Entertainment and Something Weird.
19 I am quoting the English subtitles in the Italian version of the film distributed by Arrow Video in 2013.
20 As Curti notes, comics and super heroes in general had a big impact on Italian cinema of the mid-to-late-1960s (2015: 140).
21 In *Il boia scarlatto*, this connection is spelled out for the viewer when the voice-over explains that the executioner's 'castle will stand throughout the centuries as a reminder of the barbarism committed within its walls'.
22 I am quoting the English dubbing in the Spanish version of the film distributed by Grapevine Video in 2016.

23 The scene recalls the opening of a much-earlier film, Luigi Batzella's *Nuda per Satana* (*Nude for Satan*, 1974), where Rita Calderoni's character, wearing nothing but an open nightgown, runs through some dark woods.
24 The company Profilmes even specialised in horror cinema for a short while (1972–76) during the dying years of Franco's dictatorship (Pulido 2012: 65–67). This steady investment in horror cinema was new to Spain.
25 I write that there are at least eight films in the Waldemar series because there was a ninth now lost film, apparently made in 1968, named *Las noches del hombre lobo* (*Nights of the Werewolf*). Despite the fact that the film has not been found, Naschy claimed it was definitely shot.
26 I am quoting the English dubbing in the version of the film distributed by Anchor Bay in 2005.
27 For some reason, the dubbed American version of the film changes Roger's key line in the Spanish 'estamos en pleno siglo veinte' ('this is the twentieth century') to 'I want to look into this myself'.
28 It is perhaps important to point out that de Ossorio denied both that his characters were derived from Bécquer's works or that they were zombies, suggesting instead that they felt closer to mummies and vampires (Rigby 2016: 242).
29 Although *Vampyres* is technically a British film, it is often included in histories of Spanish fantaterror due to its Spanish director.
30 One of the versions of the film even includes extraneous pornographic inserts (Curti 2017: 210).
31 For more on this topic, see Rhodes (2003), Fisher and Walker (2016) and Waddell (2018).

BIBLIOGRAPHY

Abad, J. (2014) *Mario Bava: El cine de las tinieblas*, Madrid: T&B Editores.
Agudo, Á. (2009) *Paul Naschy: La máscara de Jacinto Molina*, Pontevedra: Scifiworld.
Aguilar, C. (2011) *Jesús Franco*, Madrid: Cátedra.
Curti, R. (2015) *Italian Gothic Horror Films, 1957–1969*, Jefferson, NC: McFarland.
Curti, R. (2017) *Italian Gothic Horror Films, 1970–1979*, Jefferson, NC: McFarland.

Di Chiara, F. (2016) 'Domestic Films Made for Export: Modes of Production of the 1960s Italian Horror Film', in S. Baschiera and R. Hunter (eds) *Italian Horror Cinema*, Edinburgh: Edinburgh University Press.

Fisher, A. and J. Walker (eds) (2016) *Grindhouse: Cultural Exchange on 42nd Street, and Beyond*, London and New York: Bloomsbury.

Gómez Rivero, A. (2009) *Cine zombi*, Madrid: Calamar Ediciones.

Hawkins, J. (2000) *Cutting Edge: Art-Horror and the Horrific Avant-Garde*, Minneapolis: University of Minnesota Press.

Heffernan, K. (2004) *Ghouls, Gimmicks, and Gold: Horror Films and the American Movie Business, 1953–1968*, London and Durham, NC: Duke University Press.

Hinds, D. (2016) *Fascination: The Celluloid Dreams of Jean Rollin*, London: Headpress.

Howarth, T. (2014) *The Haunted Worlds of Mario Bava*, rev. and exp., London and Baltimore, MD: Midnight Marquee Press.

Hunter, I. Q. (2009) 'Exploitation as Adaptation', in I. R. Smith (ed.) *Cultural Borrowings: Appropriation, Reworking, Transformation*, Nottingham: Scope.

Hunter, I. Q. (2013) *British Trash Cinema*, London: BFI.

Hunter, R. (2016) 'Domestic Films Made for Export: Modes of Production of the 1960s Italian Horror Film', in S. Baschiera and R. Hunter (eds) *Italian Horror Cinema*, Edinburgh: Edinburgh University Press.

Kowalski, D. (2004) 'Rated S: Softcore Pornography and the Spanish Transition to Democracy, 1977–1982', in A. Lázaro-Reboll and A. Willis (eds) *Spanish Popular Cinema*, Manchester: Manchester University Press.

Krämer, P. (2006) *The New Hollywood: From Bonnie and Clyde to Star Wars*, London and New York: Wallflower.

Lázaro-Reboll, A. (2012) *Spanish Horror Film*, Edinburgh: Edinburgh University Press.

Lucas, T. (2007) *Mario Bava: All the Colors of the Dark*, Cincinnati, OH: Video Watchdog.

Luigi, C. (2011) *Mario Bava: Master of Horror*, Roma: Profondo Rosso.

Marinone, I. (2015) *Surrealism in the Service of the Fantastic: Jean Rollin, a 'Parallel' Director in Libertarian French Cinema*, Hastings: Christie Books.

Matellano, V. (2009) *Spanish Horror*, Madrid: T&B Editores.

Mathijs, E. and J. Sexton (2011) *Cult Cinema: An Introduction*, Oxford and Malden, MA: Wiley-Blackwell.

Mesnildot, S. du (2004) *Jess Franco: Énergies du fantasme*, Aix-en-Provence: Rouge Profond.

Naschy, P. (1997) *Memorias de un hombre lobo*, Madrid: Alberto Santos Editor.

Odell, C. and M. Le Blanc (2004) 'Jean Rollin: Le Sang d'un Poète du Cinema', in E. Mathijs and X. Mendik (eds) *Alternative Europe: Eurotrash and Exploitation Cinema since 1945*, London and New York: Wallflower Press.

Pezzotta, A. (2013) *Mario Bava*, Milan: Il Castoro Cinema.

Pulido, J. (2012) *La década de oro del cine de terror español (1967–1976)*, Madrid: T&B Editores.

Pulido, J. (2015) 'El espanto surge de la tumba', in R. Higueras (ed.) *Cine fantástico y de terror español: De los origines a la edad de oro (1912–83)*, Madrid: T&B Editores.

Rhodes, G. D. (2003) *Horror at the Drive-In: Essays in Popular Americana*, Jefferson, NC: McFarland.

Rigby, J. (2016) *Euro Gothic: Classics of Continental Horror Cinema*, Cambridge: Signum Books.

Serrano Cueto, J. M. (2011) *Jess Franco: Tutto sul suo cinema spiazzante. Da Orson Welles alla pornografia*, Roma: Profondo Rosso.

Shaefer, E. (1999) *'Bold! Daring! Shocking! True!': A History of Exploitation Films, 1919–1959*, London and Durham, NC: Duke University Press.

Thrower, S. and J. Grainger (2015) *Murderous Passions: The Cinema of Jesús Franco*, London: Strange Attractor Press.

Tohill, C. and P. Tombs (1995) *Immoral Tales: Sex and Horror Cinema in Europe 1956–1984*, London: Titan Books.

Waddell, C. (2018) *The Style of Sleaze: The American Exploitation Film, 1959–1977*, Edinburgh: Edinburgh University Press.

7

LATE DISPERSIONS

The Gothic aesthetic had manifested in genres other than horror well before the 1980s. It had appeared in the women-led melodramas of the 1940s, in Abbott and Costello's monster parodies and in 1970s sexploitation flicks, to name a few. The 1960s also saw significant developments of the non-horrific Gothic on television, especially in the shape of the new 'magicom' or 'fantastic family sitcom' (Wheatley 2006: 126). The Addams Family (1964–66), adapted from the cartoons by Charles Addams, turned what were once grotesque characters into an endearing bunch. Their signature mansion and, as the show's song put it, 'kooky', 'all-together ooky' quirks were played for laughs, rather than screams. The similarly benign protagonists in The Munsters (1964–66) were even more evidently in debt to horror's history, with their costumes and appearances deliberately looking back to Universal films.[1] Scooby-Doo, Where Are You? (1969–70), an animated cartoon series for children following the adventures of a group of four teenagers and a talking dog as they investigate hauntings and other horrific mysteries, also routinely revealed its chills to be nothing more than hoaxes. But perhaps the show that best captured the Gothic's tonal shift was Dark Shadows (1966–71), whose classical-looking vampire

Barnabas Collins (Jonathan Frid) gradually transformed from fearful antagonist to helpful, charismatic hero over the course of the show's life. For a while, these new likeable Gothic monsters from another time, their clothes and rituals rickety, happily cohabitated with those of exploitation cinema. They would eventually overtake their sombre cousins following horror's modernisation.

Film critic Kim Newman has suggested that, with 'Count Yorga and Carl Kolchak, American gothic horror died' (2011: 46) and that, '[c]ommercially, the gothic mode has been dead since *The Exorcist*' (49). These are both interconnected and complex statements. The success of Friedkin's film evinced that there was an audience for big-budget horror, a product against which smaller independent films and industries could not compete, as well as for a horror cinema set in the present. The success of other urban and occult-themed horrors, such as *Rosemary's Baby* (1968) and *The Omen*, as well as the rise of the *giallo* in Italy and, eventually, of the slasher in the States, pointed to important changes in audience taste. Viewers and filmmakers started to favour a type of horror decoupled from the Gothic aesthetic that had long contained its libidinal undercurrents. Gothic horror began to recede because its aesthetic cues and temporal retrojections were no longer necessary; its distancing techniques had become somewhat unnecessary.[2] The vampires in *Count Yorga, Vampire* and the television film *The Night Stalker* (1972), not to mention Dracula himself in *Dracula A.D. 1972*, are relics of the past, cape-wearing aristocrats set in stark opposition to a liberated world with much more relaxed attitudes towards drugs and sexuality.[3] Throughout the late 1970s, and especially in the 1980s, bloodsuckers would become modern, edgy and subcultural (even underground) in *The Hunger* (1983), *Vamp* (1986) and *The Lost Boys* (1987). These new horror films also incorporated references to popular culture, humour and rock, pop or goth music in a bid to appeal to a teenage audience. Vampires became conspicuous next-door-neighbours in the television miniseries *Salem's Lot* and in *Fright Night* (1985), and even suave seducers in John Badham's adaptation of *Dracula* (1979) and Francis Ford Coppola's *Bram Stoker's*

Dracula (1992). All manner of monsters, from werewolves and mummies to Frankenstein monsters, cultists and reinvigorated, intestine-guzzling zombies, would roam modern horrors, their conditions and proclivities adapted to a genre that, although still indebted to its Gothic roots, was now reneging its origins in favour of new scenarios and characters.

The 'old' Gothic has manifested most consistently since the 1980s at the level of setting, in the chronotopes of the secluded Gothic castle and the secret-ridden cathedral, both of which are still connected to ideological regression and diseased states of mind. The medieval castle turns up in films like *Howling V: The Rebirth* (1989), where a Hungarian fortress is opened to a group of people harbouring a mystery werewolf descended from a family who committed suicide 500 years ago in order to stop the spread of a lycanthropic curse. The castle also appears, as a citadel, in *The Keep* (1983). Probably built by the Turks or the ancient Wallachians, its recesses contain supernatural entity Radu Molasar (Michael Carter), a creature that concretises the threat posed by the Nazis currently occupying the Romanian pass. In a telling speech by conflicted anti-fascist Captain Woermann (Jürgen Prochnow), he labels their mission a 'psychotic fantasy' and accuses his colleagues of 'hav[ing] released the foulness that dwells in all men's minds'. The Gothic castle also acts as an insane asylum for military personnel in the psychological drama *The Ninth Configuration* (1980), where the building also channels anxieties about the casualties of war, becoming a metaphor for the bottling up of psychological trauma. Brought over from Germany in 1900, the castle explicitly references the history of the Gothic on screen. A big poster of Bela Lugosi playing his most iconic role presides over the main hall and, upon being told that the place is not particularly 'therapeutic', one of the characters comments that 'that is what Dracula said about it'. As the film progresses and the real Jekyll and Hyde nature of the medical experiment comes to light, the place becomes another receptacle for the 'madness [that] grows out of evil'. Evil is aligned with the cruelty that fuelled the Vietnam war and, implicitly, humanity. Secluded, like the repressed murderous memories of Colonel Kane (Stacy Keach), the Gothic space emerges as a proxy for the inscrutable recesses of the psyche.

As for the cathedral, it plays a major role in the Gothic-inflected historical mystery *The Name of the Rose* (1986), where a medieval Benedictine abbey is eventually discovered to be housing Aristotle's second book of *Poetics*, dedicated to comedy. Venerable Jorge (Feodor Chaliapin, Jr.) perceives laughter as ungodly, so he poisons the pages of the coveted book with the intention that future readers shall pay for their sacrilegious indulgence with their lives. The abbey is connected to forbidden wisdom and, in its labyrinthine, booby-trapped library, with the need for its preservation and seclusion. It is, however, in *La Chiesa* (*The Church*, 1989) that the cathedral gets its most aesthetically horrific treatment as receptacle of buried and dangerous secrets. This luscious film, partly shot in Budapest's Matthias Church, kicks off in medieval Germany. There we are introduced to a band of Teutonic knights, 'a military religious order that defended the pilgrims traveling to the Holy Land at the time of the Crusades' and whose 'cruelty became legendary'.[4] These men slaughter a coven of 'witches' and then build a church over their mass grave, apparently to subdue their powers. In the 1980s, however, a new librarian (Tomas Arana) accidentally breaks the spell and lets loose the demonic forces, which take the shape of Catholic and occult-influenced hallucinations and creatures connected to the esoteric world. An earlier scene shows Lisa (Barbara Cupisti) reading Fulcanelli's *Le Mystère des Cathédrales* (*The Mystery of the Cathedrals*, 1926), a book that famously decoded the symbols used in the Gothic cathedrals of Europe, all of which purportedly display the secrets of alchemy. The bishop (Fiodor Chaliapin, Jr.) is also shown reading a Latin inscription on a tomb, 'depositum custodi' (keep that which is committed to thee), a message protecting a security mechanism that can hermetically seal the building.[5] A flashback scene involving the abbey's original architect discloses that a bout of the plague is possibly what was mistaken for 'evil' by the knights and that their theories regarding witches are nothing more than 'lies generated by sick evil minds'. The ending of *La chiesa* is impervious to literal readings: the discovery of the abbey's weak spot eventually prompts the rise of a cross made out of the corpses of heretics as well as the collapse of the building. There is a strange reparatory circularity to the events, with both Father Gus (Hugh Quarshie) and the sacristan's daughter, Lotte (Asia Argento), having previously appeared in different guises, as knight and victim, in the medieval sequences. Lotte's survival and Father Gus's sacrifice right the wrongs of the past and restore balance. *La chiesa* thus ostensibly suggests that the unleashed forces are not mystical but metaphorical, 'the evil that men do in the name of religion and nationhood' (Balmain 2007: 45), the crimes committed in the name of faith.

Religion and cults, although often not in themselves enough to conjure up the Gothic, have been recuperated for the anachronistic values of the ideologies and beliefs behind them. These are portrayed as cruel, merciless and sometimes the product of psychoses, ideas mirrored by the terrible spaces which accommodate the perpetrators' misdeeds. In *The Pit and the Pendulum* (1991), Stuart Gordon's loose adaptation of Poe's

Figure 7.1 In *La chiesa* (*The Church*, 1989), a cross made out of murdered heretics symbolises religion-fuelled cruelty.

short story, events are set in 1492 in Spain, a country under the stronghold of zealous Inquisitors like Torquemada (Lance Henriksen). The film takes place almost exclusively in the dungeons of the castle, where the tortures visited upon victims are the focus of the horrific scenes. As Torquemada gradually succumbs to the beauteous Maria (Rona de Ricci), a woman accused of witchcraft, his descent into lascivious sin follows the path of Father Lorenzo (Paul McGann) and Ambrosio (Vincent Cassel) in the two adaptations of *The Monk* made during this period.[6] The work of H. P. Lovecraft, best remembered for its sects and cosmic deities that go back to time immemorial, has long been the subject of modern adaptations. *Dark Waters* (1994), with its story of a young woman (Louise Salter) who visits an island monastery only to discover her own non-human origins, ventriloquises 'The Shadow over Innsmouth' (1936). Stuart Gordon's *Dagon* (2001) replaces Innsmouth with Imboca, an invented Galician counterpart to the coastal town in Lovecraft's story harbouring a breed of fish-like people. The church, which has been transformed into a temple to the God Dagon, is as important in creating the Gothic atmosphere in this film as the atavistic return to the sea implied by Paul's (Ezra Godden) amphibian transformation. The dark arts and ceremonials practised by cults are key to this strand of the Gothic, an aspect that makes it resonates with the witchcraft film. In *The Witch* (2015), the retrojection to 1630s New England serves precisely to explore the patriarchal core of Puritanism through Thomasin's (Anya Taylor-Joy) journey from law-abiding young girl to happy member of a coven. The setting, a forbidding, dark and untamed wilderness, echoes the American Gothic's obsession with the forest as a 'vast, lonely and possibly hostile space that ... resists any rational explanation' (Lloyd-Smith 2004: 93).

Traditional Gothic horror was in retreat by the early-to-mid-1980s, with only a temporary surge of interest in Gothic-inflected 'prestige horror' (Abbott 2010) in the 1990s exemplified by the successes of *Bram Stoker's Dracula* and *The Mummy* (1999). Yet the Gothic as an aesthetic marker did not stop existing or serving a function. Instead, it began to undergo a cultural transvaluation that would continue into the twenty-first century. This process relied heavily on consumer knowledge of formulas that meant its stock monsters, settings and tropes could become vessels for socio-political messages, arenas for the analysis of injustice, discrimination or the human predicament. The Gothic could, at this point, be decoupled from horror, its very underlying structures, responses (terror, disgust, suspense) and history experimented with. As the rise of the sympathetic zombie in the post-millennial period in films like *Wasting Away* (2007) and *Warm Bodies* (2013) and in the television series *In the Flesh* (2013–14) and *iZombie* (2015–19) demonstrates, this procedure need not rely on Gothic aesthetics, but on the more general alterity of the monstrous Other as constructed by incumbent ideological structures. Even then, the Gothic often provides a perfect stage upon which to question normative ideas about gender, sexuality, race, class and religion. Because the Gothic as an aesthetic correlates isolation and its temporal dynamics allow for explorations of regressive and retrograde codes of behaviour, its mystery-ridden narratives encourage the manifestation of the return of the repressed. For example, *The Elephant Man* (1980) gives the real story of Joseph Merrick (John Hurt), a nineteenth-century man with severe deformities, a thorough Gothic treatment that demonises those who mock or monetise his body. In another film, the histrionic *Gothic*, centred on the events that inspired Mary Shelley's *Frankenstein*, the Villa Diodati becomes a hotbed of sexual desire.

The Gothic's master myths (Dracula, Frankenstein, Jekyll and Hyde) probe the very boundaries of what it means to be human and this has kept them relevant. As palimpsestic figures that have given rise to a veritable legion of adaptations, parodies and paratexts, their contemporary Gothic re-imaginings tend to be influenced by previous cinematic adaptations. Hence the profusion of self-aware references in *Bram Stoker's Dracula* to the performances of Bela Lugosi and Christopher Lee and even to old visual effects techniques like back projection, miniatures, silhouettes and superimposed sequences, rendered in an artificial and knowing manner that homages the history of cinema. As

Stacey Abbott has argued, tributes and acknowledgements aside, the two main qualities that distinguish contemporary adaptations of *Dracula* are both their humanisation of the count and his association, especially since the publication of Raymond T. McNally and Radu Florescu's *In Search of Dracula* (1972) and its 1975 docu-drama adaptation *Vem var Dracula?* (*In Search of Dracula*, Calvin Floyd, 1975), with his historical inspiration, Vlad Țepeș, or Vlad the Impaler (2018: 201–202). In *Bram Stoker's Dracula*, the television film *Dark Prince: The True Story of Dracula* (2000), *Dracula: The Dark Prince* (2013) and *Dracula Untold* (2014), Dracula gains a love interest that humanises him, the reincarnated version of a beloved who tragically kills herself.[7] Importantly, he also becomes the focal narrative point. He is elevated to hero and martyr in *Dracula Untold*, where the curse of vampirism becomes the price to pay for the survival of his people. Led by CGI-heavy battle scenes and a narrative closer to high fantasy texts like *Game of Thrones* (2011–19), *Dracula Untold* shows how vampires have broadly, although not exclusively, become figures of sympathy and identification and how the Gothic past is being recuperated for nostalgic purposes. Issues of nationality, family honour and the barbaric nature of war have interestingly returned the Dracula myth to the chivalric origins of the Gothic romance.

As for Frankenstein and his creature, *The Rocky Horror Picture Show* (1975), a musical with a roster of memorable songs and performances, is a good early indication of how the Gothic would transform to encompass societal changes. Its parodic Dr. Frank-N-Furter (Tim Curry), the 'sweet transvestite from Transsexual, Transylvania', offered an innovative, if not wholly unproblematic, challenge to normative masculinity and, in his capacity to create life without women, championed a queer politics premised on the rejection of heteronormative reproduction. Similarly, *The Bride* (1985), which begins with the reanimation scene of the creature's wife-to-be, appeared interested in gender politics. Eva (Jennifer Beals) is raised by the doctor (Sting) not to become a 'pliable mistress', as suggested by his friend Clerval (Anthony Higgins), but 'as equal in thought and reasoning'. As Eva begins to develop feelings of love for other men, the doctor's philanthropic pretensions are put to the test, his possessive wish to keep the woman to himself eventually getting the best of him. *Mary Shelley's Frankenstein* (1994), despite its bid to faithfulness, included a new head-grafting scene that turned the creature into a monster-maker himself. It also shortened the distance between the doctor and his creation, suggesting that the latter may partly operate as a projection of his psyche. *Victor Frankenstein* (2015) devoted a significant amount of screen time to Igor (Daniel Radcliffe), who becomes a fully fleshed-out character. The film's most innovative feature is the humanisation of what was previously a grotesque, but its commercial failure, one that follows a string of unsuccessful cinematic rethinkings of Frankenstein in the twenty-first century, suggests that Shelley's novel may have most productively evolved outside of the horror genre, for example in AI tales of cyborgs and robots or in films incorporating 'hybrid creations and once-dead organisms brought back to life' (Friedman and Kavey 2016: 147). As I have argued elsewhere, it is possible to see in the rise of the viral zombie narrative and its preoccupation with science and the thin layer separating the living from the reanimated infected the latest manifestation of Frankencinema (Aldana Reyes 2018: 174–180).

Since Jekyll and his alternative personality, Hyde, are the quintessential embodiment of the universal and transhistorical repression of human urges that go against social propriety, they have, like *Frankenstein*, transcended their fin-de-siècle origins. They have appeared in modern times in, among others, the comedy *Dr. Jekyll and Ms. Hyde* (1995), the television film *Dr. Jekyll and Mr. Hyde* (2000), the horror film *The Strange Case of Dr. Jekyll and Mr. Hyde* (2006), the direct-to-video *Jekyll + Hyde* (2006) and the melodrama *Madame Hyde* (*Mrs. Hyde*, 2017), where the doctor becomes a timid physics teacher (Isabelle Huppert) struggling for recognition and respect at a French technical high school. These adaptations foreground the magical properties of science, which stimulate radical temperamental and physical (sometimes even gendered) transformations in the main characters. Again, as in *Frankenstein*, the stories revolve around the side effects and consequences of disrupting the natural order, commenting on technological development and the dangers of unbridled scientific discoveries that threaten to disintegrate traditional notions of the self. Although a box office disappointment, Mary Reilly is perhaps the most interesting of the modern refashionings of the Jekyll and Hyde myth. In it, Julia Roberts plays Jekyll's maid, Mary, who enters the household and ends up falling in love with both the doctor and his alter ego. Like the source 1990 Valerie Martin novel, this film is interesting because it puts a maid at the heart of a story almost exclusively populated by middle- and upper-class men. Mary's introspection, best captured by the motif of the rat teeth marks on her wrist and neck, casts her as a character with a troubled past who is nevertheless able to empathise with and understand Jekyll/Hyde. One of the defacing scribbles on Jekyll's notebook, which reads '[p]ain begins in understanding', underscores this idea. Mary, tortured by her alcoholic father, is able to forgive him. She explains that '[d]rink turned [her dad] into a different man', to which Jekyll (John Malkovich), tongue firmly in cheek, retorts that maybe alcohol simply set free another person inside him. Wrongdoing, Mary Reilly suggests, is a question of judgement and of sociohistorical and economic pressures. In this respect, the film illustrates the modern Gothic's ambiguous position towards evil.

Beyond the main three myths, the Gothic has travelled to the small screen in the shape of made-for-television films based on the literary canon. James L. Conway's The Fall of the House of Usher, shot in 1979 but not released in the United States until 1982, expanded upon Poe's story by adding a new character, Jonathan's wife (Charlene Tilton), who acts as the candelabrum-holding Gothic heroine, and by explaining the Usher curse as a consequence of devil worship. There were also two American adaptations of The Phantom of the Opera, one in 1983, with the action set in Budapest, and another in 1990, a part-musical television miniseries.[8] Following the acclaim of the British-American Frankenstein: The True Story (1973), a new television adaptation that gave the monster his voice back appeared in 1984. The Female

Gothic also experienced a resurgence. Charlotte Brontë's *Jane Eyre* was adapted as a serial in 1983 and again in 2006, and as a television film in 1997, with the melodramatic and romance elements of the original foregrounded.[9] Wilkie Collins's *The Woman in White* was turned into a similarly classic five-part serial in 1982; into a Marian-focused narrative BBC television film in 1997 and into another five-part miniseries in 2018. Of these, the only adaptation to receive a traditional Gothic treatment was the David Pirie-scripted 1997 version, which, in a self-referential nod, has Marian (Tara Fitzgerald) admit that the sisters are 'so fond of Gothic novels that we sometimes act as if we're in them'. Even darker was the television miniseries *The Dark Angel* (1989), based on Sheridan Le Fanu's *Uncle Silas* (1864). In the novel, Madame de la Rougierre and Silas Ruthyn are Victorian updates of Madame Cheron and Signor Montoni in Ann Radcliffe's *The Mysteries of Udolpho*, plotting against the heroine, young Maud, and coveting her inheritance. Played in a flamboyant style by Jane Lapotaire and Peter O'Toole, these characters are threatening presences that complement the deteriorating, hostile house they inhabit. Another 1989 production adapted *The Woman in Black* (1983), a more recent novel written by Susan Hill that has since become part of the Gothic canon. Directed by Herbert Wise, this television film is more clearly a traditional ghost story, a tale about a female figure dressed in black whose presence presages the death of children. It includes a bedroom scene where the screaming apparition (Pauline Moran) hovers over the camera, aligned in this case with a cowering Arthur (Adrian Rawlins). To the short films made as part of *A Ghost Story for Christmas* (1971–78, 2005–18), which included many adaptations of the works of M. R. James and Charles Dickens, one must add *Schalcken the Painter* (1979), a television horror film based on the Le Fanu short story of the same name, and the grandiose *Gormenghast* (2000), developed from Mervyn Peake's Gothic fantasy novels.

Many of these costume dramas and ghost stories hint at another distinctive feature of the contemporary Gothic: the retrojection of the barbaric past to the nineteenth and early twentieth centuries. If the

Gothic was once associated with the medieval period from which first wave Gothic novels drew architectonic inspiration, the late Victorian and Edwardian eras have become what Robert Miles calls the 'Gothic cusp', the perceived 'transitional phase' 'when the Gothic epoch came to an end, and the modern one began' (1995: 87). For contemporary filmmakers, these periods are now the 'site of struggle between incipient modernity and an unenlightened past' (Spooner 2007: 44) that the Gothic returns to compulsively. As the Gothic travelled to contemporary times in the sensation novel and in fin-de-siècle classics such as *Strange Case of Dr Jekyll and Mr Hyde* and *The Picture of Dorian Gray*, the Gothic's temporal dislocations found new representations in the form of fears of reversion. Since many of the Gothic texts that have been most prominently adapted to cinema were written in the nineteenth century, it is also the case that its indicators (the vast mansion fallen into disrepair, the dark underbelly of the urban metropolis) have become associated with the Gothic by proxy. The recent obsession with the Victorian and Edwardian periods, apart from reflecting the legacy of determined beliefs and mores on current social attitudes towards, for example, sexuality, also makes sense in terms of the Gothic's temporal tensions. Reducing the distance between the modern present and the barbaric past allows filmmakers to investigate how modernity and its many technological and social developments hint at (and even mask) a continuation of 'uncivilised' behaviours, desires and repressions assumed forsaken, left behind or superseded. *The Haunting* (1999), a remake of the 1963 British film of the same name; *The Woman in Black* (2012), so far the most successful of the films made by Hammer Films in their revival period (2007–); and *Crimson Peak*, Guillermo del Toro's homage to the Female Gothic, are all examples of this trend. In *The Haunting*, Nell (Lily Taylor) discovers that the forces behind the supernatural events in Hill House, a nineteenth-century manor belonging to a textile tycoon, are the children once exploited and tortured in its cotton mills. The remake of *The Woman in Black* is set in 1906 in the fictional town of Crythin Gifford, where superstitions country folk are pitted against the secular utilitarianism of London-based lawyer Arthur (Daniel Radcliffe). Eel Marsh House, cut off from the mainland by the rising tide, is a great metaphor for the ideological distance between the two worlds. In *Crimson Peak*, Allerdale Hall similarly sits atop an initially precarious and eventually sinking clay pit that turns into a Bluebeard nightmare for budding writer Edith (Mia Wasikowska). After escaping the machinations of husband Thomas (Tom Hiddleston) and sister-in-law Lucille (Jessica Chastain), who intend to kill her for her money, Edith becomes a fiction writer, effectively finding the voice and confidence denied her due to her sex. The desolate and decaying states in these films become modern-day surrogates for the castles of the late eighteenth-century Gothic and the morals that enslave the characters reminders of inflexible customs and patriarchal tyranny.

As important as temporality and historical locale is the fact that the past, often in the shape of a curse or horrific presence, returns to either exert its evil grasp or impose a revision of forgotten, repressed or unknown events or memories. For Chris Baldick, who describes the 'Gothic effect' as a combination of 'a fearful sense of inheritance in time with a claustrophobic sense of enclosure in space, these two dimensions reinforcing one another to produce an impression of sickening descent into disintegration', the present time can be the setting of a Gothic tale 'provided that [the latter] focuses upon a relatively enclosed space in which some antiquated barbaric code still prevails' (Baldick 2009: xix, xv). Naturally, Baldick's description applies to the haunted house film more generally, but individuals and communities can be equally trapped in cycles of retributive trauma. In Spain, for example, the Gothic has been evoked in *Los otros* and *El orfanato* (*The Orphanage*, 2007), films interested in the difficulty of coming to terms with loss. Perhaps most noticeably, and distinctly, the Gothic has become an aesthetic means through which to explore the legacy of silence surrounding the Spanish Civil War (1936–39) and Francisco Franco's dictatorship imposed by the 'pacto del olvido' (pact of forgetting), written after his death in 1975 and given legal basis in 1977. Although the pact was drafted with the aim of facilitating the transition to a democratic state, it has become a symbol for the country's struggling relationship with its modern history. As I have argued elsewhere, the ghosts and monsters in *El espinazo del diablo* (*The Devil's Backbone*, 2001), *El laberinto del fauno* (*Pan's Labyrinth*, 2006), *NO-DO* (*The Haunting*, 2009) and *Insensibles* (*Painless*, 2012) negotiate concerns about the processes of 'acknowledgement and reparation' that have followed the 'memory boom' of the late 1990s (Aldana Reyes 2017: 217). Their plots about acceptance and attempts to redress the past resonate with the founding of the 'Asociación para la Recuperación de la Memoria Histórica' (Association for the Recovery of Historical Memory) and the introduction in 2007 of the 'Ley de Memoria Histórica' (Historical Memory Law), which finally extended rights to the victims of persecution or violence during the War and subsequent dictatorship.

Naturally, the fact that both international co-productions and home market films are reaching wider audiences is a sign of the effects of globalisation. As Byron suggests, the contemporary period is marked by the supersession of the national by the transnational as well as by a decentring of the West as the main site of Gothic production (2013: 1–4). As happened in the 1960s and 1970s, a sure-fire approach for filmmakers has been to capitalise on monsters that have mass appeal.

Since tales of the returning dead are not exclusive to Europe and America, spectres have been key to the cultural spread of the Gothic in countries like Russia and Korea.[10] These 'monsters' of superstition are perhaps the oldest, most universally recognisable, yet the sensibilities of the ghost story resonate with the Gothic's aesthetic and thematic preoccupations. As Susan Owens argues, '[i]n binding together ancient history, old buildings, ruins and ghosts with the glue of psychological horror', Horace Walpole's *The Castle of Otranto* did 'invent ... a new, highly charged way of looking at the world – one that has had consequences for the way in which ghosts have been thought of ever since' (2017: 124). The familiarity and malleability of the ghost, its capacity to be attached to all forms of horror and transgression and its inextricability from the notion of a compulsive comeback are the main reasons ghost stories may be perceived as one of the most straightforward and discernible descendants of the classical Gothic in the contemporary period. At a time when the Gothic has fragmented and dispersed, films about hauntings have remained relatively unchanged. Western viewers may not have been entirely cognisant of the intricacies of the 'onryō' in *Ringu* (Ring, 1998) and *Ju-on: The Grudge* (2002), and may even have been taken by surprise by the former's innovative ghost coming out of a television screen, but the films' basic plotlines (circling around curses and retributive reparation) do not differ greatly from those of more classical ghost stories like *Kaidan* (2007). As with the Mexican 'la llorona', the specific national significance in Japanese culture of the 'onryō' has not stopped it from having a global appeal.[11] Another monster to have reached a similar level of popularity is the zombie (Luckhurst 2015: 167–196). While ghosts are still attached to buildings and settings that connote instability, derangement or repression, zombies have been freer to roam the open spaces of post-apocalyptic urban centres, effectively standing in for the human condition in times of rampant and mindless consumerism.

Figure 7.2 The vengeful ghost, a central figure in *Kaidan* (2007), continues to be one of the most enduring and transnational monsters associated with the Gothic.

The Gothic's socio-political investment, its utilisation as catalyst for economic, systemic and ideological oppression, is not necessarily incompatible with whimsy and an appreciation of the playfulness of its aesthetic qualities. The celebratory nature of the Gothic in the contemporary period goes beyond the parody and the homage of films like *Carry on Screaming!* (1966). It embraces the notion of the surface, and even prioritises it over narrative, because it is riven with types of affective and emotional power that rest on intertextual connections and on a long history of Gothic images and settings endlessly recycled and remediated. The durability of certain motifs makes them more valuable and their material quality more obviously open to merchandising. Tim Burton's work is the quintessential example of this type of postmodern Gothic. It is intrinsically personal at the visual level, yet simultaneously marked by its pastiching of the past, by its dark reimagining of existing characters, franchises and texts. Burton has reinvigorated Gothic formulae through stunning, festive and carnivalesque aesthetic displays that, with a few exceptions, cannot be considered horror despite the fact that they contain horrific elements. In fact, his films bring together a series of interrelated, but also vastly different, genres (fantasy, science fiction, horror, comedy, melodrama and children's literature), media (comics, animated cartoons and television) and myths (fairy tales and folkloric legends). Equally eclectic are Burton's inspirations, which range from purportedly low-brow cultural products like Hammer and Dr. Seuss to high-brow cinema directors like Federico Fellini. For Jeffrey Andrew Weinstock, the undercutting of Gothic's horrors 'through humour and sentimentality' necessarily leads to a citational form of the Gothic, to a 'Gothic lite' that is 'the consequence of two interconnected modes of storytelling: Gothic nostalgia, on the one hand, and Gothic irony, on the other' (2013: 26). Their combination creates a type of distancing that emphasises self-referentiality, metatextuality, a re-evaluation of 'camp' and an appreciation of cinema history (26–27). This turn to self-consciousness and quotation has been noted by other critics too. Writing about vampire cinema, Ken Gelder suggests that what distinguishes contemporary films from previous offerings is that they cite previous texts 'in a particularly visible, performative way' (2012: vi). Tim Burton films explore Gothic cinema, its histories and mythologies. The burden of the past, and of influence, can now be a measure of pride for filmmakers and even become necessary for viewers. It is, for example, hard to laugh at the jokes in *What We Do in the Shadows* without an awareness of the vampiric canon it references.

Burton's oeuvre is very varied and heterogenic, but it is visually consistent in its Gothic investment, with skulls, stitches, black and white stripes and bats acting as the main motifs and sequences often shot using chiaroscuro, when not black-and-white cinematography.[12] The director's quirks, partly a result of his training as an animator for Disney, suggest an acquaintance with Gothic horror that would be mapped out in his early stop-motion animation film *Vincent* (1982) and his short film *Frankenweenie* (1984), both of which owe a debt to Universal's horrors, especially to James Whale's *Frankenstein*, and to the work of actor Vincent Price, in particular his Poe films with Roger Corman. The erasure of the boundary between the living and the dead, between the normal and the monstrous, permeates his most straightforwardly Gothic films, principally *Sleepy Hollow* (1999) and *Corpse Bride* (2005), as does the figure of the misunderstood or forgotten loner. Importantly, there is a strong relationship between this imagery and the messages in his films, which investigate rejection and the roots of suburban maladjustment. Burton himself has acknowledged the similarities between Bruce Wayne, from *Batman* (1989) and *Batman Returns* (1992), the eponymous anti-hero in *Edward Scissorhands* (1991), Ed Wood in the 1994 biopic and Willie Wonka from *Charlie and the Chocolate Factory* (2005), admitting that they all exhibit the same 'anti-social' traits and strong 'fear of human contact and interaction' (quoted in Salisbury 2006: 227). The isolation of these characters is often mirrored by the empty, derelict spaces they inhabit, with the attic and the Gothic mansion recurring throughout Burton's oeuvre. The ambiguity of the Gothic space in his cinema, halfway between the dreadful and the comforting, between the nostalgic nod and its re-appropriation, correlates with the modern Gothic's recasting of the monster as lovable outsider. Although, as in *Edward Scissorhands*, the creature (Johnny Depp) may not ultimately be able to happily coexist with humans and find himself forced to retreat into obscurity, he can be pitied, cared for and, for doe-eyed teenager Kim (Winona Ryder) and bored housewife Joyce (Kathy Baker), even actively pursued as a love interest.

Romance became prominent in the contemporary Gothic, especially following the furore over Stephenie Meyer's *Twilight* novels (2005–8) and their film adaptations (2008–12).[13] 'Paranormal romance', a subgenre of romantic and speculative fiction involving sentimental relationships between supernatural characters and sometimes humans, became a force to be reckoned with and prompted discussions about the Gothic's value. The 'defanged' (Clements 2011) or conscientious vampire (Tenga and Zimmerman 2013: 73), although not, as Stacey Abbott (2016) has shown, the exclusive manifestation of this creature in the post-millennial period, is still interesting for what it tells us about the tonal changes the Gothic has undergone. The friendly Eli (Lina Leandersson) in *Låt den rätte komma in* (*Let the Right One In*, 2008) and Edward Cullen (Robert Pattinson) in *Twilight* (2008), a 'vegetarian' vampire who registers more as a magical version of the 'rebellious biker boy' (Botting 2014: 200) than as a corpse-like Count Orlok, attest to the fact that the Gothic is increasingly manifesting outside the traditional parameters of horror cinema. Whether the romantic vampire is modern or indeed a bowdlerised figure is debatable, given that John Polidori's Lord Ruthven in 'The Vampyre' (1819) could be considered the first in a long line of Byronic vampires travelling all the way into late twentieth-century films like *Interview with the Vampire* (1994). It has also been argued that romance has been historically intertwined with the Gothic (Botting 2008: 9–20) and that the role it has played in reshaping some of its major myths constitutes less a change than a return to form (Crawford 2014: 5). The point is not that romantic monsters did not exist before the twenty-first century, but that they have become more numerous and command a greater attention. Their profusion cannot be understood without the type of dispersion that has removed Gothic aesthetics from their origins in horror media and allowed them to appeal to different demographics.

Some of these new audiences are children and young adults. As covered in Chapter 1, animation is no stranger to the Gothic and short films such as Jan Švankmajer's *Otrantský zámek* and *Zánik domu Usherú* (*The Fall of the House of Usher*, 1980), Jiří Barta's *Krysař* (*The Pied Piper*, 1986) and the Brothers Quay's *Street of Crocodiles* (1986) are clear signs that animation for adults has not ceased exploring uncanny, surreal scenarios. Yet big-budget computer-animated and (sometimes 3D) stop-motion animated comedies aimed primarily at children and containing Gothic characters are a pretty modern phenomenon that has seen a boom of interest in the early twenty-first century. To Burton and Burton-related projects *The Nightmare Before Christmas* (1993), *Corpse Bride* and the remake of *Frankenweenie* (2012), one could add *Wallace & Gromit: The Curse of the Were-Rabbit* (2005), *Monster House* (2006), *Coraline* (2009), based on the Neil Gaiman novella of the same name, *ParaNorman* (2012) and *Hotel Transylvania* (2012) and its sequels. In these films, Gothic aesthetics mingle with other less threatening elements, like light-hearted musical interludes or humour, that betray their target market. Generically, these animation films could be categorised as dark fantasy comedies and, in this respect, handle the Gothic as irreverently and cheerfully as child-friendly films like *The Addams Family* (1991), *Addams Family Values* (1993) and *Hocus Pocus* (1993). Since films like *Frankenweenie* include many references to classical horror, they are also intended to appeal to adults through nostalgic evocation.

The intimate acquaintance with cinematic history required by the new Gothic may arguably have led to what Fredric Jameson, writing about the depthlessness of postmodern art, names the 'waning of affect' (1991: 10, 11). For Fred Botting, modernity's obsession with consumption and technology have changed the nature of the Gothic: '[i]n a situation of real-time global media screens and febrile heralding of novelty … what is to come is increasingly anticipated, predicted, named' (2013: 499). 'As

Figure 7.3 The light-hearted pastiche of animated films like *Frankenweenie* (2012) illustrates the Gothic's postmodern evolution.

monsters', he claims, 'are sought out, radical difference is diminished: they become familiar, recognized, expected ... domesticated to the point of becoming pets' (500). This is quite literally the case in *Frankenweenie*, where Sparky, Victor's dog, is scary only to the apprehensive members of the sleepy community in which the boy and his family live. Botting's point is, naturally, less literal and connected to the effects of the redundancy of narrative formulas constantly exploited for commercial gain. This is perhaps the reason why *Dracula*, *Frankenstein* and *Dr Jekyll and Mr Hyde* adaptations have generally struggled to make much of an impact since Francis Ford Coppola's *Bram Stoker's Dracula*, while the market for vampires, zombies and other monsters, much more able to renew its premises substantially, has continued to find ways to adapt and soar, to repeat without replicating. Even the success of Ford Coppola's film may be attributed to what Thomas Austin, *pace* Richard Maltby, calls its '"commercial aesthetic" of aggregation', whereby the film's 'diverse textual components' are first amalgamated and 'subsequently disaggregated' (2002: 114) in promotional campaigns to appeal to the biggest number of audience sectors.[14] As the Gothic disperses, it can be one of the many elements that coalesce into successful popular films more solidly rooted in genres with mass appeal like fantasy, in *Harry Potter and the Half-Blood Prince* (2009); supernatural drama, in television series like *Buffy the Vampire Slayer* (1997–2003) and the monster mash-up *Penny Dreadful* (2014–16); and the action adventure, in the case of the Gothic superheroes in *The Crow* (1994), *Blade* (1998), *Underworld* (2003) and *Nochnoy Dozor* (*Night Watch*, 2004).

As Dan Hassler-Forest has suggested, perhaps the post-millennial interest in the superhero is politically minded, with this figure acting 'as a potent placeholder for the conflicting fantasies, anxieties and desires that typify the age of intensified neoliberalism that was ushered in under the George W. Bush presidency' (2012: 4). Yet, if the upholding of ideological, and implicitly or explicitly American, understandings of justice, peace and what is morally right are part and parcel of the superhero's crusader rhetoric, the Gothic's turn to these characters is also clearly financially motivated. Superhero films since *Iron Man* (2008) and *The Dark Knight* (2008) are responsible for some of the biggest successes in post-millennial box office history.[15] Universal studios, emboldened by the popularity of the Marvel Cinematic Universe and by the moderate interest generated by *Dracula Untold*, introduced its own Dark Universe in 2017. This venture planned to resurrect old monsters from its property vaults in the shape of new versions of classics like *Bride of Frankenstein*. Universal was, however, forced to rethink its strategy after *The Mummy* (2017) was critically panned and failed to meet ticket sale projections. Teaming up with Blumhouse Productions, responsible for some of the most profitable low-budget horror films of the twenty-first century, for a series of 'singular, director-driven films that will be unique in terms of budget, rating, and tone' (Newby 2019), the studio appears to be on the brink of a similar, more modest, rescue plan. Universal's repeated attempts and struggles to modernise its icons according to the zeitgeist are a good indication of just how far the Gothic has travelled since the 1890s, of how deeply it has pervaded the popular imagination and transcended traditional ideas of genre, audiences and identification.

They are also a reminder of how the Gothic's socio-cultural role as a cinematic aesthetic is still as important as the dominant market forces that dictate the viability of films.

FILMOGRAPHY

Addams Family Values (Barry Sonnenfeld, 1993, USA)
Batman (Tim Burton, 1989, USA)
Batman Returns (Tim Burton, 1992, USA)
Blade (Stephen Norrington, 1998, USA)
Bram Stoker's Dracula (Francis Ford Coppola, 1992, USA)
Bride of Frankenstein (James Whale, 1935, USA)
Carry on Screaming! (Gerald Thomas, 1966, UK)
Charlie and the Chocolate Factory (Tim Burton, 2005, UK/USA/Australia)
Coraline (Henry Selick, 2009, USA)
Corpse Bride (Mike Johnson and Tim Burton, 2005, USA)
Count Yorga, Vampire (Bob Kelljan, 1970, USA)
Crimson Peak (Guillermo del Toro, 2015, USA/Canada)
Dagon (Stuart Gordon, 2001, Spain)
Dark Prince: The True Story of Dracula (Thomas Baum, 2000, USA)
Dark Waters (Mariano Baino, 1994, Russia/UK)
Dr. Jekyll and Mr. Hyde (Colin Budds, 2000, Canada/Australia)
Dr. Jekyll and Ms. Hyde (David Price, 1995, UK/Canada/USA)
Dracula (Dan Curtis, 1974, UK)
Dracula (John Badham, 1979, UK/USA)
Dracula A.D. 1972 (Alan Gibson, 1972, UK)
Dracula: The Dark Prince (Pearry Reginald Teo, 2013, USA)
Dracula Untold (Gary Shore, 2014, USA)
Ed Wood (Tim Burton, 1994, USA)
Edward Scissorhands (Tim Burton, 1990, USA)
El espinazo del diablo (*The Devil's Backbone*, Guillermo del Toro, 2001, Spain/Mexico)
El laberinto del fauno (*Pan's Labyrinth*, Guillermo del Toro, 2006, Spain/Mexico)

El orfanato (*The Orphanage*, J. A. Bayona, 2007, Spain)
Frankenstein (James Whale, 1931, USA)
Frankenstein (James Ormerod, 1984, UK/USA)
Frankenstein: The True Story (Jack Smight, 1973, UK/USA)
Frankenweenie (Tim Burton, 1984, USA)
Frankenweenie (Tim Burton, 2012, USA)
Fright Night (Tom Holland, 1985, USA)
Goongnyeo (*Shadows in the Palace*, Mi-jung Kim, 2007, South Korea)
Gothic (Ken Russell, 1986, UK)
Harry Potter and the Half-Blood Prince (David Yates, 2009, UK/USA)
Hocus Pocus (Kenny Ortega, 1993, USA)
Hotel Transylvania (Genndy Tartakovsky, 2012, USA)
Howling V: The Rebirth (Neal Sundstrom, 1989, USA)
Iron Man (Jon Favreau, 2008, USA)
Insensibles (*Painless*, Juan Carlos Medina, 2012, Spain/France/Portugal)
Interview with the Vampire (Neil Jordan, 1994, USA)
Jane Eyre (Julian Amyes, 1983, UK)
Jane Eyre (Franco Zeffirelli, 1996, France/Italy/UK/USA)
Jane Eyre (Robert Young, 1997, UK)
Jane Eyre (Susanna White, 2006, UK)
Jane Eyre (Cary Fukunaga, 2011, UK/USA)
Janghwa, Hongryeon (*A Tale of Two Sisters*, Jee-woon Kim, 2013, South Korea)
Jekyll + Hyde (Nick Stillwell, 2006, USA/Canada)
Ju-on: The Grudge (Takashi Shimizu, 2002, Japan)
Kaidan (Hideo Nakata, 2007, Japan)
Krysař (*The Pied Piper*, Jiří Barta, 1986, Czechoslovakia/West Germany)
La chiesa (*The Church*, Michele Soavi, 1989, Italy)
Le Moine (Dominik Moll, 2011, Spain/France)
Los otros (*The Others*, Alejandro Amenábar, 2001, Spain)
Madame Hyde (*Mrs. Hyde*, Serge Bozon, 2017, France/Belgium)
Mary Reilly (Stephen Frears, 1996, USA)
Mary Shelley's Frankenstein (Kenneth Branagh, 1994, USA/Japan/UK)
Monster House (Gil Kenan, 2006, USA)
Nevesta (*The Bride*, Svyatoslav Podgaevskiy, 2017, Russia)

Nochnoy Dozor (*Night Watch*, Timur Bekmambetov, 2004, Russia)
NO-DO (*The Haunting*, Elio Quiroga, 2009, Spain)
Otrantský zámek (*Castle of Otranto*, Jan Švankmajer, 1979, Czechoslovakia)
ParaNorman (Sam Fell and Chris Butler, 2012, USA)
Ringu (*Ring*, Hideo Nakata, 1998, Japan)
Rosemary's Baby (Roman Polanski, 1968, USA)
Salem's Lot (Tobe Hooper, 1979, USA)
Schalcken the Painter (Leslie Megahey, 1979, UK)
Sleepy Hollow (Tim Burton, 1999, USA)
Street of Crocodiles (Brothers Quay, 1986, UK)
The Addams Family (Barry Sonnenfeld, 1991, USA)
The Bride (Franc Roddam, 1985, UK/USA)
The Crow (Alex Proyas, 1994, USA)
The Dark Angel (Peter Hammond, 1989, UK)
The Dark Knight (Christopher Nolan, 2008, USA/UK)
The Elephant Man (David Lynch, 1980, UK/USA)
The Exorcist (William Friedkin, 1973, USA)
The Fall of the House of Usher (James L. Conway, 1982, USA)
The Haunting (Jan de Bont, 1999, USA)
The Hunger (Tony Scott, 1983, UK/USA)
The Keep (Michael Mann, 1983, UK/USA)
The Lost Boys (Joel Schumacher, 1987, USA)
The Monk (Francisco Lara Polop, 1990, Spain/UK)
The Mummy (Stephen Sommers, 1999, USA)
The Mummy (Alex Kurtzman, 2017, USA/China/Japan)
The Name of the Rose (Jean-Jacques Annaud, 1986, Italy/West Germany/France)
The Night Stalker (John Llewellyn Moxey, 1972, USA)
The Nightmare Before Christmas (Henry Selick, 1993, USA)
The Ninth Configuration (William Peter Blatty, 1980, USA)
The Omen (Richard Donner, 1976, UK/USA)
The Phantom of the Opera (Robert Markowitz, 1983, USA)
The Phantom of the Opera (Tony Richardson, 1990, USA/France/Italy/Germany)

The Pit and the Pendulum (Stuart Gordon, 1991, USA/Italy)
The Rocky Horror Picture Show (Jim Sharman, 1975, UK/USA)
The Strange Case of Dr. Jekyll and Mr. Hyde (John Carl Buechler, 2006, USA)
The Witch (Robert Eggers, 2015, UK/Canada/USA)
The Woman in Black (Herbert Wise, 1989, UK)
The Woman in Black (James Watkins, 2012, UK/USA/Sweden/Canada)
The Woman in White (John Bruce, 1982, UK)
The Woman in White (Tim Fywell, 1997, USA/UK)
The Woman in White (Carl Tibbetts, 2018, UK)
Twilight (Catherine Hardwicke, 2008, USA)
Underworld (Len Wiseman, 2003, UK/Germany/Hungary/USA)
Vamp (Richard Wenk, 1986, USA)
Vem var Dracula? (*In Search of Dracula*, Calvin Floyd, 1975, Sweden/West Germany/France)
Vincent (Tim Burton, 1982, USA)
Viy 3D (*Forbidden Empire*, Oleg Stepchenko, 2014, Russia/Ukraine/Czech Republic)
Wallace & Gromit: The Curse of the Were-Rabbit (Nick Park and Steve Box, 2005, UK/USA)
Warm Bodies (Jonathan Levine, 2013, USA)
Wasting Away (Matthew Kohnen, 2007, USA)
What We Do in the Shadows (Jemaine Clement and Taika Waititi, 2014, New Zealand/USA)
Zánik domu Usherú (*The Fall of the House of Usher*, Jan Švankmajer, 1980, Czechoslovakia)

NOTES

1 In the case of Herman Munster (Fred Gwynne), the copyrighted version of the Frankenstein creature was used for the design because the series was produced by Universal (Stoker 1980: 104).

2 As the routine banning of snuff-themed films in the 1970s and the video nasties debacle in the early 1980s show, the mainstreaming of extreme horror is not a smooth history (Kerekes 2000; Egan 2012). Horror has

always had to pay a price for its pushing of the boundaries of the acceptable and to contend with moral and literal censorship, especially where brutal depictions of death or sexualised violence are concerned (Jones 2013; Jackson et al. 2016; Kerekes and Slater 2016).

3. Arguably, this is also the case for Dracula in Stoker's novel, but my point is that these vampires look out of place, even anachronistic.

4. I am quoting from the dubbed DVD version of *The Church* released by Shameless in 2016.

5. The Latin inscription most famously appears in 'The Treasure of Abbott Thomas' (1904), a short story by M. R. James. Given that James's academic and antiquarian characters often die because they are incapable of leaving the past alone, the quote resonates with *La chiesa*'s emphasis on hermetism.

6. These adaptations were *The Monk* (1990) and *Le Moine* (2011).

7. As Abbott points out, the trope of the reincarnated beloved originates in Dan Curtis's television adaptation *Dracula* (1974), which was penned by Richard Matheson (2018: 201).

8. There have been a very significant number of film adaptations of *The Phantom of the Opera* since the 1980s, especially following Andrew Lloyd Webber's musical drama of 1986. For a detailed analysis, see Hall (2009: 95–170).

9. The novel was also made into two feature films, one directed by Franco Zeffirelli in 1996 and the other by Cary Fukunaga in 2011.

10. I am referring to films such as *Viy 3D* (*Forbidden Empire*, 2014) and *Nevesta* (*The Bride*, 2017) or *Goongnyeo* (*Shadows in the Palace*, 2007) and *Janghwa, Hongryeon* (*A Tale of Two Sisters*, 2013). Little has been written on contemporary Russian horror, although see Dolgopolov (2015). For Korean horror cinema, see the essays in Peirse and Martin (2013).

11. I mean, specifically, how the 'onryō' speaks to traditionally Japanese '"appropriate" sex and gender roles' (McRoy 2015: 202). For more on the national particularities of Japanese horror, as well as previous manifestations of the 'onryō', see McRoy (2005) and Balmain (2008).

12. The inconsistencies in Burton's oeuvre are, in part, a result of the tension between his auteur inclinations, especially at the level of design, and his circumstance as a director who has struggled with the many compromises involved in working in the Hollywood production system.

13 For a survey of the fictional phenomenon, see Crawford (2014: 181–236). For a survey of the cinematic one, see Clayton and Harman (2014) and Jancovich (2014).
14 In this case, *Bram Stoker's Dracula* was promoted as an auteur film, as a star vehicle, as an adaptation of a classic, as a horror film, as a romance and as an art film (Austin 2002: 114).
15 I do not mean to suggest that superhero films have not undergone their own commercial ups and downs (Clark 2018), but rather that they are a much more noticeable cinematic force in the twenty-first century.

BIBLIOGRAPHY

Abbott, S. (2010) 'High Concepts Thrills and Chills: The Horror Blockbuster', in I. Conrich (ed.) *Horror Zone: The Cultural Experience of Contemporary Horror Cinema*, London and New York: I.B.Tauris.

Abbott, S. (2016) *Undead Apocalypse: Vampires and Zombies in the Twenty-First Century*, Edinburgh: Edinburgh University Press.

Abbott, S. (2018) 'Dracula on Film and TV from 1960 to the Present', in R. Luckhurst (ed.) *The Cambridge Companion to Dracula*, Cambridge: Cambridge University Press.

Aldana Reyes, X. (2017) *Spanish Gothic: National Identity, Collaboration and Cultural Adaptation*, Basingstoke: Palgrave Macmillan.

Aldana Reyes, X. (2018) 'Promethean Myths of the Twenty-First Century: Contemporary *Frankenstein* Film Adaptations and the Rise of the Viral Zombie', in C. M. Davison and M. Mulvey-Roberts (eds) *Global Frankenstein*, Basingstoke: Palgrave Macmillan.

Austin, T. (2002) *Hollywood, Hype and Audiences: Selling and Watching Popular Film in the 1990s*, Manchester: Manchester University Press.

Baldick, C. (2009) [1992] 'Introduction', in C. Baldick (ed.) *The Oxford Book of Gothic Tales*, Oxford: Oxford University Press.

Balmain, C. (2007) 'The Church (*La Chiesa*, aka *Cathedral of Demons*)', in S. J. Schneider (ed.) *100 European Horror Films*, London: BFI.

Balmain, C. (2008) *Introduction to Japanese Horror Film*, Edinburgh: Edinburgh University Press.

Botting, F. (2008) *Gothic Romanced: Consumption, Gender and Technology in Contemporary Fictions*, London and New York: Routledge.

Botting, F. (2013) 'Post-millennial Monsters: Monstrosity-no-more', in G. Byron and D. Townshend (eds) *The Gothic World*, London and New York: Routledge.

Botting, F. (2014) *Gothic*, 2nd edn, London and New York: Routledge.

Byron, G. (2013) 'Introduction', in G. Byron (ed.) *Globalgothic*, Manchester: Manchester University Press.

Clark, T. (2018) '14 Superhero Movies Whose Successes and Failures Have Shaped the Genre since 2008, from the Grit of *The Dark Knight* to the Dominance of MCU', *Business Insider*, 18 July. Available at: www.businessinsider.com/superhero-movies-whose-successes-and-failures-have-shaped-the-genre-2018-7?r=US&IR=T (accessed 26 February 2019).

Clayton, W. and S. Harman (eds) (2014) *Screening Twilight: Critical Approaches to a Cinematic Phenomenon*, London and New York: I.B.Tauris.

Clements, S. (2011) *The Vampire Defanged: How the Embodiment of Evil Became a Romantic Hero*, Grand Rapids, MI: Brazos Press.

Crawford, J. (2014) *The Twilight of the Gothic? Vampire Fiction and the Rise of Paranormal Romance, 1991–2012*, Cardiff: University of Wales Press.

Dolgopolov, G. (2015) 'Horror', in B. Beumers (ed.) *Directory of World Cinema: Russia 2*, Bristol: Intellect.

Egan, K. (2012) *Trash or Treasure? Censorship and the Changing Meanings of the Video Nasties*, Manchester: Manchester University Press.

Friedman, L. D. and A. B. Kavey (2016) *Monstrous Progeny: A History of the Frankenstein Narratives*, London and New Brunswick, NJ: Rutgers University Press.

Gelder, K. (2012) *New Vampire Cinema*, London: BFI.

Hall, A. C. (2009) *Phantom Variations: The Adaptations of Gaston Leroux's Phantom of the Opera, 1925 to the Present*, Jefferson, NC: McFarland.

Hassler-Forest, D. (2012) *Capitalist Superheroes: Caped Crusaders in the Neoliberal Age*, Alresford: Zero Books.

Jackson, N., S. Kimber, J. Walker and T. J. Watson (eds) (2016) *Snuff: Real Death and Screen Media*, London and New York: Bloomsbury.

Jameson, F. (1991) *Postmodernism: Or, the Cultural Logic of Late Capitalism*, Durham, NC: Duke University Press.

Jancovich, M. (2014) '"Cue the Shrieking Virgins?": The Critical Reception of the *Twilight Saga*', in W. Clayton and S. Harman (eds) *Screening Twilight: Critical Approaches to a Cinematic Phenomenon*, London and New York: I.B.Tauris.

Jones, S. (2013) *Torture Porn: Popular Horror after Saw*, Basingstoke and New York: Palgrave Macmillan.

Kerekes, D. (2000) *See No Evil: Banned Video and Film Controversy*, Manchester: Critical Vision.

Kerekes, D. and D. Slater (2016) *Killing for Culture: From Edison to Isis: A New History of Death on Film*, London: Headpress.

Lloyd-Smith, A. (2004) *American Gothic Fiction: An Introduction*, London and New York: Continuum.

Luckhurst, R. (2015) *Zombies: A Cultural History*, London: Reaktion Books.

McNally, R. T. and R. Florescu (1975) *In Search of Dracula: A True History of Dracula and Vampire Legends*, Greenwich, CT: New York Graphic Society.

McRoy, J. (ed.) (2005) *Japanese Horror Cinema*, Edinburgh: Edinburgh University Press.

McRoy, J. (2015) 'Spectral Remainders and Transcultural Hauntings: (Re)iterations of the Onryō in Japanese Horror Cinema', in M. Leeder (ed.) *Cinematic Ghosts: Haunting and Spectrality from Silent Cinema to the Digital Era*, London and New York: Bloomsbury.

Miles, R. (1995) *Ann Radcliffe: The Great Enchantress*, Manchester: Manchester University Press.

Newby, R. (2019) 'How Blumhouse Can Rehab Universal's Monsters', *The Hollywood Reporter*, 29 January. Available at: www.hollywoodreporter.com/heat-vision/invisible-man-can-blumhouse-save-universals-monsters-1180478 (accessed 26 February 2019).

Newman, K. (2011) *Nightmare Movies: Horror on Screen since the 1960s*, rev. edn, London and New York: Bloomsbury.

Owens, S. (2017) *The Ghost: A Cultural History*, London: Tate Publishing.

Peirse, A. and D. Martin (eds) (2013) *Korean Horror Cinema*, Edinburgh: Edinburgh University Press.

Salisbury, M. (ed.) (2006) [1995] *Burton on Burton*, rev. edn, London: Faber & Faber.

Spooner, C. (2007) 'Gothic in the Twentieth Century', in C. Spooner and E. McEvoy (eds) *The Routledge Companion to Gothic*, Abingdon and New York: Routledge.

Stoker, J. (1980) *The Illustrated Frankenstein*, Newton Abbot: Westbridge Books.

Tenga, A. and E. Zimmerman (2013) 'Vampire Gentlemen and Zombie Beasts: A Rendering of True Monstrosity', *Gothic Studies*, 15.1: 76–87.

Weinstock, J. A. (2013) 'Mainstream Outsider: Burton Adapts Burton', in J. A. Weinstock (ed.) *The Works of Tim Burton: Margin to Mainstream*, Basingstoke: Palgrave Macmillan.

Wheatley, H. (2006) *Gothic Television*, Manchester: Manchester University Press.

INDEX

Films have been alphabetised both in their original and main export titles. Page references in italics refer to figures.

5 tombe per un medium (1965) 190
13 Ghosts (1960) 166

Abbott, Bud 118, 209
Abbott, Stacey 113, 215–216, 226, 234n7
Abbott and Costello Meet Frankenstein (1948) 118
adaptations 12–13
Addams Family, The (1964–66) 209
Addams Family, The (1991) 227
Addams Family Values (1993) 227
Adivina quién soy (2006) 84
aesthetics: German expressionism 73, 81, 82, 90–1
aesthetics, Gothic 3, 6, 7, 9, 12, 13–26, 28, 61; Amicus productions 163; *The Bat* 131–132; *The Cat and the Canary* 129; *Crimson Peak* 11; *Dracula's Daughter* 112; explained supernatural 144; Female Gothic 126–127; Hammer films 158; *Le Manoir du diable* 44, 53–54; Méliès, Georges, films 44, 49, 53–54; old dark house mysteries 108, 126–127; playfulness 224; post-1970s films 210, 214–215, 226–227, 230; *Son of Frankenstein* 110; Universal Studios 112, 119–120; *I vampiri* 186
AIP (American International Pictures) 167, 184
alchemy 46, 50, 58, 61, 81, 114, 212; *Der Golem, wie er in die Welt kam* 81, 82; *Le Manoir du diable* 43
Alcofribas, The Master Magician (1898) 50
Alien 9
amante del vampiro, L' (1960) 183
Amanti d'oltretomba (1965) 21
Amicus Productions 162–163
And Now the Screaming Starts! (1973) 162, 163–164

Andalusian Superstition (1912) 46, 56
Anglo-Amalgamated 161
animation 225, 227, 228
anthology films 86–87, 162–163
Antre des esprits, L' (1901) 50
anxieties, social and cultural 8, 15, 28
Arcane Sorcerer (1996) 25
arcano incantatore, L' (1996) 25
architecture: American trick films 51; Gothic and 14, 16, 19, 91, 110, 113; women and 141; *see also* buildings; sets
Argento, Dario 190–191, 197, 198
Asociación para la Recuperación de la Memoria Histórica 222
Asylum (1972) 163–164
Auberge ensorcelée, L' (1897) 46
aullido del diablo, El (1987) 198
aural effects: early sound cinema 105–106
Avenging Conscience, The (1914) 49, 68n19
Awakening of the Beast (1970) 166
Awful Dr. Orlof, The (1962) 181–182

Baldick, Chris 17–18, 221
barbarism 44
Barbe-bleue (1901) 53
Barbot, Gabrielle-Suzanne 145
Baron Blood (1972) 192
Baron fantôme, Le (1943) 145
Barrymore, John 57
Bat, The (1926) 126–127, 130–133, 136
Bat Whispers, The (1930) 130–131
Báthory, Elizabeth 185, 204n9
Batman (1989) 225
Batman Returns (1992) 225
Bava, Mario 167, 184, 186–188, 189–190, 192
Baxter, Les 168
Bay of Blood, A (1971) 192
Bear's Wedding, The (1925) 87
Beauty and the Beast (1946) 145
Bécquer, Gustavo Adolfo 194, 196, 206n28

Belle et la Bête, La (1946) 35n37, 145
Benét, Stephen Vincent 115
Bernard, James 154–155
Bewitched Inn, The (1897) 46
Bildnis des Dorian Gray, Das (1917) 76
bisexual monsters: *Dracula's Daughter* 112
black and white 20; *13 Ghosts* 166; Burton, Tim, films 225; ...*Et mourir de plaisir* 165; decline 158–159, 172, 197; *La maschera del demonio* 187
Black Castle, The (1952) 116, 117
Black Cat, The (1934) 108, 157
'Black Cat, The' (Poe) 86
Black Narcissus (1947) 25
Black Pearl, The (1908) 46, 47
Black Room, The (1935) 115–116
Black Sleep, The (1956) 18
Black Sunday (1960) 167, 184, 187
Black Torment, The (1964) 164
Blackenstein (1973) 198
Blacula (1972) 198
Blancheville Monster, The (1963) 185
blaxpoitation 198
Bloch, Robert 162, 163
blood: *El espanto surge de la tumba* 196; ...*Et mourir de plaisir* 165; Hammer films 156, 159; *House of Usher* 169; *The Masque of the Red Death* 171; *Lo spettro* 190
Blood and Roses (1960) 165
Blood Feast (1962) 160
Blood of Dracula (1957) 167
Blood on Satan's Claw (1971) 164
Blood Spattered Bride, The (1972) 185
Bloody Pit of Horror (1964) 191–192
Bluebeard 23–24, 35n35, 53, 138, 140, 151n17, 193, 221
Bluebeard (1901) 53
Blumhouse Productions 229
Body Snatcher, The (1945) 116
Body Snatcher, The (1957) 119
Boese, Carl 56, 73
Bogart, Frank 191
boia scarlatto, Il (1964) 191–192
Bonnie and Clyde (1967) 24, 196

Botting, Fred 14, 227–228
Bram Stoker's Dracula (1992) 210–211, 214, 215, 216, 228, 235n14
Brewster, Ben 57
Bride, The (1985) 216–217
Bride of Darkness (1945) 145
Bride of Frankenstein (1935) 109, 111, 133–134, 229
Brides of Dracula, The (1960) 158, 181–182
British Film Institute (BFI) 1, 2
British Film Producers Association (BFPA) 161, 177n8
British Library 1–2
Broadway 130–131
Brontë, Charlotte 23–24, 35n35, 57, 137–138, 219
Bryce, Allan 164
Bucket of Blood, A (1959) 167
Buffy the Vampire Slayer (1997–2003) 228–229
buildings 17, 18, 25, 61; *see also* architecture, Gothic; cathedrals; castles; houses
Buñuel, Luis 89
Burton, Tim 224, 225, 227, 234n12
Bustillo Oro, Juan 89
Butterfly Murders, The (1979) 18

Cabinet des Dr. Caligari, Das (1920) 61, 73, 74, 78–80, 87, 88, 95n9
Cabinet of Dr. Caligari, The (1920) 61, 73, 74, 78–80, 87, 88, 95n9
Caltiki – Il mostro immortale (1959) 186–187
'Carmilla' (Le Fanu) 88, 112, 161, 185
Carrère, Emilio 181
Carry on Screaming! (1966) 224
'Case of Charles Dexter Ward, The' (Lovecraft) 178n20
Case, David 162
'Cask of Amontillado, The' (Poe) 58
Castle of Otranto (1977) 3, 32n3, 227
Castle of Otranto, The (Walpole) 10, 21, 31n2, 134, 169, 222

Castle, William 67n12, 160, 161–162, 166
castles 16, 135, 221; *The Bat* 131–132; *The Black Castle* 117; *The Black Room* 115–116; *The Cat and the Canary* 134–135; *Dracula* (1931) 104–105, 106, 130; *Dracula's Daughter* 112; *Frankenstein* (1931) 106, 107, 130; *The Ghost Breaker* 129; *Howling V: The Rebirth* 211; *The Keep* 211; *La maschera del demonio* 187–188; *Malombra* 145; Méliès, Georges, films 50, 53; *The Most Dangerous Game* 115; *The Ninth Configuration* 211–212; *The Pit and the Pendulum* (1991) 214; post-1980s films 211; punisher movies 192–193; *Rapsodia satanica* 60; *Son of Frankenstein* 109–110; *The Strange Door* 116–117; Tigon films 165; Tower of London 115; Universal Studios 114, 115; *I vampiri* 186
Cat and the Canary, The (1927) 72, 105, 126–127, 129, 130–131, 133–136
Cat Creeps, The 105, 130–131
cathedrals 100, 211, 212–213
Caught (1949) 141
Cavallaro, Dani 19
Cendrillon (1899) 46, 53
censorship: Hammer films 161, 177n8; Tigon films 164–165
Chaney, Lon 100, 101
Chaplin, Sue 15, 16
Château de la peur, Le (1912) 58
Chevalier mystère, Le (1899) 50
chiaroscuro lighting 19–20, 80–81, 90–91, 128, 172, 197; Burton, Tim, films 225; decline of 197; *Frankenstein* (1931) 107; *Der Golem* (1920) 82; *The Innocents* 10; *Nosferatu* (1922) 83; old dark house mysteries 128; *The Telltale Heart* 88
Chibnall, Steve 165
chiesa, La (1989) 212–213

children: animation 227
Chinese Gothic cinema 18
choreutoscope 49
Church, The (1989) 212–213
Chute de la maison Usher, La (1928) 89, 186
Cinderella (1899) 46, 53
CinemaScope 161, 168
cinematography 19; Burton, Tim, films 225; colour 160, 168, 170; Frankenstein (1931) 107; Nosferatu (1922) 83
Circular Staircase, The (1915) 131
Circus of Horrors (1960) 162
City of the Dead, The (1960) 162
City of the Living Dead (1980) 198
Clarens, Carlos 134
Clark, Alfred 44
claustrophobic spaces 25, 82, 90–91, 127, 142–143, 168, 221
clavo, El (1944) 145
Clery, E. J. 21
Coffin Joe 166
Collins, Wilkie 57, 219
colour 160, 170; 13 Ghosts 166; British horror 162, 172; continental Europe 181–182; Corman, Roger, films 167–168, 168–169, 170–172, 178n19; Hammer films 155, 156, 157–158, 158–159, 160, 172; silent movies 55–56; supernatural as 166; Tales of Terror 170–171; see also Technicolor
comedy 18, 132, 136–137, 182–183, 212
Compton Films 164
Confessional of the Black Penitents, The (1977) 31n3
Confessionnal des pénitents noirs, Le (1977) 31n3
contemporary settings 114, 126–127
Conway, James L. 218
co-productions 184, 190, 194
Corman, Roger 127, 167–172, 177n14, 178nn19, 21, 182, 225

Corpse Bride (2005) 225, 227
Corpse Vanishes, The (1942) 60, 114, 186
Costello, Lou 118, 209
Count Yorga, Vampire (1970) 160–161, 210
Crane, Wilbur 130
Creeping Flesh, The (1973) 164
Crime and Punishment (1923) 80–81
Crimes at the Dark House (1940) 156–157
Crimson Peak (2015) 10–11, 23, 220, 221
cripta e l'incubo, La (1964) 185
Crosby, Floyd 168
Cross of the Devil (1975) 194
cruz del diablo, La (1975) 194
Crying Woman, The (1960) 20
cults: post-1980s films 213
Curse of Frankenstein, The (1957) 20, 155–157, 164, 176n2, 187
Curse of the Crimson Altar (1968) 164
Cushing, Peter 154, 156, 158, 162, 184

Dagon (2001) 214
Damnation de Faust, La (1903) 46, 67n10
Damnation of Faust, The (1903) 46, 67n10
danse macabre 49
Dark Angel, The (1989) 219
Dark City (1998) 19
Dark Eyes of London, The (1939) 156–157
Dark Knight, The (2008) 229
Dark Prince: The True Story of Dracula (2000) 216
Dark Shadows (1966–71) 209–210
Dark Universe (Universal Studios) 229
Dark Waters (1994) 214
darkness 19–20
Daughters of Darkness (1971) 185
Davis, Rhidian 2
Dead of Night (1945) 86, 157
Deane, Hamilton 57, 87
de Chomón, Segundo 55, 56, 67n14
de Ossorio, Amando 194, 196, 206n28

del Toro, Guillermo 220
Destiny (1921) 86
Devil and Daniel Webster, The (1942) 115
Devil in a Convent, The (1899) 51, 53–54
Devil Rides Out, The (1968) 159
Devil's Possessed (1974) 193
Devils, The (1971) 25, 196
Diable au couvent, Le (1899) 51, 53–54
Dickens, Charles 57, 219
Dickey, Paul 129
Die bian (1979) 18
Doctor X (1932) 114, 157
doppelgängers *see* double, the
Dos monjes (1934) 89–90, 91
Dostoevsky, Fyodor 80–81
double, the 5, 20, 74–76, 77, 79, 94n5; Female Gothic 142; witches and female reincarnations 188
Dr. Black, Mr. Hyde (1976) 198
Dr. Jekyll and Mr. Hyde (1920) 57
Dr. Jekyll and Mr. Hyde (1931) 186
Dr. Jekyll and Mr. Hyde (2000) 217
Dr. Jekyll and Ms. Hyde (1995) 217
Dr. Mabuse, der Spieler (1922) 81
Dr. Mabuse, The Gambler (1922) 81
Dr. Terror's House of Horrors (1965) 163
Dracula: continental Gothic 184–185
Dracula (1931) 12, 21, 57, 87, 102–106, 108, 130, 133–134; influence on later films 114–115, 118–119, 130, 133–134
Dracula (1958) 20, 154–155, 156, 176n2, 182, 204n4
Dracula (1974) 234n7
Dracula (1979) 210–211
Dracula (Stoker) 83, 84, 87, 215–216
Dracula: Prince of Darkness (1966) 159
Dracula: The Dark Prince (2013) 216
Dracula A.D. 1972 (1972) 160–161, 210
Dracula Has Risen from the Grave (1968) 159, 196
Dracula Untold (2014) 216, 229
Dracula's Daughter (1936) 109, 111–113
Dracula's Death (1921) 87–88

Dragonwyck (1946) 137, 142–143
Drake, Nathan 127
Drakula halála (1921) 87–88
dread 6–7, 10, 21, 131, 188; German expressionist cinema 90; phantasmagorias 48; *see also* fear; terror
Dreyer, Carl Theodor 88
du Maurier, Daphne 23–24, 137–138, 151n16
dungeons 18, 101, 108, 115, 185, 191, 214

Eady Levy 162, 199
Eastmancolor 160, 176n2
EC comics 163
Edward Scissorhands (1991) 225, 226
Edwardian era 25, 185, 219–220
Eerie Tales (1919) 86
Eisner, Lotte 82
Elephant Man, The (1980) 215
Eloísa está debajo de un almendro (1943) 145
Eloísa Is Under an Almond Tree (1943) 145
Enchanteur Alcofribas, L' (1903) 50
Epstein, Jean 89
eroticism: continental Gothic 182–183, 188–189, 190, 192–193, 194, 204n6; …Et mourir de plaisir 165; Hammer films 157–158; Tigon films 164–165; vampires and 112
espanto surge de la tumba, El (1973) 193, 195–156
Esta noite encarnarei no teu cadáver (1967) 166
…*Et mourir de plaisir* (1960) 165–166, 185
Euro horror 198
Evil of Frankenstein, The (1964) 159
Ewers, Hanns Heinz 74, 75, 77
excursion incohérente, Une (1909) 55
Execution of Mary, Queen of Scots (1895) 44
Exorcist, The (1973) 25–26, 164, 198, 210

INDEX 243

exploitation cinema 183–184, 189–190, 192, 197–198, 204n7, 210; see also punisher, the; sexploitation; specific films
expressionism 88
expressionist cinema: Germany 73–74, 78, 80, 87, 90–91, 110; Mexico 89–90
Eyes Without a Face (1960) 185

Fall of the House of Usher, The (1928) 89, 186
Fall of the House of Usher, The (1979) 218
'Fall of the House of Usher, The' (Poe) 88–89
fangs, vampire 119, 123n17
fantasma del convento, El (1934) 90
fantastic, the, 15–16, 46, 48, 127–128; explained supernatural 141; *Der Golem* 77; *Der Student von Prag* 75; trick films 53, 67n9
Fantôme de l'Opéra, Le (Leroux) 76
Faust 43, 46, 60, 67n10, 74, 75, 115
Faust: Eine deutsche Volkssage (1926) 75, 81
fear 7–8, 11, 12, 17, 25, 27, 61, 72, 113, 127; *The Bat* 132; *Das Cabinet des Dr. Caligari* 80; *Dracula* (1931) 106; *Frankenstein* (1910) 59–60; *Frankenstein* (1931) 106; *Der Golem* (1915) 78, 82; sex and 183, 205n14; Tigon films 164; see also dread; terror
Fée Carabosse, ou Le Poignard fatal, La (1906) 53, 54
féeries 52–53, 53–54, 69nn24–26
Female Gothic 23–24, 25, 27, 126, 137–138, 140–147, 197; impact on continental Gothic 188; post-1980s films and serials 218–219, 220; see also specific films
Fengriffen (Case) 162
Fiancée des ténèbres, La (1945) 145
filoni 188, 205n12
Fisher, Terence 158, 181–182

flashbacks 20
Florescu, Radu 216
Fogazzaro, Antonio 144–145
folklore 47, 52, 67n10, 77, 196, 224; Central Europe 12, 67n13, 106; Germany 43; Jewish 77; Poland 67n13
Ford Coppola, Francis 210–211, 228
Forshaw, Barry 4–5
Fowler, Alastair 13
Franco, Francisco 181, 206n24, 221–222
Franco, Jesús (Jess) 182, 189
Frankenstein (myth) 215, 217; continental Gothic 184–185
Frankenstein (1910) 58–60
Frankenstein (1931) 12, 57, 99, 106–107, 123nn10–11, 130; influence of earlier films 61, 81, 87, 106–107, 133–134; influence on later films 109, 158, 225
Frankenstein: The True Story (1973) 218
Frankenstein and the Monster from Hell (1974) 176n4
Frankenstein Created Woman (1967) 159
Frankenstein Meets the Wolf Man (1943) 113, 118
Frankenstein Must Be Destroyed (1969) 159
Frankenstein's Bloody Terror (1968) 185, 204n9
Frankenweenie (1984) 225
Frankenweenie (2012) 227, 228
Freda, Riccardo, 181, 187
French Gothic 51, 90, 52–53, 145, 189; see also specific films
Fright Night (1985) 210
Frightmare (1974) 161, 165
From Morn to Midnight (1920) 80–81
Fulci, Lucio 190–191, 198–199
Fuseli, Henry 58–59, 79

Gainsborough Pictures 141, 156
Galeen, Henrik 77
Gamer, Michael 14
Gaslight (1940) 140–141
Gaslight (1944) 140–141, 142–143

Gaspard-Robertson, Étienne 48, 68n16
Gaston de Blondeville (Radcliffe) 150n3
Gelder, Ken 224–225
German film industry, development of 72–73
German folklore 43
German Gothic 5, 22, 56, 99, 128, 172; expressionist cinema 73–74, 78, 80, 87, 90–91, 110; *see also specific films*
German Romanticism 72, 74, 77, 81–82, 86
Gertner, Richard 158–159
Geung si sin sang (1985) 18
Ghost, The (1963) 190
Ghost Breaker, The (1914) 52, 129
ghost films 90, 107–108, 137, 222–223; *see also specific films*
Ghost of Yotsuya, The (1959) 18
Ghost Story for Christmas, A (1971–78, 2005–18) 219
ghosts: phantasmagorias 47–48, 49, 61–62
giallo genre 182, 190–191, 192, 197, 210
Gilling, John 194
globalisation 222
Goddard, Charles W. 129
Goethe, Johan Wolfgang von 74
Gogol, Nikolai 57, 187
Golem, Der (1915) 77–78
Golem, Der (Meyrink) 74
Golem, The (1915) 77–78
Golem, Der; wie er in die Welt kam (1920) 26, 56, 73, 81–83, 87
Golem, The: How He Came into the World (1920) 26, 56, 73, 81–83, 87
Golem and the Dancing Girl, The (1917) 78
Golem und die Tänzerin, Der (1917) 78
Gómez Rivero, Ángel 196
Gordon, Stuart 213–214
gore cinema 160
Gorilla, The (1927) 130
Gormenghast (2000) 219
Gothic (1986) 109, 215

Gothic Studies 16
'Gothic': definition of term 2
Gothic: The Dark Heart of Film 1, 5
Grand Guignol 10, 45, 66n3, 132
Great Gabbo, The (1929) 157
Griffith, D. W. 49, 58, 130
Gritos en la noche (1962) 181–182
Gulick, Paul 134

Hall, Charles D. 133–134
Haller, Daniel 168
Hamilton, Patrick 140
Hammer Film Productions 3–5, 32n8, 127, 154–162, 163, 220; Corman, Roger and 167, 170 impact on continental cinema 182, 183;
Hand, Richard J. 59
Hands of Orlac, The (Renard) 76
Happy Skeleton (1898) 49
Harper, Sue 161
Harry Potter and the Half-Blood Prince (2009) 228–229
Haskell, Molly 143–144
Hassler-Forest, Dan 229
Haunted Castle, The (1896) 43–44, 53–54
Haunted House, The (1906) 55
Haunted Palace, The (1963) 178n20
Haunting Shadows (1919) 129–130
Haunting, The (1963) 8, 147, 159
Haunting, The (1999) 220
Hawthorne, Nathaniel 57, 162–163
Häxan (1922) 49, 68n19
Hays Code 112, 123n13
Head of Janus, The (1920) 76
Hearn, Lafcadio 162–163
heroines: Female Gothic 23–24, 138, 140, 141–146
Hexen bis aufs Blut gequält (1970) 189
Hill, Susan 219
Hitchcock, Alfred 137, 145, 190
Hocus Pocus (1993) 227
Hoffmann, E. T. A. 74, 81–82, 86
Hoffmanns Erzählungen (1916) 86
Hogan, David J. 90
homosexuality, vampires and 112

Homunculus (1916–17) 81–82
Hopkins, Lisa 5
Hopwood, Avery 130
Horner, Avril 151n16
Horrible Dr. Hichcock, The (1962) 188–189
Horror (1963)
horror, Gothic and 4–5, 6–13
Horror Express (1974) 184
horror genre 151n14, 233n2; decline of Gothic 163–164; decoupling from Gothic 215, 217, 224, 226–227; Euro horror 198; *Frankenstein* (1910) 59; impact of Hammer films 158–159, 160–161; post-Gothic 210–211, 214
Horror of Frankenstein, The (1970) 159
Horror Rises from the Tomb (1973) 193, 195–196
Horrors of the Black Museum (1959) 161, 162
Hostel 8
House by the Cemetery, The (1981) 198–199
house mysteries, old dark *see* old dark house mysteries
House of a Thousand Candles, The (1915) 129–130
House of Dracula (1945) 113, 114
House of Fear, The (1939) 102
House of Frankenstein (1944) 113
House of Mortal Sin (1975) 165
House of Terrors (1965) 18
House of the Seven Gables, The (1910) 57
House of the Seven Gables, The (1940) 115
House of the Tolling Bell, The (1920) 129–130
House of Usher (1960) 166–167, 167–170, 171, 177n18, 178n19
House of Wax (1953) 157
House of Whipcord (1974) 165
House on Bare Mountain (1962) 205n13
House on Haunted Hill (1959) 16, 162
House That Dripped Blood, The (1971) 163

houses: *Crimson Peak* 221; *House of Usher* 168, 170; *The Woman in Black* (2012) 220–221
houses, haunted 10, 18, 166, 221; *see also* old dark house mysteries
Howl of the Devil (1987) 198
Howling V: The Rebirth (1989) 211
Hugo, Victor 57, 100, 122n1
Huli jing 18
Hunchback of Notre Dame, The (1911) 57
Hunchback of Notre Dame, The (1923) 100–101, 122n1
Hunchback of Notre Dame, The (1939) 115
Hunchback of the Morgue (1972) 194
Hund von Baskerville, Der (1929) 76
Hunger, The (1983) 210
Hutchings, Peter 9
'Hypnovista' 161

I Was a Teenage Frankenstein (1957) 167
I Was a Teenage Werewolf (1957) 167
I, Monster (1971) 162
Ibáñez Serrador, Narciso 190–191
'Illusion-O' 166
Imp of the Bottle, The (1909) 51
In Search of Dracula (McNally and Florescu) 216
In the Days of Witchcraft (1909) 51
In the Flesh (2013–14) 215
Inferno (1980) 198
Innocents, The (1961) 10, 147, 159
Inquisición (1976) 189
Inquisition (1976) 189
Interview with the Vampire (1994) 20, 226
Invisible Man, The (1933) 107
Invisible Ray, The (1936) 107
Iron Man (2008) 229
Irving, Washington 115
Italian Gothic 181, 182, 185–188, 190, 191–193, 197, 199, 204n2; *see also specific films*
Italian, The (Radcliffe) 4, 32n3, 79
iZombie (2015–19) 215

Jack the Ripper 24, 80–81
Jacobs, Leah 57
James, M. R. 219
Jameson, Fredric 13, 227
Jane Eyre (1910) 57
Jane Eyre (1934) 115
Jane Eyre (1943) 141
Jane Eyre (1983, 1997 and 2006) 219
Jane Eyre (Brontë) 23–24, 35n35, 57, 137–138
Januskopf, Der (1920) 76
Japanese Gothic cinema 18
Jardiel Poncella, Enrique 145
Jaws (1975) 164, 198
Jazz Singer, The (1927) 105
Jekyll + Hyde (2006) 217
Jekyll and Hyde 215, 217; *see also* Dr. Jekyll and Mr. Hyde
Jewish folklore 77
jiangshi 18
Ju-on: The Grudge (2002) 223
jorobado de la morgue, El (1972) 194

Kaidan (1964) 18, 162–163
Kaidan (2007) 223
Kaidan semushi otoko (1965) 18
Karloff, Boris 103, 106, 109, 111, 115–116, 117, 164; golem as forerunner 81; influence on later films 158
Karnstein trilogy 161
Kasten, Jürgen 87
Kavka, Misha, 90–91
Keep, The (1983) 211
kinetograph 45, 66n4
kinetoscope 45, 66n4
Kiss of the Vampire, The (1963) 159
Klimovsky, León 190–191
knights Templar 194–195, 196
Kolchak, Carl 210
Korda, Alexander 87
Körkarlen (1921) 49, 68n19
Kosofsky Sedgwick, Eve 20
Kracauer, Siegfried 74
Kramer, Heinrich 49, 68n19

Ladrón de cadáveres (1957) 119
Laemmle, Carl, Jr. 102
Lagerlöf, Selma 49, 68n19
Lahaie, Brigitte 205n14
Lajthay, Károly 87
Lake of Dracula (1971) 18
landscape 17
Lang, Fritz 72, 73, 89
Last Warning, The (1929) 102, 105, 130
Låt den rätte komma in (2008) 226
Latidos de pánico (1983) 193–194
Le Fanu, Sheridan 88, 112, 161, 219
Lee, Christopher 156, 158, 162, 164, 182, 184, 215
Leeder, Murray 166
Legend of Hell House, The (1973) 18
Légende du fantôme, La (1908) 46, 47
Leni, Paul 72, 86, 129, 133, 134
Leroux, Gaston 76, 101
lesbianism 112, 189
Let the Right One In (2008) 226
Lèvres rouges, Les (1971) 185
Lewis, Matthew 2, 4, 10, 32n3
Ley de Memoria Histórica 222
lighting 25, 45, 113; *The Bat* 131–132; *The Cat and the Canary* 134–135; *Dracula* (1931) 104; *Nosferatu* (1922) 83–84; *Der Student von Prag* 75; *see also* chiaroscuro lighting
lightning 19, 61, 110–111, 113, 169
literature, Gothic 2, 4, 7, 12, 13, 21, 48–49, 57, 76, 100, 107–108; *see also specific works and related films*
Little Shop of Horrors, The (1960) 167
Liveright, Horace 102–105
Llácer, Teresa 168
Loïe Fuller (1905) 55
Lokis: A Manuscript of Professor Wittembach (1970) 21
Lokis: Rękopis profesora Wittembacha (1970) 21

London After Midnight (1927) 114, 123n17, 130
Lord Feathertop (1908) 57
Lost Boys, The (1987) 210
Lost Shadow, The (1921) 75
lost youth 60
Lovecraft, H. P. 178n20, 194, 195, 214
Lowe, Edward T., Jr. 113–114
Lugosi, Bela 102–103, 105, 108, 109, 114–115, 118–119, 211, 215
Lumière brothers 49

llorona, la 119, 223
llorona, La (1960) 20
Lloyd Webber, Andrew 234n8

M – Eine Stadt sucht einen Mörder (1931) 24, 73
Macabre (1958) 162
mad scientists 12, 34n27, 60, 114, 118, 119, 156, 204n6
Madame Hyde (2017) 217
madness 10, 24; *Das Cabinet des Dr. Caligari* 78–80; *The Creeping Flesh* 164; Female Gothic 144, 145; *Gaslight* 140–141; *House of Usher* 168, 170; *Malombra* 145; *El mariscal del infierno* 193; *The Ninth Configuration* 211; *The Telltale Heart* 88–89; see also psychological disturbance; scientists, mad
Mágia (1917) 87
magic 28, 46–47, 55, 67nn8,12; Frankenstein (1910) 58, 60; Jekyll and Hyde films 217; Méliès, Georges, films 43, 49, 50, 52–53; Son of Frankenstein 110; see also trick films
Magic (1917) 87
magic lanterns 49
magic shows 44–45; see also phantasmagorias
Magician's Cavern, The (1901) 50
Mahal (1949) 151n21
Mains d'Orlac, Les (Renard) 76
Maison ensorcelée, La (1906) 55

Malabimba (1979) 198
Malicious Whore, The (1979) 198
Malombra (1917) 204n7
Malombra (1942) 144–145
Man in Grey, The (1943) 141
Man Who Laughs, The (1928) 100–101, 122n1
Man Who Wouldn't Die, The (1942) 114
Man-Made Monster (1941) 107
Manoir du diable, Le (1896) 43–44, 53–54
Mansion, The 151n21
marca del hombre lobo, La (1968) 185, 204n9
mariscal del infierno, El (1974) 193
Mark of the Devil (1970) 189
Mark of the Vampire (1935) 114
Martin, Valerie 218
Martini, Fausto Maria 60
Mary Reilly (1996) 20, 218
Mary Shelley's Frankenstein (1994) 217
maschera del demonio, La (1960) 184, 186–188
maschera di Frankenstein, La (1957) 187
Masque of the Red Death, The (1964) 171
'Masque of the Red Death, The' (Poe) 58, 89
Matheson, Richard 167, 234n7
Matray, Ernst 76
Maturin, Charles 2, 4, 10, 31n2, 115, 127
McNally, Raymond T. 216
medieval, the 17–18, 21, 43, 52, 115; *Das Cabinet des Dr. Caligari* 79; punisher movies 192, 193, 194–195
Medvezhya svadba (1925) 87
Méliès, Georges 43, 45, 49–51, 52–54, 58, 67nn7–8,10, 69n25
Melmoth the Wanderer (Maturin) 4, 32n3, 115, 127
melodrama 10, 16
memento mori 49, 60, 86, 139
Menzies, William Cameron 131
Mephistopheles 43–44, 45–46, 60, 74

Metempsyco (1963)
Metropolis (1927) 73, 81, 107
Mexico: expressionist cinema 89–90; horror films 118–119
Meyer, Stephenie 226
Meyrink, Gustav 74
Mill of the Stone Women (1960) 188
mio amico Jekyll, Il (1960) 185
miracle sous l'inquisition, Un (1904) 51
Miracle Under the Inquisition, A (1904) 51
Miró decree 199
mirror images 75
mirrors 45, 58, 68n15, 80, 105
mise-en-scène 12, 23, 100; *Das Cabinet des Dr. Caligari* 80; *Dracula* (1931) 106; *Frankenstein* (1910) 58; *Frankenstein* (1931) 106–107; *House of Usher* 168; *The Innocents* 10; *Nosferatu* (1922) 84, 85; *The Phantom of the Opera* (1925) 102; *Son of Frankenstein* 110; story films 52; *Viy* 22; *Wachsfigurenkabinett* 86–87; *see also* set design
mode, Gothic as aesthetic 13–17
Moers, Ellen 150n12
Moine, Le (1972) 31–32n3
Moine, Le (2011) 31–32n3
Molina, Jacinto 118 *see also* Naschy, Paul
Monk, The (1990) 31–32n3, 214
Monk, The (Lewis) 4, 21, 32n3, 48, 127, 189, 214
Monster of Fate, The (1915) 77
Monster, The (1903) 68n21
Monster, The (1925) 130
Monstre, Le (1903) 68n21
monstrosity 15, 22–24, 33n23, 72, 81; *Abbott and Costello Meet Frankenstein* 118; Amicus productions 163; atomic monster films 119; *Bride of Frankenstein* 109; continental Gothic 191; *Dracula* (1931) 102–103, 104, 105; *Dracula's Daughter* 112; franchise Gothic 100; *Frankenstein* (1931) 106; German expressionist cinema

90; *Der Golem* (1915) 77–78; *Der Golem* (1920) 81–82; Hammer films 157–158; *The Phantom of the Opera* (1925) 101; *Son of Frankenstein* 110–111; trick films 54–55; twenty-first-century films 215, 222, 225–227, 228; Universal Studios 113–114; *see also specific monsters, types of monster*
mood 8, 17, 19; *The Bat* 131; *The Cat and the Canary* 133; colour 55; *The Fall of the House of Usher* 89; German expressionist cinema 82, 90; Universal Studios 105–106
Most Dangerous Game, The (1932) 115, 117
Mr. Sardonicus (1961) 18
Mr. Vampire (1985) 18
Mrs. Hyde (2017) 217
müde Tod, Der (1921) 86
mulino delle donne di pietra, Il (1960) 188
mummies 54–55, 60, 100, 176n5, 194
Mummy, The (1932) 107, 113
Mummy, The (1959) 157–158, 159
Mummy, The (1999) 214
Mummy, The (2017) 229
Mummy's Revenge, The (1975) 194
Munsters, The (1964–66) 209, 233n1
Murders in the Rue Morgue (1932) 108, 157
Murnau, F. W. 73, 75, 76, 81, 83–84
My Friend, Dr. Jekyll (1960) 185
Myers, Henry 116
Mysteries of Udolpho, The (Radcliffe) 4, 10, 21, 23–24, 79, 127–128, 219
Mysterious Knight, The (1899) 50
mystery genre: *The Bat* 132–133; *The Cat and the Canary* 135; Radcliffe, Ann 128
Mystery of Edwin Drood, The (1914) 57

Nächte des Grauens (1917) 95n17
Nail, The (1944) 145

Name of the Rose, The (1986) 212
narrative 17, 19, 20–21; Corman, Roger, films 170; explained supernatural 128, 141; Female Gothic 23, 141–142, 144, 146, 197; *Gaslight* 140, 141; German expressionist cinema 90; *House of Usher* 168; old dark house mysteries 128; post-1970s Gothic 197, 228; punisher movies 192; *Rapsodia satanica* 61; *Rebecca* 12, 138; *Der Student von Prag* 75; transitional period 52, 56–57, 58, 59; trick films 46, 67n9; Universal Studios 113, 118
Naschy, Paul 118, 189–190, 193–194, 198, 204n9, 206n25
Natural Born Killers (1994) 24
Necronomicon (Lovecraft) 195
New Hollywood 196
Newman, Kim 18
nickelodeons 56
night 19
Night of Horror, A (1917) 95n17
Night of the Living Dead (1968) 196
Night of the Seagulls (1975) 195
Night of the Werewolf (1980) 198
Night Stalker, The (1972) 210
'Nightmare, The' (Fuseli) 58–59, 79
Nightmare Before Christmas, The (1993) 227
Nightmare Castle (1965) 21
Ninth Configuration, The (1980) 211–212
noche de las gaviotas, La (1975) 195
noche de Walpurgis, La (1971) 185, 204n9
noche del terror ciego, La (1972) 194–195, 196
Nordisk 73
Noroi no yakata: Chi o sû me (1971) 18
Nosferatu, eine Symphonie des Grauens (1922) 73, 77, 81, 83–86, 99, 102–103; influence on later films 89, 123n17, 135
Nosferatu a Venezia (1988) 84
Notre-Dame de Paris (1911) 57
novel, Gothic *see* literature, Gothic

novia ensangrentada, La (1972) 185
nudity 161, 189, 190, 197, 205n13

Offenbach, Jacques 86
old dark house mysteries 91, 108, 126–127, 128–130, 135–136, 137, 145–146, 172; influence on Hammer films 159; *see also specific films*
Old English Baron, The (Reeve) 13
Omen, The (1975) 164, 210
'On the Supernatural in Poetry' (Radcliffe) 6–7
One Exciting Night (1922) 130
Onibaba (1964) 18
'onryō' 223
Opera (1987) 198
opera house sets 101–102
optical illusions 2, 44–45, 46, 52–53, 61, 66n1
orfanato, El (2007) 221
Orgy of the Dead (1965) 205n13
Orlacs Hände (1924) 76
Orphanage, The (2007) 221
orribile segreto del Dr. Hichcock, L' (1962) 188–189
orrori del castello di Norimberga, Gli (1972) 192
Oswald, Richard 76, 86
Other, the 28; Frankenstein's monster 60, 106
Others, The (2001) 20, 221
Otrantský zámek (1977) 3, 32n3, 227
otros, Los (2001) 20, 221
Owens, Susan 222

Pan Twardowski (1921) 67n13
Pan Twardowski (1936) 67n13
Panic Beats (1983) 193–194
Pánico en el Transiberiano (1974) 184
paranormal romance 226
Pardy, George T. 132
parodies, horror 117–118
pathetic fallacy 113
patriarchy: Female Gothic 23, 139, 142, 144, 146; old dark house mysteries 135, 139

Paura nella città dei morti viventi (1980) 198
Peake, Mervyn 219
Peeping Tom (1960) 4–5, 162
Penny Dreadful (2014–16) 228–229
Perrault, Charles 23
Petit Poucet, Le (1909) 46
phantasmagorias 47–49, 61–62, 67n14, 68nn15–16, 85
Phantom (1922) 80–81
Phantom Baron, The (1943) 145
Phantom Carriage, The (1921) 49, 68n19
Phantom der Oper, Das (1916) 76
Phantom of the Convent, The (1934) 90
Phantom of the Opera, The (1925) 53, 101–102, 103, 122n5, 157
Phantom of the Opera, The (1983) 218
Phantom of the Opera, The (1986) 234n8
Phantom of the Opera, The (1990) 218
Phillips, Kendall R. 51–52
Picture of Dorian Gray, The (1917) 76
Picture of Dorian Gray, The (1945) 157
Picture of Dorian Gray, The (Wilde) 76, 219
'Pikovaya dama' (Pushkin) 76
Pique Dame (1918) 76
Piranesi, Giovanni Battista 107, 123n10
Pirie, David 4, 32n8
Pit and the Pendulum, The (1909) 58
Pit and the Pendulum, The (1912) 58
Pit and the Pendulum, The (1961) 16, 168, 170
Pit and the Pendulum, The (1991) 213–214
'Pit and the Pendulum, The' (Poe) 58
Pitt, Ingrid 161, 162
Plague-Stricken City, The (1912) 58
Playgirls and the Vampire, The (1960) 183
Poe, Edgar Allan 57–58, 88–89, 167–171, 178n21; *see also specific adaptations, works*
Poelzig, Hans 82
Polidori, John 103, 226
Polish folklore 67n13

portmanteau films 86–87; horror 157, 162–163
portraits: Female Gothic 142, 143; *House of Usher* 169
Poverty Row Studios 118
Powell, Dylis 167
Powell, Michael 162
Prana Film 102
Premature Burial, The (1962) 170
Price, Vincent 225
Profilmes 206n24
Psycho (1960) 190
psychological disturbance 8, 13–14, 15, 20, 24–25, 88; *see also* madness
psychology: Burton, Tim, films 225–226; *Das Cabinet des Dr. Caligari* 78–80; Corman, Roger, films 167, 170, 171; Female Gothic 138, 140; *Dos monjes* 90; *The Ninth Configuration* 211; *Der Student von Prag* 75; *Vampyr* 88
Puits et le Pendule, Le (1909) 58
punisher, the 191–196
Punter, David 7
Pushkin, Alexander 76

Quatermass Xperiment, The (1955) 177n8
Queen of Spades, The (1949) 156
Quella villa accanto al cimitero (1981) 198–199

Radcliffe, Ann 2, 6–7, 10, 127–128, 134, 150nn3,12, 219; Female Gothic 23–24, 145, 146; Hammer films 4; old dark house mysteries 126, 136; *see also specific adaptations, works*
Rais, Gilles de 193
Rapsodia satanica (1917) 60–61
Raskolnikow (1923) 80–81
Raven, The (1935) 108, 157
Raven, The (1963) 171
Real Friend, A (2006) 84

realism, Gothic 126, 128, 129, 144, 145
Reazione a catena (1971) 192
Rebecca (1940) 11–12, 108, 112, 126–127, 137–140, 142–143, 144, 151nn17,21
Rebecca (du Maurier) 23–24, 137–138
red 55, 154, 163, 166, 169, 171, 178n19, 191
Red Spectre, The (1907) 55, 56
Reeve, Clara 13
Reinhardt, Max 82
Rękopis znaleziony w Saragossie (1965) 20
religion: post-1980s films 213
Renard, Maurice 76
repression 20, 23, 198, 215, 220, 223
repression: exploitation cinema 165; expressionist cinema 75–76, 78, 80, 88, 94n6; Female Gothic 139, 142, 144; Jekyll and Hyde 217; New Hollywood 197; *The Phantom of the Opera* 101; punisher movies 192–193
retorno del hombre lobo, El (1980) 198
retrojection: contemporary Gothic 219; *Crimson Peak* 11; *The Curse of Frankenstein* 155–156; decline of 163, 197, 210; *Execution of Mary, Queen of Scots* 44; Japanese films 20; medieval 21, 25, 52, 192; *The Witch* 214; *see also* temporality
Revenge of Frankenstein, The (1958) 158
Rhodes, Gary D. 54–55
Rigby, Jonathan 5
Ring, The (1998) 223
Ringu (1998) 223
Rippert, Otto 89
Roberts, Julia 218
Roberts Rinehart, Mary 130, 131
Rocky Horror Picture Show, The (1975) 216
Rollin, Jean 189–190, 205n14
romance 13, 16, 17–18, 55, 216; *The Bat* 136; *The Cat and the Canary* 136; Female Gothic 136, 137; twenty-first-century Gothic 226–227
Romance of the Forest, The (Radcliffe) 79
Romanticism 4, 32n9, 61, 100, 194, 226; German 72, 74, 77, 81–82, 86
Romero, George A. 196
Rosemary's Baby (1968) 210
Rosen, Marjorie 144
Rosenberg, Max 162

sadism: continental Gothic 189
Salazar, Abel 119
Salem's Lot (1979) 84, 210
Salò o le 120 giornate di Sodoma (1975) 196
Santo Versus the Vampire Women (1962) 119
Santo vs. las mujeres vampiro (1962) 119
Saragossa Manuscript, The (1965) 20
Satan's Rhapsody (1917) 60–61
Satanic Rites of Dracula, The (1973) 160–161
Scars of Dracula (1970) 159, 176n4
Schalcken the Painter (1979) 219
Schatten – Eine nächtliche Halluzination (1923) 81
Scheunemann, Dietrich 74
Schiller, Friedrich 74
science 81, 107, 217–218
science fiction, Gothic 6, 16–17, 46; continental Gothic 190–191, 196; Hammer films 177n8; Roger Corman films 167; trick films 46
scientists, mad 12, 34n27, 60, 114, 118, 119, 156, 158
Scooby-Doo, Where Are You? (1969–70) 209
scores 106, 109, 113, 154–155, 168, 190
Scream and Scream Again (1970) 163–164
Sealed Room, The (1909) 58
Searle Dawley, J. 58
Secret Beyond the Door (1947) 72, 142

seltsamer Fall, Ein (1914) 76
serial format 52, 69n23
serial killers 24
sets: *L'Antre des esprits* 50; *The Bat* 131; *Das Cabinet des Dr. Caligari* 78–79; *The Cat and the Canary* 133–134, 135; Corman, Roger, films 168; *Dracula* (1931) 103, 104; *Frankenstein* (1931) 107, 123n10; *Der Golem* (1920) 79, 82; *House of Usher* 168, 169, 171; *The Hunchback of Notre Dame* (1923) 100; *The Phantom of the Opera* (1925) 101–102, 103; Universal Studios' reuse of 113, 115; *see also* mise-en-scène:
sex: 1970s Gothic 197–198; *see also* eroticism
sex-horrors 198
sexploitation 160, 198, 209; *see also* exploitation cinema
shadows 8, 19–20, 61–62; *The Bat* 131, 132; Bava, Mario, films 186, 188; *The Cat and the Canary* 72, 134–135; decline of 197; *The Fall of the House of Usher* (1928) 89; German Gothic 73, 74–75, 80, 83, 88, 90–91; *La maschera del demonio* 188; *The Phantom of the Opera* (1925) 101; *Rebecca* 139; stolen 75; Universal Studios 106, 110, 113, 114
Shelley, Mary 58, 59, 79, 106, 109, 215, 217
Shonberg, Burt 169
Siodmack, Curt 113–114
Skull, The (1965) 162
'Skull of the Marquis de Sade, The' (Bloch) 162
slasher horror 141, 151n19, 192, 199, 210
Slaughter, Tod 24
Slaughter of the Vampires (1962) 185
Sleep, My Love (1948) 141
Sleepy Hollow (1999) 225
slide show 49
Son of Frankenstein (1939) 109–111

Sorry, Wrong Number (1948) 141
sound: early aural effects 105–106
spaces, claustrophobic 25, 82, 90–91, 127, 142–143, 168, 221
Spadoni, Robert 105
Spanish Civil War 221–222
Spanish Gothic 181–182, 184–185, 188, 190, 193–196, 198, 199, 204n2, 221–222
special effects 45–46, 188
spectacle pictures 100
Specta-Color 162
Spectre rouge, Le (1907) 55, 56
Spellbound (1945) 56, 142
Spence, Ralph 130
spettro, Lo (1963) 190
Spiral Staircase, The (1946) 137, 141
Spirit of Evil (1967) 22
splatter movies 189, 193
Spooks Run Wild (1941) 137
Spooner, Catherine 14, 128
Squelette joyeux, Le (1898) 49
star system, emergence of 56
Steele, Barbara 164
Stevenson, Robert Louis 2, 51, 76, 86, 116, 220
Stewart, Carl 51
Stoker, Bram 83, 84
Stoker, Florence 102
storms 16, 19, 61, 107, 113, 117, 130, 169
strage dei vampiri, La (1962) 185
Strange Case, A (1914) 76, 94n7
Strange Case of Dr. Jekyll and Mr. Hyde, The (2006) 217
Strange Case of Dr Jekyll and Mr Hyde (Stevenson) 76, 162, 220
Strange Door, The (1951) 116–117
Strashnaya mest (1913) 57
Strawn, Arthur 116
Student of Prague, The (1913) 74–75, 76–77, 94n6
Student of Prague, The (1926) 75, 77
Student von Prag, Der (1913) 74–75, 76–77, 94n6
Student von Prag, Der (1926) 75, 77

studio system, emergence of 56
sublime, the 7, 9, 48, 127
Subotsky, Milton 162
'Suicide Club, The' (Stevenson) 86
superheroes 229
supernatural, the 7, 16, 21–22, 25–26, 49, 61, 157; colour 56, 166, 170–171; explained 126–151; 'féerie' plays 52–53; German cinema 72, 78, 82, 83, 90; Méliès, Georges, films 43, 52, 55; Nosferatu (1922) 83; Superstition andalouse 56; trick films 46, 51, 55
superstition 18, 21, 25, 48, 61, 222; La noche del terror ciego 194, 196; Nosferatu (1922) 85–86; old dark house mysteries 129, 136–137; punisher movies 192, 196; Spain 127–128; Tigon films 164; trick films 47, 51–52; Universal Studios 112
Superstition andalouse (1912) 46, 56
surrealism 24–25
suspense 7, 17, 21, 56, 127, 197, 215; Female Gothic 11–12, 126–127; German expressionist cinema 90; old dark house mysteries 126–127, 128, 132, 135
Suspicion (1941) 141, 151n20
Suspiria (1977) 188
Svengali (1931) 102
Sweeney Todd: The Demon Barber of Fleet Street (1936) 156–157
Sweeney Todd: The Demon Barber of Fleet Street (2007) 25
Syder, Andrew 119

Tales from the Crypt (1972) 163–164
Tales of Hoffmann, The (1916) 86
Tales of Terror (1962) 162–163, 170–171
Taste the Blood of Dracula (1970) 159, 196
Technicolor 102, 165, 176n6, 157, 159, 160

television 160, 177n7, 209, 218; see also specific films, series
Telltale Heart, The (1928) 88
Tempi duri per i vampiri (1959) 182–183
temporality 13, 17–18, 25, 126, 146, 163, 215, 220; The Curse of Frankenstein 155–156; Universal Studios 146; see also retrojection
Temptation of Saint Anthony, The (1898) 50
Tempter, The (1913) 86
Tenser, Tony 164
Tentation de Saint Antoine (1898) 50
Terrible Vengeance, A (1913) 57
terror 2, 61; horror and 6–7, 127; phantasmagorias 48; see also fear; dread
Terror, The (1963) 170
Terror-Creatures from the Grave (1965) 190
Terror in the Crypt (1964) 185
theatre: influence on film during transitional period 57
This Night I Will Possess Your Corpse (1967) 166
Tierney, Dolores 119
Tigon British Film Productions 164
Tingler, The (1959) 162
Todorov, Tzvetan 16
Tôkaidô Yotsuya kaidan (1959) 18
Tom Thumb (1909) 46
Tomb of Ligeia (1964) 170, 171
Tomb of Torture (1963) 185
Tombs of the Blind Dead (1972) 194–195, 196
tonality 20
torre de los siete jorobados, La (1944) 181
Torture Garden (1967) 163
Tower of London (1939) 108, 115
Tower of London (1962) 170, 178n20
Tower of the Seven Hunchbacks, The (1944) 181
Townshend, Dale 6
trick films 45–56, 66n1, 67nn9,14, 68n22, 119
Twice Told Tales (1963) 162–163
Twilight (2008) 226

Two Monks (1934) 89–90, 91
Two Mrs. Carrolls, The (1947) 142
Tybjerg, Casper 75

ultima preda del vampiro, L' (1960) 183
uncanny, the 8
Uncle Josh in a Spooky Hotel (1900) 51
Uncle Josh's Nightmare (1900) 51
Uncle Silas (1947) 145
Uncle Silas (Le Fanu) 145, 219
Uncle Was a Vampire (1959) 182–183
undead, the 22
Undead, The (1957) 167
Unheimliche Geschichten (1919) 86
Universal Studios 22, 61, 87, 91, 100–101, 133–134, 146; Hammer films and 156, 157, 158; horror films 113–114, 118, 119–120; horror parodies 117–118; influence on Mexican horror cinema 118–119; influence on *The Munsters* 209; middle-Europe 112, 113; modernisation 229–230; sound technology 105–106; *see also specific films*
urban settings 112, 114, 186, 210, 220, 223

Vadim, Roger 165
Vallet, Joaquín 168
Vamp (1986) 210
Vampire and the Ballerina, The (1960) 183
Vampire for Two, A (1965) 185
'vampire' in film titles 69n26
Vampire in Venice (1988) 84
Vampire Lovers, The (1970) 161
vampires 22, 23, 54–55, 100; 1970s and 1980s period 209–210, 210–211; conscientious 226; eroticism and 112; …*Et mourir de plaisir* 165; fear, violence and sex 183; *Mágia* 87; *Nosferatu* (1922) 83, 84, 85, 86; *Vampyr* 88; *What We Do in the Shadows* 84, 225; *see also* Dracula

Vampires, The (1957) 60, 181, 185–186, 187
vampiri, I (1957) 60, 181, 185–186, 187
vampiro, El (1957) 118–119
vampiro para dos, Un (1965) 185
Vampyr (1932) 88
'Vampyre, The' (Polidori) 226
Variety 101, 129
Varma, Devendra P. 4
venganza de la momia, La (1975) 194
vergine di Norimberga, La (1963) 191, 192
verlorene Schatten, Der (1921) 75
Victor Frankenstein (2015) 217
Victorian era 25, 108, 126–127, 158, 219–220; British Gothic 159, 163, 164; Female Gothic 139, 140–141, 142–143
Vieira, Mark A. 12, 34n24
Vincent (1982) 225
violence: eroticism and 188–189, 190, 192–193, 194, 196, 197–198; Hammer films 157–158, 176n4; *Peeping Tom* 162
violence in film 136
Virgin of Nuremberg, The (1963) 191, 192
Viy (1967) 22
Vlad the Impaler 216
voluntad del muerto, La (1930) 105, 130–131
Von morgens bis mitternachts (1920) 80–81

Wachsfigurenkabinett (1924) 72, 77, 80–81, 86–87
Walker, Pete 164–165
Walpole, Horace 2, 4, 31n2, 169, 222
Walsh, Andrea S. 144, 146
Warm Bodies (2013) 215
Warner, Marina 48
Warning Shadows (1923) 81
Warwick, Alexandra 10
Wasting Away (2007) 215
Waxman, Franz 109
Waxworks (1924) 72, 77, 80–81

weather 19
Webling, Peggy 57
Wegener, Paul 56, 73, 74, 76, 77–78, 81, 82, 94n8
Weinstock, Jeffrey Andrew 224
Werewolf of London (1935) 107
Werewolf Versus the Vampire Woman, The (1971) 185, 204n9
werewolves 22, 54–55, 100, 194, 211
Whale, James 3–4, 81, 87, 99, 106, 158, 225
What We Do in the Shadows (2014) 84, 225
Wheatley, Dennis 159
Wiene, Robert 76, 80–1, 87
Wilde, Oscar 76, 220
Will of the Dead Man, The (1930) 105, 130–131
Willard, John 130
Wise, Herbert 219
Witch, The (1906) 53, 54
Witch, The (2015) 214
Witchcraft Through the Ages (1922) 49, 68n19
Witches, The (1966) 159
Witchfinder General (1968) 164
wolf man 185
Wolf Man, The (1941) 107, 113
Woman in Black, The (1989) 219
Woman in Black, The (2012) 18, 220–221
Woman in White, The (1912) 57
Woman in White, The (1948) 20, 137
Woman in White, The (1982, 1997, 2018) 219
women, depiction of: continental Gothic 188–189, 192; Female Gothic 138, 139–144, 145–146; old dark house mysteries 135–136; Tigon films 165; *see also* heroines

X Rays, The (1897) 49
X the Unknown (1956) 177n8

Yeux sans visage, Les (1960) 185
You'll Find Out (1940) 137

Zlosnik, Sue 151n16
zombies 196, 215, 217, 223

For Product Safety Concerns and Information please contact our EU representative GPSR@taylorandfrancis.com
Taylor & Francis Verlag GmbH, Kaufingerstraße 24, 80331 München, Germany

www.ingramcontent.com/pod-product-compliance
Lightning Source LLC
Chambersburg PA
CBHW051518230426
43668CB00012B/1650